English in Europe

# BILINGUAL EDUCATION AND BILINGUALISM

**Series Editors**
Professor Nancy H. Hornberger, *University of Pennsylvania, Philadelphia, USA*
Professor Colin Baker, *University of Wales, Bangor, Wales, UK*

**Other Books in the Series**
Becoming Bilingual: Language Acquisition in a Bilingual Community
  Jean Lyon
Bilingual Education and Social Change
  Rebecca Freeman
Building Bridges: Multilingual Resources for Children
  Multilingual Resources for Children Project
Child-Rearing in Ethnic Minorities
  J.S. Dosanjh and Paul A.S. Ghuman
Curriculum Related Assessment, Cummins and Bilingual Children
  Tony Cline and Norah Frederickson (eds)
Foundations of Bilingual Education and Bilingualism
  Colin Baker
Japanese Children Abroad: Cultural, Educational and Language Issues
  Asako Yamada-Yamamoto and Brian Richards (eds)
Language Minority Students in the Mainstream Classroom
  Angela L. Carrasquillo and Vivian Rodriguez
Languages in America: A Pluralist View
  Susan J. Dicker
The Languages of Israel: Policy, Ideology and Practice
  Bernard Spolsky and Elana Shohamy
Multicultural Children in the Early Years
  P. Woods, M. Boyle and N. Hubbard
Multicultural Child Care
  P. Vedder, E. Bouwer and T. Pels
A Parents' and Teachers' Guide to Bilingualism
  Colin Baker
Policy and Practice in Bilingual Education
  O. García and C. Baker (eds)
Teaching and Learning in Multicultural Schools
  Elizabeth Coelho
Teaching Science to Language Minority Students
  Judith W. Rosenthal
Working with Bilingual Children
  M.K. Verma, K.P. Corrigan and S. Firth (eds)
Young Bilingual Children in Nursery School
  Linda Thompson

**Other Books of Interest**
Beyond Bilingualism: Multilingualism and Multilingual Education
  Jasone Cenoz and Fred Genesee (eds)
Encyclopedia of Bilingualism and Bilingual Education
  Colin Baker and Sylvia Prys Jones

**Please contact us for the latest book information:**
**Multilingual Matters, Frankfurt Lodge, Clevedon Hall,
Victoria Road, Clevedon, BS21 7HH, England
http://www.multilingual-matters.com**

**BILINGUAL EDUCATION AND BILINGUALISM 19**
Series Editors: Nancy Hornberger and Colin Baker

# English in Europe

## The Acquisition of a Third Language

Edited by
Jasone Cenoz and Ulrike Jessner

**MULTILINGUAL MATTERS LTD**
Clevedon • Buffalo • Toronto • Sydney

To Our Mothers – María Victoria and Emma

**Library of Congress Cataloging in Publication Data**

English in Europe: The Aquisition of a Third Language
Edited by Jasone Cenoz and Ulrike Jessner
Bilingual Education and Bilingualism: 19
Includes bibliographical references and index
1. English language–Study and teaching–Foreign speakers.
2. English language–Study and teaching–Europe. 3. Languages in contact–Europe.
I. Cenoz, Jasone. II. Jessner, Ulrike. III. Series.
PE1128.A2 E483 2000
428'0071'04–dc21   99-054935

**British Library Cataloguing in Publication Data**

A CIP catalogue record for this book is available from the British Library.

ISBN 1-85359-480-6 (hbk)
ISBN 1-85359-479-2 (pbk)

**Multilingual Matters Ltd**

*UK*: Frankfurt Lodge, Clevedon Hall, Victoria Road, Clevedon BS21 7HH.
*USA*: UTP, 2250 Military Road, Tonawanda, NY 14150, USA.
*Canada*: UTP, 5201 Dufferin Street, North York, Ontario M3H 5T8, Canada.
*Australia*: P.O. Box 586, Artarmon, NSW, Australia.

Copyright © 2000 Jasone Cenoz, Ulrike Jessner and the authors of individual articles.

All rights reserved. No part of this work may be reproduced in any form or by any means without permission in writing from the publisher.

Typeset by Bookcraft, Stroud.
Printed and bound in Great Britain by WBC Book Manufacturers Ltd.

# Contents

Introduction
*Jasone Cenoz and Ulrike Jessner* .................................... vii

**Part I    English in Contact with Other Languages in the European Context: Sociolinguistic Perspectives**

1   The Spread of English and the Growth of Multilingualism with English in Europe
    *Charlotte Hoffmann* .............................................. 1
2   English as a European *Lingua Franca*: Current realities and existing dichotomies
    *Allan R. James* ................................................. 22

**Part II   Issues in Third Language Acquisition**

3   Research on Multilingual Acquisition
    *Jasone Cenoz* ................................................... 39
4   Putting Language Proficiency in its Place: Responding to critiques of the conversational/academic language distinction
    *Jim Cummins* .................................................... 54
5   The Dynamics of Third Language Acquisition
    *Philip Herdina and Ulrike Jessner* .............................. 84

**Part III  Studies in the Acquisition of English as L3: Psycholinguistic Perspectives**

6   Metaphorical Competence in Trilingual Language Production
    *Istvan Kecskés and Tunde Papp* .................................. 99
7   Word-fragment Completions in the Second (German) and Third (English) Language: A contribution to the organisation of the trilingual speaker's lexicon
    *Ute Schönpflug* ................................................. 121
8   Towards the Construction of a Theory of Cross-linguistic Transfer
    *Christine Bouvy* ................................................ 143

## Part IV Studies in the Acquisition of English as L3: Educational Perspectives

9  Bilingualism and Trilingualism in School Students in Catalonia
   *Carmen Muñoz* .............................................. 157
10 Three Languages and Three Linguistic Models in the Basque Educational System
   *David Lasagabaster* ........................................ 179
11 The Role of English as L3 in a Swedish Immersion Programme in Finland: Impacts on language teaching and language relations
   *Siv Björklund and Irmeli Suni* ............................. 198
12 Trilingual Primary Education in Friesland
   *Jehannes Ytsma* ............................................ 222
13 Teaching English as a Third Language to Hungarian-Romanian Bilinguals
   *Tatiana Iatcu* ............................................. 236

## Conclusion

14 Expanding the Scope: Sociolinguistic, psycholinguistic and educational aspects of learning English as a third language in Europe
   *Ulrike Jessner and Jasone Cenoz* ........................... 248

The Contributors ............................................... 261

Index .......................................................... 264

# Introduction

JASONE CENOZ AND ULRIKE JESSNER

It is the combination of British colonial power in the nineteenth and early twentieth centuries and North American dominance of the twentieth century that has made English into the most important language of wider communication in the world. English is also the main language of global science and technology, and is expanding into many countries and regions where it has not traditionally been spoken before.

The spread of English has been visualised in terms of three concentric circles or rings that represent its historical and sociolinguistic profile in different parts of the world (Kachru, 1985; 1992). The innermost circle includes those countries that are traditionally considered the bases of English, where it is the first language for the majority of the population: the UK, USA, Ireland, Canada, Australia, New Zealand. Nevertheless, English is not the only language spoken in these countries; it is also in contact with heritage languages or those spoken as the result of immigration. The second or 'outer' ring includes those countries where English is not the first language of the majority but is established as a second language used at an institutional level as the result of colonisation, such as India, Nigeria and the Philippines. The expanding outermost ring includes those countries where English has no official status and is taught as a foreign language, such as continental Europe, Japan, China and South America.

The degree of contact between English and other languages in the three circles and the spread of English in the outer and expanding rings both carry important sociolinguistic and psycholinguistic implications. At the sociolinguistic level, the spread of English has significant implications for the ownership of the language and also for its different varieties. Its spread as a *lingua franca* threatens its traditional status as the property of native speakers. At the same time, new non-native varieties (for example Indian English, Nigerian English) have developed as the result of contact between English and other languages in different parts of the world. At the psycholinguistic level, both this contact and the spread of English have further implications. English is being learnt by many individuals not only as a second but as a third or even a fourth language and now forms part of many multilingual repertoires.

This book is about the acquisition of English in continental Europe, which bear similarities to the way the language has spread in other parts of the world. Most European countries are located in the expanding ring of Kachru's diagram, where English is identified as a foreign language that has no official status but is increasingly used as a language of wider communication. Nevertheless, the spread of English in Europe is not uniform. It has a long tradition in most northern European countries, but is still expanding in the south and east where the foreign languages learnt have traditionally been others. The European Union is helping to change the status of English as a foreign language; because it is now the main channel of communication among European citizens, English is really becoming the EU's second language. However, in the European context the combined influence of American English and the increasing use of the language among non-native speakers is beginning to challenge the pre-eminence of British English as the only model, and a European non-native variety called 'Euro-English' seems to be emerging (Modiano, 1996; Crystal, 1995). This variety shares characteristics of British and American English but presents some differences when compared to native varieties.

English is in contact with other languages in the European context because most European countries are bilingual or multilingual. It is a second language for a large number of Europeans, but there are several situations that are common in the European context where it is learned as a third language. These include:

- Native speakers of minority autochthonous languages who are also proficient in the majority language and study English as a third language. This is the case with native speakers of, for example, Basque, Breton, Sardinian, Catalan, Frisian and Sàmi.
- Native speakers of a majority language who learn a minority autochthonous language at school and study English as a third language. This applies to native speakers of Spanish who learn Catalan or Basque at school, or native speakers of Dutch who learn Frisian at school, and who study English as a foreign language.
- Native speakers of less widespread European languages who acquire a second and a third language; for example, native speakers of Dutch in Belgium who learn French as a second language and English as a third, or native speakers of Swedish in Vaasa/Vasa who learn Finnish and English.

- Native speakers of widespread European languages whose language is a minority one at the national level and who also learn English as a third language; for example, German-speakers in France, Italy or Belgium.
- Immigrants from non-European countries who learn the official language of the new country and study English as a third language; for example, Turkish immigrants in Germany or the Netherlands.
- Other Europeans who learn English as a third language; for example, an Italian who learns French and English or German and English.

The acquisition of English as a third language or L3 is also common in other parts of the world. For example, English is the L3 for many schoolchildren living in Central America, South America or French-speaking Canada who are speakers of heritage languages such as Guarani, Quechua and Mohawk. It is the L3 for many speakers of African languages living in countries where French is widely used as a second language or L2 (Mozambique, Mauritius) and also for those children who live in African countries where English is widely used at the institutional level (Kenya, Nigeria) but who already speak two heritage languages before they go to school. It is the L3 for many speakers in other parts of the world such as Asia or the Pacific where many languages are spoken but English is needed for wider communication. And it is the L3 for a large number of immigrants who have established themselves in countries where English is learned as an L2 (French-speaking Canada, Israel, Japan) and for those who already spoke two languages before they established themselves in English-speaking countries (the US, Australia, New Zealand).

The acquisition of English as L3 shares many characteristics with the acquisition of English as L2 but it also presents differences. Third language acquisition or TLA is a more complex phenomenon than second language acquisition (SLA) because, apart from all the individual and social factors that affect the latter, the process and product of acquiring a second language can themselves potentially influence the acquisition of a third. Third language learners have more experience at their disposal than second language ones do, and have been found to present more strategies and a higher level of metalinguistic awareness. The acquisition of English as a third language also raises issues such as multilingual competence and linguistic interdependence. The educational aspects of the acquisition of English as a third language differ from those of English as a second language, too, and have more implications regarding the optimal age for the introduction of the different languages and the desired level of proficiency in each. Another distinction between the acquisition of an L2 and an L3 is related to terminology. In talk about L1 and L2 it is implicitly assumed that L1 is the dominant language and that the level of proficiency in L2 must necessarily be lower than in L1. When a third language is acquired, however, the chronological order in which the three languages have been learnt does not necessarily correspond to the frequency of use by or level of competence in the trilingual speaker. In this book, English as a third language is understood chronologically: it is the third language that a speaker comes into contact with in his or her biography.

The purpose of this book is to provide an up-to-date overview of the sociolinguistic, psycholinguistic and educational aspects of the acquisition of English as a third language in Europe. Although the book is focused on Europe it provides relevant information for many other contexts where English is acquired as a third language and in general for all those involved in the study of multilingualism at the individual, social and educational levels. Specifically, it should be of interest to:

- language planners and administrators in the spread of English, bilingualism and multilingualism;
- researchers interested in the English language, second language acquisition, multilingual acquisition, bilingualism and multilingualism;
- teacher educators and language teachers; and
- university students of English linguistics, psycholinguistics or applied linguistics.

The book is divided into four parts. In Part 1, English in Contact with Other Languages in the European Context: Sociolinguistic Perspectives, readers will be introduced to the sociolinguistic situation of English in Europe, the spread of English as a *lingua franca* and its relationship to bilingualism. In the opening chapter, Charlotte Hoffmann provides an account of the spread of English in Europe and the development of bilingualism and multilingualism as the result of contact between English and other languages. In Chapter 2 Allan James examines the use of English as a *lingua franca* by focusing on the characteristics of communicative interactions in micro-contexts and their implications for future research in this area.

Part 2, Issues in Third Language Acquisition, includes three chapters concerned with the development of proficiency in a third language. In Chapter 3, Jasone Cenoz provides an overview of the main areas of research in multilingual acquisition, including third language acquisition, by focusing on early multilingualism, the outcomes of bilingualism, bilingual competence and cross-linguistic influence in multilingual acquisition.

In the next chapter, Jim Cummins focuses on language proficiency as related to bilingualism and trilingualism and discusses his original distinction between basic interpersonal communicative skills (BICS) and cognitive academic language proficiency (CALP). He also relates this distinction to the grade of cognitive involvement and the range of contextual support in different tasks, and responds to the critiques made of the BICS/CALP distinction. In Chapter 5, Philip Herdina and Ulrike Jessner adopt a holistic approach to the study of language acquisition, present the main features of multilingual development and describe the characteristics of the dynamic model of multilingualism.

Part 3, Studies in the Acquisition of English as L3: Psycholinguistic Perspectives, consists of three chapters that report on research studies on the acquisition of English as a third language, involving different language combinations. In Chapter 6 Istvan Kecskés and Tunde Papp focus on the acquisition of metaphorical competence by learners of English who have Hungarian as their first language and have also studied Russian. The chapter by Ute Schönpflug explores the organisation of the multilingual lexicon in learners of English as an L3 who have Polish as their first language and German as their second. In the last chapter in this section Christine Bouvy examines cross-linguistic influence in the acquisition of English as a third language by learners with French as their first language, German or Dutch as their second and English as their third.

Part 4, Studies in the Acquisition of English as L3: Educational Perspectives, comprises five chapters on the acquisition of English as a third language in different educational contexts. In Chapter 9, Carmen Muñoz reports the results of a research study on the introduction of English as an L3 to Catalan–Spanish bilingual students at different ages. In the next chapter, David Lasagabaster explores the relationship between proficiency in three languages (Basque/Spanish/English), comparing Basque students who are in different bilingual educational programmes. In Chapter 11, Siv Björklund and Irmeli Suni describe the situation in Vaasa/Vasa where English is introduced as a third language from a very early age in bilingual educational programmes in Swedish and Finnish. They also discuss the specific pedagogical strategies used to teach English to young learners. In the next chapter, Jehannes Ytsma discusses the situation in Frisian primary schools where English is introduced as a third language in bilingual programmes in Dutch and Frisian. In Chapter 13 Tatiana Iatcu provides a description of the teaching of English in Romania and focuses on the teaching of English as a third language to the Hungarian speech community.

As Conclusion, the final chapter, 'Expanding the Scope: Sociolinguistic, psycholinguistc and educational aspects of learning English as a third language in Europe' summarises the main ideas of the book and discusses future perspectives.

## References

Crystal, D. (1995) *The Cambridge Encyclopedia of the English Language*. Cambridge: Cambridge University Press.

Kachru, B.B. (1985) Standards, codification and sociolinguistic realism: The English language in the outer circle. In R. Quirk and H.G. Widdowson (eds) *English in the World* (pp. 11–30). Cambridge: Cambridge University Press.

Kachru, B.B (1992) Models for non-native Englishes. In B.B Kachru (ed.) *The Other Tongue* (pp. 48–74). Urbana: University of Illinois Press.

Modiano, M. (1996) The Americanization of Euro-English. *World Englishes* 15, 207–15.

*Chapter 1*
# The Spread of English and the Growth of Multilingualism with English in Europe

CHARLOTTE HOFFMANN

When asked what, in his opinion, was the most decisive event in modern history the 84-year-old German statesman Otto von Bismarck is said to have replied, 'The fact that the North Americans speak English'. That was in the year 1898, and quite what the politician had in mind we do not know, but today one has to admit that certainly one of the most remarkable linguistic developments of the twentieth century has been the phenomenal spread of the English language to all parts of the globe.

Many studies have been undertaken outlining the extent of that spread and proposing factors which have facilitated it. Often such accounts focus on parts of the world which in the past fell under British and later North American rule, where English was used as the language of colonial administration and later became established as a second language, often enjoying official status as a co-official or even national language or as an administrative language.

The spread of English in Europe has followed a slower and somewhat different path which only started to gather momentum after the Second World War. Although the dispersion of a language does not necessarily result in bilingualism or multilingualism, the spread of English has been a powerful promoter of both societal and individual bilingualism and multilingualism, and, in Europe at least, this is a new phenomenon. Since 1945 Europe's political, economic, social and cultural conditions have undergone far-reaching changes, some of which have altered the linguistic landscape quite considerably. For example, we have seen a long overdue recognition of indigenous minority languages in countries such as the Netherlands, Spain, and Britain, among others, and large-scale migration and immigration which has affected virtually all member states within the European Union. Both these developments have resulted in multilingualism and brought about a change in language behaviour and policy. A further major development affecting twentieth-century Europe is internationalisation, which means in effect the spread of English and its increased use for a variety of communicative functions by non-native speakers (see also James, Chapter 2). Influential factors in this respect have been the many effects that increased mobility, multinational business and international co-operation in many diverse fields have had on the means and media of communication between people with different mother tongues, and the implications of these. But does all this amount to a new kind of multilingualism?

These post-war changes in language use have affected different parts of Europe at different times, with varying intensity and speeds. They started in northern and western Europe, then spread to the southern part of the continent, and we are now witnessing a similar development beginning to take shape in central and eastern Europe. From a macrolinguistic point of view we can see the spread of English resulting in a form of societal bilingualism (or multilingualism in communities which are already bilingual), as an ever-increasing number of people use it as a vehicle of communication, not only with native speakers of English but also as a *lingua franca* in their own contacts with speakers of other languages. Indeed, the presence of and need for English have become so widespread, and access to and provision for it so varied, that it is now possible to talk about 'bilingualism with English' rather than just the use of English as a foreign language. The expression 'bilingualism with English' is ambiguous: it could mean either two languages, or three, as in the case of someone who was already bilingual (for instance by birth or by immigration) who then added English to the repertoire of languages they needed for frequent communication. The term 'multilingualism' is therefore the preferred one here, as it allows for a variety of linguistic constellations involving two or more languages in speakers and communities.

My aim in this chapter is twofold: first, to examine, from a sociolinguistic viewpoint, the spread of English in Europe, which for this purpose is defined mainly as the member states of the European Union. Secondly, I will look at the impact of the language from a microlinguistic angle, considering some aspects of the linguistic influence which English has had on Europe's other languages, as well as at the individual forms of bilingualism or multilingualism which result from language contact. There are clearly different patterns of contact with English; how multilingualism develops will depend on the way English is acquired and used and the role it plays for the individual, for bilingual families and for whole communities.

As will become evident, education and schooling play a significant role in establishing and maintaining the type of bilingualism we shall be looking at, and in the acquisition of biliteracy. Although different patterns of multilingualism with English exist in Europe today, one is justified in saying, I believe, that in the majority of cases it is of one particular kind: it is *achieved* bilingualism, i.e. it is not naturally acquired, although it goes beyond school bilingualism; it is neither 'élite' bilingualism (although it may have started off as such), nor can it be labelled 'popular' bilingualism, i.e. found among large numbers of the population (see again James, Chapter 2). Differing from the type of bilingualism found in bilingual areas or in bilingual families, it has its own particular characteristics. It is being embraced by growing numbers of people who need to be bilingual or multilingual in their daily communicative functions or who consider that they, or their children, have a potential need for it.

My working definition of bilingualism/multilingualism here will be 'the habitual use of two (or more) languages by individuals or speech communities'. In what follows I shall approach the subject of multilingualism with English by looking first at settings where it consists of English plus another language, with English being the dominant one. Then I shall look at the topic from the opposite perspective, discussing a number of aspects regarding contact with a second language plus English, addressing questions such as where, how, for what purpose and in which ways is English used? How is it acquired and what are the consequences, both for it and for the non-native language(s)? The answers to these questions will allow us to identify the particular characteristics of this new type of bilingualism/multilingualism.

## Areas where English is the Main Language

Apart from the British Isles there have been, and still are, territories in Europe where English is the official language. Gibraltar is, in effect, a multilingual territory due to its geographical location, its military and commercial history and its present-day position as a tourist and business centre. Spanish is spoken by virtually everybody as the language of general communication, but English is the official language. There are areas where English is co-official with one or two other national languages, as in Malta and the Republic of Ireland. But whereas in the Irish Republic everybody uses English and only a small proportion of the population use Irish Gaelic for most or some of their communicative needs, in Malta the position is that Maltese has been gaining ground at the cost of English. In some territories English is widely used in official circles but without enjoying official status, as for example in Cyprus or in the enclaves of the American or British Armed Forces in Germany and elsewhere. Societal and individual multilingualism with English is widespread in many of these areas, but since most of them involve only relatively small numbers of speakers they are of little concern for the present discussion, except to note that their continued existence reflects how the status of English has allowed it to survive in spite of being surrounded by other, more popular languages.

In Britain itself, sizeable communities use English alongside another language. Here we find different patterns of bilingualism, of both the individual and the societal variety. In Wales bilingualism has official status and legislation guarantees the use of Welsh in public life and as a language used in education, either together with English, or as the sole medium of instruction, or as an optional subject for study. Bilingualism is usually acquired in the home and reinforced in the community; schools play an important role in its further development and maintenance, and in the establishment of biliteracy. It is probably true to say that attitudes towards Welsh and towards bilingualism itself among the mainstream English-speaking society are more positive today than they were some 30 or 40 years ago. More young people are undergoing education in Welsh than ever before, and by comparison with earlier statistics there are now greater numbers of young people who know the language. However, the overall number of habitual users of Welsh and hence bilinguals (there are no Welsh monolingual speakers any more in Wales) is still declining.

Britain's new, non-indigenous minorities, i.e. the groups of people who were born elsewhere and settled there mainly during the second half of this century, and their descendants, are in a different position from that of the older minorities like the Welsh. Some of their members may be monolingual, either in English or in the community language (for example Cantonese or Panjabi), but many may be bilingual or multilingual, with varying degrees of competence in their two or three languages. They may have acquired English from a variety of sources: as a second language in their countries of origin, or simply from being exposed to English in their new country of residence, or as a result of school attendance. If they want to survive and progress in society they need to become proficient in English, but at the same time they may also be under considerable pressure from members of their families or communities to continue to use their home language. What distinguishes them from the older minorities is that the British state, although it is under an obligation to support their children in the acquisition of English, makes no provision for them to maintain their mother tongue, which means that their children do not normally receive schooling in their home language or achieve literacy in it unless their parents make private arrangements. The maintenance of both individual and societal bilingualism thus depends totally on individual or collective volition and effort. Minority or, as they are called, 'community' languages do not enjoy much prestige among British mainstream society, and any bilingualism in these languages plus English tends to be taken for granted rather than seen as something to which special merit might be attached.

The examples presented so far have involved English in contact with one or more other languages in different settings. In most cases English has been the dominant language which, for historical reasons, has forced speakers of other tongues to become bilingual or multilingual. For the remainder of this chapter the focus will be on a new type of multilingualism where considerations of geography and historical antecedent are unimportant or can perhaps be seen as incidental.

## The growth of English in parts of Europe where it has no official status

Language spread is defined as an increase in the number of users and functions of a language beyond the boundaries of the area where it was originally spoken. Many different factors may cause a language to spread, ranging from military conquest and colonisation to careful planning and perception of the prestige and material advantage that its acquisition may bestow on its speakers. The growth of English as a world language has been examined from a variety of angles focusing on causes as well as effects (e.g. Brosnahan, 1973; Fishman et al., 1977; Wardhaugh, 1987; Kachru, 1992a). The factors that trigger the initial momentum may not be the same as those which maintain the spread or propel it further in later years. In the case of English, this was originally imposed by colonial administrators in the territories that had been taken over, but many post-colonial nations, after independence and as a result of sociopolitical events such as the rise of the United States in world affairs, economic dependence and internationalisation, retained it. This in itself in terms of colonial history is not unusual. What makes the case of English unique, as compared to other former colonial languages such as French or Spanish, is the speed and extent of its growth also in mainly monolingual countries in the Middle and Far East, and in many parts of Europe. English has become the *lingua franca* for trade, tourism, air travel, popular media, sport, science, technology and many other fields of importance in contemporary life; and English is a *sine qua non* if one wants to gain access to international electronic information networks.

As described in the Introduction, Kachru (1992b) categorises types of English-user in terms of a model consisting of three concentric circles showing 'world Englishes', where each circle or ring represents the kinds of spread-pattern, acquisition and functional domain of the English use typical for that category. First there is the 'inner circle' of native speakers (e.g. the British, Americans, Canadians, Australians) for whom English is the mother tongue and also the only one they employ. Then there is the 'outer circle' comprising second language speakers who use English as their 'other' tongue in everyday communication, for instance administrators in former British colonies. And thirdly there is the 'expanding circle' of people who use English as 'another' tongue. Fishman (1992) refers to this phenomenon, which is encountered in many monolingual countries, as the use of English by 'third parties'. In the continental European context, English represents 'another' language in the expanding circle, and this circle has become a highly significant one. With regard to multilingualism in Europe the second or 'outer' circle is relevant only in officially bilingual areas such as Wales or Gibraltar; and the inner circle, the one consisting of native speakers, may well also be expanding, containing a growing number of people who are bilingual by upbringing or whose living and working conditions require the use of two or more languages.

Typically, members of the 'expanding' circle are those people who make up the international communities that have sprung up everywhere in Europe wherever international organisations, companies or institutions have become established. There are multinational commercial concerns in virtually every European country, and there are also the many institutions of NATO, the UN, the Council of Europe and, most prominently, the European Union. Major cities like Geneva, Brussels, Luxembourg, Paris and Copenhagen have international communities with many thousands of members, and there are many other regions where such communities are also found – perhaps fewer in number but still amounting to thousands of people with different mother tongues. More often than not English, and not the language of the country where they find themselves, is used as a working language, either the sole one or as one of several. Apart from these groups of people there are many ordinary European nationals for whom the use of English has become an indispensable part of their linguistic repertoire. So internationalisation, co-operation and mobility, both within Europe and without, have led to the expansion in the European use of English.

Whereas English spread into other continents centuries ago in the wake of conquests and immigration, it is 'a veritable newcomer in the European continent', as McArthur (1996: 24) puts it. One might add that this newcomer has only really begun to leave its mark in the second half of the twentieth century, or even later in the case of certain eastern and southeastern European countries. Many interrelated factors have contributed to this situation and one would need to go to the historians, the political, economic and social scientists, the experts in popular culture, mass communication and technology in order to gain a comprehensive understanding of British, and above all American, influence in post-war Europe. Nevertheless as linguists we too may observe, and try to account for, the many diverse types of settings in which non-native speakers use English on a regular basis, either for professional or recreational purposes, or both. It seems that peoples' linguistic needs and behaviour have been changing faster than in earlier times. One explanation is likely to be the 'snowball effect' visible nowadays: the more widely English is used in terms of functions and speakers, the greater its prestige and association with instrumental reward and consequently the incentive to acquire it. This in turn has had repercussions on the role English plays in education, as will be shown later.

## English and Its Uses

In this section I shall first look at the varieties of English involved in language spread and then go on to examine in which domains, and for what functions, English is used in Europe. In most European countries English was traditionally associated with the variety of the language spoken in England, and even today many teaching materials and teachers use British English. Yet the kind of English which is most influential, because of its widespread presence, is American English. After World War II the American occupying forces had a much greater impact on people in Germany and Austria than did the British, and this was soon reinforced by the increasingly dominant economic, political and scientific position of the United States in world affairs. Today Europeans are exposed mainly to American English in the many spheres where English is used, and Britain's (late) entry into the Common Market has had no particular effect on this situation. Indeed, one could even argue that in many instances 'internationalisation' or 'globalisation', or even 'modernisation', are terms which could just as well be read as meaning 'Americanisation'. Also on a microlinguistic level there is evidence that the most recent loan material on, for instance, German or Dutch or the Scandinavian languages, is of American origin – just as all other varieties of English are influenced by American English, too. The English, or rather Englishes, of 'third party' users will obviously show great variation owing to the different models they are exposed to when acquiring and gaining experience of the language, especially in terms of pronunciation patterns. But with regard to lexical characteristics one does find stronger leanings towards Americanism.

In a study on English in Europe, and especially Austria, Denison (1991: 5) makes the strong claim that with regard to English in western Europe 'a stage has now been reached, for a growing proportion of the population, in which a diglossic situation is rapidly approaching or already exists'. Denison is mainly concerned with considering the consequences of the growth of English for the functions and structure of the mother tongue (in this case Austrian German), and he does not return to the issue of diglossia. He is certainly right in pointing out the increasing inroads that English is making in a number of areas of daily communication, and the resulting linguistic effect on German. Perhaps in the broadest possible interpretation of diglossia (i.e. setting aside Ferguson's notion of functional separation of high and low varieties) one can see English as involved in a 'diglossic situation', since it is being used for an increasing number of communicative purposes. However these can be extremely varied, occurring both inside countries and across frontiers and ranging from passive understanding, through the use of some words and expressions, often of a highly specialised technical nature, to productive fluency – and such gradients are not normally present in discussions of diglossic situations.

As pointed out earlier, the position of English as a medium in national life varies from country to country. In Scandinavia, Belgium and the Netherlands the English language has acquired a higher profile than anywhere else in Europe, due to their relatively small size and their dependence on international trade and collaboration; and also, as Clyne maintains, to the predominance of subtitled, rather than dubbed English programmes on their television channels, 'which are seen even by children who cannot read their first language!' (1995: 202). In Germany and Austria the functions English fulfils are expanding, even if they have not yet reached the position they have in Scandinavia and the Benelux countries. However, there is ample evidence to show that German is the European language which has been influenced more than any other by English (see for example Clyne, 1995; Denison, 1991; Wandruszka, 1979). Thus in his discussion of the various forms this influence has taken Denison remarks on the 'leading place occupied by German in its openness to microlinguistic penetration by English'.

In the countries with Romance languages English has been expanding at a slower rate, but its presence can be felt there just as in less developed countries such as Turkey where, according to a study by Dogançay-Aktuna (1998) on the current sociolinguistic profile of English, it is acquiring growing significance in education and the job market. Similar studies are likely to emerge soon from central and eastern European nations now that they are so frontally exposed to internationalisation, and there has been an almost universal adoption of teaching English as a first foreign language in schools, a position held previously by Russian. Obviously the number of speakers one would consider as bilinguals with English is much lower in these countries than in northern and western Europe, even though it is perhaps disproportionately high among academics and scientists.

If we allow then for a certain degree of variation from one European country to another, we can observe some degree of penetration of the English language in a number of the functional domains typically associated with ex-colonial territories. For instance, it serves as a neutral medium in multilingual countries such as Belgium, where a certain amount of tension exists between the country's main two languages, or between countries with similar languages such as Denmark, Sweden and Norway, or Belgium and the Netherlands, for speakers who want to avoid encountering negative linguistic attitudes. Other parts of Europe, such as for instance Catalonia or the Basque Country in Spain, seem to be moving in the same direction.

In most European countries English is also of considerable importance in higher education. For many academic careers, particularly in medicine, the natural and social sciences, not to mention linguistics, a degree of competence in English is a prerequisite, as extensive use must be made of material published in this language. The case of Turkey may stand as an example for a country that has undergone modernisation in this respect relatively recently. Dogançay-Aktuna (1998) describes the rapid demand for English which emerged in the 1980s as a result of Turkey's more liberal import policy and influenced the country's education as well as the workforce. He refers to an analysis by Ahmad (1993) of the country's sociopolitical development where, as he writes, higher education in Turkey had been reorganised so as to respond to the demands of the growing private sector. A two-tier system was created, with a small number of top universities which taught through the medium of English. These:

> Were expected to produce the growing managerial and technocratic class. Advertisements for such positions began to appear in English even in Turkish-language newspapers; the message was clear: those who cannot read this advertisement need not apply. (Ahmad, 1993: 210, quoted in Dogançay-Aktuna, 1998: 28)

I am not aware of other English-medium universities, except for the European University in Florence, and this one caters for postgraduate students only. But individual courses taught in English have existed in many

European universities for some time, and are growing in number. Postgraduate education may be imparted through the medium of English and students are encouraged, or indeed obliged, to write their dissertations or theses in English, in order to facilitate examinations which may involve international panels and to enable the dissemination of results to a wider circle of interested readers. In such cases students, and especially members of university staffs, need to be at least receptive bilinguals with English, although of course very many of them are also highly efficient users of standard written English and competent oral communicators in the language.

This use of English in higher education has created its own momentum, in that more and more academics are choosing to publish their research in English in the first place. It has been pointed out (e.g. by Viereck, 1996) that the bulk of scientific publishing is nowadays in English, just as English seems to have become the *lingua franca* for scientific debate. While such scientific interchange of ideas may be greatly assisted by a fairly uniform use of technical terms and expressions, this development may also seriously affect the mother tongue. For instance, according to Denison (1991: 7), 'at the frontiers of knowledge, it is often the case that generally recognised and unambiguous technical terms in languages other than English are simply not available', with the result that the European languages 'are in danger of becoming terminologically underdeveloped'. If this type of replacement of linguistic terms were to happen on a wide scale – and it is still too early to judge – bilingualism with English in Europe would have a particular subtractive feature of the kind which is often found in settings where a dominant majority language is in contact with a minority language.

English has now become visible throughout Europe and beyond in a large number of domains such as commerce, sport, entertainment, youth culture and tourism. It has become most evident in the media, and in many countries seems to be the dominant language of advertising, especially for consumer goods such as clothes, cosmetics, cigarettes and cars. Its increased status is also reflected in the fact that in many professional environments knowledge of English is considered to be an essential requirement for a career with an international (European or global) component, be it in an international organisation or a national one with multinational links, or in the area of entertainment and, above all, the media – films, television, music, computers, telecommunications and many areas of information technology, as well as the press, radio and TV. One of the big growth areas of our times is information technology, and in their article about the global information society Laver and Roukens (1996) vividly describe the new linguistic challenges created by the acceleration in the development of information networks, which is leading to an increase in internationally oriented services. A command of English is a *sine qua non* for anyone who uses the tools and media of communication and wants to benefit from electronic information retrieval systems such as the Internet or other electronic storage systems. The desire to become a participant in all these fields of activity may provide the initial motivation to acquire English, or the spur to become more proficient. It does not, of course, necessarily lead to active bilingualism, but in many instances it may constitute a first step towards it.

The European Union is probably the European institution with the most explicit language policy, as it specifies the status and use of the languages of its member states. Fluency in English is a prerequisite for its employees since this is one of its two main working languages. According to Dollerup (1996), who writes about English within the European Union, French is the language employed by permanent staff, and English is used by delegates from national countries attending meetings. In particular, English has gained considerable ground since the 1995 expansion of the Union, not so much as a result of political decisions taken by the member states but simply because members prefer to use English.

The spread of English can be traced both at the sociolinguistic level, where an increasing number of uses and functions have been described, and on a linguistic level. The latter involves examining a given European language for linguistic evidence in terms of overt and covert integration of English influences, for example in the form of loans and all manners of lexical, semantic and syntactic transfers, and even new creations, called by Clyne (1995) 'pseudo-transfers'. These occur where a new lexeme is used with a meaning which it does not have in English, such as the German *der Herren-Slip* (a fashionable word for underpants) or *das Handy* (mobile phone), or the Spanish *el footing* (jogging) or *un consulting* (a business consulting firm). Many languages have experienced penetration by English, particularly in the form of lexical transfers, and, as already mentioned, German is particularly susceptible to the influence of English in the areas of lexis as well as grammar and semantics.

Different reasons have been proposed for this German propensity (see Denison, 1991; Wandruszka ,1979). These include German's structural and semantic similarity with English, for example in terms of pronunciation and features such as predetermination. Other arguments suggest that there is a need, or at least a fondness, for short snappy English words, or that somehow the English word seems to indicate different qualities from the corresponding German equivalent, where this exists. Denison (1991: 12) concludes that of all possible explanations 'the straightforward prestige factor seems to outweigh any linguistic or rational considerations where these might be expected to militate against borrowing or popularity'. This perfectly plausible explanation tallies with the observation made earlier about underlying reasons for the choice of English on the sociolinguistic level. There is clearly a causal link between the macrostructural functions of English and its microstructural influence on individual European languages: unless English was used by an influential proportion of speakers for some communicative functions there could be no linguistic influence on the national languages. And it may well be that once this relationship has been established it works in either direction, thus further promoting the spread of English.

## The Establishment of Multilingualism

### Family bilingualism

It is probably true to say that most members of international communities and groups of individuals who use English habitually have become bilinguals or multilinguals with English through education and use, although there are, of course, also those for whom English is either the mother tongue or a language acquired naturally in childhood. Family bilingualism where one of the two languages is English can take many forms. Depending on the particular linguistic constellation and family arrangements, the patterns of language use within the family can vary widely. There are those families at one end of the scale where English is spoken by both parents within the family all the time, and also those who follow the one-parent/one-language strategy consistently, while at the other end there are those who use English only occasionally, just when they have the motivation and opportunity to do so.

The resulting type of bilingualism varies accordingly, from family to family and also from time to time within individual families. It may be more active or more passive depending on the pattern of use of the two languages; it may encompass oral and written skills in both languages, or only a small degree of literacy in the family minority language, or none at all. Unlike the case of bilingual families in Britain (whose family language may be a non-English community language), bilingual families in continental Europe who have English as a home language are unlikely to encounter any negative attitudes towards their bilingualism in the dominant outside community, since English enjoys such high prestige. So once again we find that bilingualism with English plus another language of the European Union is special, because the social and cultural attributes of English are considered to be exceptional.

## The role of education

One of the salient features of multilingualism with English in Europe is that for the majority of speakers it will have been acquired during the second and subsequent decades of their lives. Education tends to play an important part in the first learning stages. Since the end of the last war nearly all Europeans, irrespective of class and occupation, have had access to foreign language learning at school, and today the first language offered as a foreign language is nearly always English. It used to be French, but now more and more countries have changed to English, some only quite recently (e.g. Spain and Turkey) while others made the switch some 50 years ago (e.g. Scandinavia and many parts of Germany). Even in officially multilingual countries such as Belgium and Switzerland, which favour a policy of offering the other national languages as first foreign languages, English is frequently the choice parents prefer for their children. Indeed, English is now regarded as so desirable that many countries are beginning to introduce it at primary level. Experimental and pilot programmes in the Netherlands, Austria, Germany and the Basque Country have been reported on, and Italy recently announced that it will make the introduction of English compulsory in all state-maintained primary schools. A survey published in 1998 by Eurostat, the EU's statistical unit, showed that 90% of all pupils in the Union learn English as a foreign language, and most of them study it as their first foreign language. Also noted were a Europe-wide move towards introducing the first foreign language early on, and at the same time an observable trend towards starting schooling earlier. Approximately one quarter of primary school children were reported to be learning English. The United Kingdom was reported as being the only EU member state that does not automatically offer foreign languages at primary level in its state-maintained primary schools. As can be seen from the research into third language acquisition reported on in some of the other chapters in this volume, L3 acquisition in bilingual regions invariably involves English, and frequently children not yet in their teenage years; it is claimed that this is both successful and educationally sound, with some studies also suggesting that the children's bilingualism may have positive effects on their subsequent L3 acquisition.

A study mainly concerned with ascertaining schoolchildren's attitudes towards Europe in six EU states found an overwhelming dominance of English as the first foreign language offered by schools. However, the majority of the pupils interviewed (most of them were between 14 and 16 years of age) had learnt two foreign languages, except those from Spain who had learnt only one, and those from the Netherlands who had learnt three. Incidentally, on the question of attitude it was young people from the latter two countries who had the highest affirmative responses, with 68.4% and 90.4% respectively, to the question 'Do you think of yourself as European?', whereas young Britons came last with only 18.6% (Convery et al., 1997: 13). It should be remembered, though, that the learning of English for Europe's schoolchildren is different from learning any other foreign language because of the presence of English in their environment in the form of pop songs, the youth and drug cultures and, most importantly, television and the Internet. The advantages that English enjoys are obvious, as these socially prevalent sources offer varied, stimulating and therefore valuable input and provide both a support and incentive for learning the language and putting it into active use. I do not know to what extent language teachers and other producers of teaching and learning material are taking advantage of these opportunities, and it is not suggested that foreign language learning in schools should be seen as a means of fostering bilingualism among pupils. Yet it has become clear that the teaching of English in mainstream schools, when combined with additional opportunities for input and motivation, do provide a favourable basis for bilingualism with English.

There are other types of schools with a strong commitment to bilingual education which, although small in number, constitute a significant contribution towards bilingualism in Europe. Education using the minority language as the medium of instruction, or with this language being employed as a vehicle to teach part of the curriculum, provides access to a number of registers and uses of language that the young person does not otherwise experience. And there is no doubt that attitudes towards bilingualism are positively affected if the minority language is seen to be prestigious enough to be deployed as a language of education. This has been well documented in the Welsh context, where Welsh-medium schools and bilingual schools are acknowledged to have played an important role in the spread and maintenance of Welsh and also in changing attitudes towards the language (see, for example, Baker, 1992, 1993; Lyon, 1996). There are no schools in the English mainstream education system which are committed to maintaining children's bilingualism, although there are some which are either private (such as the European School), or are maintained by foreign governments (such as the French, German and Spanish schools in London) which do have this ostensible aim.

In mainland Europe conditions for bilingual education involving English seem both more varied and more favourable. There are a number of well-established institutions which use English for either all or part of their pupils' education. And it is quite exciting to see the growing number of educational projects and ventures that aim to establish a degree of bilingualism with English in national education systems that were hitherto monolingual. At the moment this trend is primarily affecting the children of people who are already economically and socially quite influential. But the process in continental European societies (which can be considered more egalitarian than the British) appears to be that, whenever an educational advantage is possessed by a privileged minority, it becomes desirable for the majority – and eventually becomes obtainable for them, at least to some extent.

Of the institutions committed to bilingual education, the International Schools are the oldest foundations. They exist in a number of countries, catering for children with international backgrounds, for instance the one in Luxembourg where a large number of pupils' parents work for multinational or European institutions. These schools are open to local children as well, if their parents are keen to provide them with an education with an international dimension in a supranational medium of instruction. But admission depends on academic ability, and school fees may have to be met by the parents. The language of instruction tends to be English and the qualification awarded after successful completion of schooling is the International Baccalaureate. There are also, sometimes running under the name of International Schools, the English Sections of mainstream national schools found, for instance, in France and Switzerland, located in the vicinity of large English-speaking commercial enterprises. This type of schooling aims to enable children to obtain English qualifications in some subjects (typically in English language and literature) alongside the national ones of their school such as the French or Swiss baccalaureates. Neither of these two types of school has the establishment of bilingualism as an explicit aim, nor is the curriculum geared specifically towards imparting biliteral and bicultural education, but most school-leavers will be fully bilingual as they will normally have acquired literacy in their home language before entering the International Schools or English Sections.

The European Schools, on the other hand, are a particularly good example of education designed to foster multilingualism. These schools grew out of parental initiatives in the 1950s after the European Coal and Steel Community was founded and employees of different nationalities went to work at its headquarters in Luxembourg. Today there are European Schools in Belgium, Germany, Italy, Luxembourg, the Netherlands and England, catering for some 15,000 children (Bulwer, 1995). Their parents usually work for one of the institutions or organisations of the European Union and tend to be fairly mobile. However, the schools are keen to point out that they are not élite institutions, and figures available show that the majority of pupils in all European Schools is not made up of children whose families are regarded as European Community personnel (Hoffmann, 1996, 1998).

There are many European children who because of their parents' mobility may well have to change school during the period of their education, perhaps within the European Union, or may be required to reinsert themselves into the education system of their country of origin. This means that they need to be educated in their native language. Hence the European School model is designed primarily as a language maintenance programme. In their primary years children receive instruction in their native language, but they are also introduced to a second language, chosen from English, French or German. In their secondary schooling they are taught partly in their native language and partly in the language they learnt as a second language, which is known as a 'vehicular' language. In addition they attend so-called 'European hours' during which the vehicular language is used among mixed groups from different linguistic backgrounds. These periods are intended to promote cross-cultural understanding and unity rather than to convey subject-specific knowledge. A third language must also be learnt. The success of these schools is measured not only in terms of a high pass-rate (90%, it is claimed) in the final examination, the European Baccalaureate, but also in the attainment of a high level of linguistic accuracy and good literacy skills in the children's two languages (Baetens Beardsmore, 1993). Clearly, schools that are designed with the linguistic and cultural needs of bilingual children in mind must be good for multilingualism. They provide a homogeneous environment in which the advantages of being bilingual are made use of. A further merit of such schools is that they cater for children with varied educational profiles and needs at the same time as having an impact on their bilingual development.

A number of newly established Montessori Schools in several European countries can be counted among the more recent developments in multilingual education, as they introduce pre-school and primary school children to a new language. They are, naturally, not very significant in terms of the numbers of bilinguals they help produce, and not all of these schools offer English, but where they exist they make a contribution to the individual child's bilingualism while at the same time reflecting the status and spread of English in the community.

A number of European countries have traditionally had American, English, French, Spanish and German schools which are maintained and run primarily by the governments of the countries concerned. Although originally intended to cater for the children of foreign nationals, these schools are open to local pupils as well and there continues to be a strong demand for them. The trend now seems to be for English-medium schools to be established and run as state-owned as well as private institutions. For example, Dogançay-Aktuna (1998) mentions statistical figures for 1987–8 which show that there were 193 such schools in Turkey, 90 of which were state-owned.

Lastly, one can mention other types of education in Europe that go beyond the traditional English as a foreign language provision and aim at exposing majority children in mainstream education to English. The fact that in a number of countries educational authorities are now willing to support the early introduction of English and bilingual projects must be seen as recognition of the importance of foreign languages – and in most cases the language in question is English. In Germany, for example, from the 1980s onwards there has been a growing number of schools that use a form of bilingual education with German and English, referred to as *bilinguale Züge*, where the children receive part of their lessons in English. The aim of these programmes, found mainly in secondary schools (but in some places, such as Berlin, also at primary level), is to encourage German-speaking pupils to see English not only as a foreign language that is an object of study, but also to learn to accept it as a vehicle for acquiring new skills and insights. To this end pupils first receive intensive tuition in English, and then English is used as the language of instruction in those subjects that are of a more practical, activity-based nature, where the language required for teaching is not too technical. The subjects judged most suitable to be taught in English are mainly in the arts/social sciences groups; biology is also increasingly being included in this kind of bilingual education, so that a subject combination of biology/geography/politics in the German–English streams is becoming the standard choice (Klapper, 1994). It is far too early to say whether such schemes will result in life-long bilingualism for those who have attended these schools, but they are interesting projects well worthy of attention.

The fact that the latter kind of provision is becoming increasingly popular among parents and pupils, and that the schools are supported by the local (or state) education authorities, is a strong indicator that there exists considerable popular interest in, as well as an official commitment to, the learning of foreign languages, especially English. What contribution do these bilingual streams make towards bilingualism? In view of the problems involved with securing adequate resources, and the artificiality of the linguistic situation that children find themselves in when English is reinforced neither in the family nor in the community around them, one ought to be cautious in one's expectations. In most cases English is taught and used as the subject language by non-native speakers, and it is not known whether it is actually being used in the classroom all the time. Yet it is not unreasonable to assume that for a significant minority of German pupils their access to English is both qualitatively and quantitatively enhanced. As a result of this, and of the motivation it probably engenders, fluency, competence and confidence in using English are more likely to develop than if the child simply attended English language classes.

## Conclusion

My aim has been to trace the rise of English in Europe and to outline the kind of multilingualism, involving one or more languages and English, which has become more prominent in the wake of this spread. As we have seen, the growth of English has, for the most part, been unplanned in the sense that it was not planned or controlled by national governments. In a number of cases states have reacted by introducing language planning, mainly in the education sector, designed to respond to the increased demand for English. Sometimes national governments have tried to stem the spread of English and have passed laws aimed at protecting their national language from too much infiltration of English, as happened, for instance, in France. Rarely have such laws proved effective, or indeed enforceable. Linguistic behaviour is not easily controllable by official decrees; language spread, in Wardhaugh's words, 'seems to have a dynamic all of its own' (1987: 16). But whichever direction language spread takes, there is obviously a causal link between it and the growth of bilingualism and multilingualism, even if this does not affect everybody to the same degree and does not involve all members of a speech community.

Multilingualism with English in Europe is very varied. Different patterns can be seen in terms of when, how, where, why and to what degree of competence English is acquired and used alongside other languages. A broad distinction needs to be made between the societal and individual bilingualism and multilingualism existing in the British Isles and that encountered elsewhere in Europe, for the simple reason that virtually everybody has exposure to the language in the former. Most bilinguals in Britain have become so by a process of natural acquisition consisting of being in contact with two (or more) languages, or through schooling, and for most of them English is the dominant language, the one for which they have most use, in which they are most proficient, and in which they possess literacy skills.

In continental Europe where the English language is not part of mainstream society, bilingualism with English is found among communities containing native speakers of English and also among international communities and individuals who choose English as the language of their own inter-group communication such as using English for special purposes in the workplace. The reason for this is, of course, that English has become established as the world's most prominent language of international communication. As such it enjoys exceptional social prestige, and one consequence of this is that any bilingualism that encompasses English is also seen as desirable and is met with positive attitudes. The high status of English, combined with its proven usefulness, naturally enhances the budding bilingual's motivation to master this language.

In Europe as a whole, English is acquired either in adulthood or in childhood, either in a natural context (family bilingualism or simply exposure) or through formal learning and schooling. School bilingualism in this case refers not only to the place where, and the manner in which, the second language is added to the mother tongue. The kind of school attended may also, to some extent, determine the linguistic models to which the non-native learner of English is exposed. Teachers and other pupils may be either native or non-native speakers of English, and their language may display varying degrees of native-speaker authenticity. The spoken varieties may have American or British or other (including non-native) features. And the resulting competence of learners spans the whole range from non-fluent to native-like. A further characteristic of school bilingualism is that the individuals involved learn to read and write in the two languages. This is quite different from the popular bilingualism found among many migrant and immigrant communities, where a large number of bilinguals or multilinguals are literate in only one of their languages. It also means that this kind of bilingualism with English implies familiarity with the written standard variety of English – in fact, it is often the case that the language use of such bilinguals is heavily dependent on the written medium. In many countries pupils and adults are in contact with English outside school, too, and for them the learning process – whether as a result of formal learning or exposure – extends well beyond school. Exposure to English language media is likely to bolster receptive skills, whereas working in an environment requiring active and passive use of English enhances productive skills.

As regards use and proficiency, many adult bilinguals and multilinguals will need English for quite specific functions in highly technical contexts and in a limited range of situations outside which they may feel uncomfortable or at a loss. So while there are many bilinguals who could be characterised as 'balanced' bilinguals, there are probably more for whom this label is not appropriate. For most Europeans, instrumental reasons are the most powerful motivator for maintaining and developing their English after schooling. English brings the promise of material gain, higher status and further prospects of mobility. An additional feature of this particular type of bilingualism is that being proficient in English does not mean that one has to be bicultural: a superficial knowledge of Anglo-Saxon culture is sufficient, there is no need to develop feelings of dual identity and shared loyalties. In this, too, the European bilingual with English differs from members of bilingual families or communities.

There is evidently a growing demand for English in Europe, and this demand is being met in various ways. For a relatively small but significant and influential minority of Europeans who are finding the habitual use of English to be either necessary or potentially necessary, bilingualism (or multilingualism) is becoming a fact of life. One may go so far as to say that in order to partake in Europe, i.e. both contribute to and benefit from the European Union politically, economically and socially, it is now highly desirable to have English. Since the number of those becoming fluent and habitual users of English is growing steadily, and access to the language is open to people from diverse social backgrounds, one can no longer refer to the outcome of this development as élite bilingualism. It is really a form of societal multilingualism, albeit a novel one. Its uniqueness lies in the particular interplay of its various features and the conditions under which it has arisen and is developing. It is a one-off phenomenon, probably unrepeatable, and as such it extends the range and typology of bilingualism. The irony is that the language that has acquired such wide currency is the tongue which originated in what is now Europe's most reluctant, and linguistically least adventurous, member.

### References

Ahmad, F. (1993) *The Making of Modern Turkey*. London: Routledge.
Baker, C. (1992) *Attitudes and Language*. Clevedon: Multilingual Matters.
Baker, C. (1993) *Foundations of Bilingual Education and Bilingualism*. Clevedon: Multilingual Matters.
Baetens Beardsmore, H. (ed.) (1993) *European Models of Bilingual Education*. Clevedon: Multilingual Matters.
Brosnahan, L.F. (1973) Some historical cases of language imposition. In R.W. Bailey and J.L. Robinson (eds) *Varieties of Present-day English* (pp. 40–55). New York: Macmillan.
Bulwer, J. (1995) European schools: languages for all? *Journal of Multilingual and Multicultural Development* 16, 459–75.
Clyne, M. (1995) *The German Language in a Changing Europe*. Cambridge: Cambridge University Press.
Convery, A., Evans, M., Green, S., Macaro, E. and Mellor, J. (1997) An investigative study into pupils' perceptions of Europe. *Journal of Multilingual and Multicultural Development* 18, 1–16.
Denison, N. (1991) English in Europe, with particular reference to the German-speaking area. In W. Pöckl (ed.) *Europäische Mehrsprachigkeit. Festschrift zum 70. Geburtstag von Mario Wandruszka* (pp. 3–18). Tübingen: Niemeyer.

Dollerup, C. (1996) English in the European Union. In R. Hartmann (ed.) *The English Language in Europe* (pp. 24–46). Oxford: Intellect.
Dogançay-Aktuna, S. (1998) The spread of English in Turkey and its current sociolinguistic profile. *Journal of Multilingual and Multicultural Development* 19, 24–39.
Fishman, J., Cooper, R.L. and Rosenbaum, Y. (1977) English the world over. A factor in the creation of bilingualism today. In P. Hornby (ed.) *Bilingualism. Psychological, Social and Educational Implications* (pp. 103–39). New York: Academic Press.
Fishman, J. (1992) Sociology of English as an additional language. In B.B. Kachru (ed.) *The Other Tongue: English Across Cultures* (pp. 19–26). Urbana/Chicago: University of Illinois Press.
Hoffmann, C. (1996) Societal and individual bilingualism with English in Europe. In R. Hartmann (ed.) *The English Language in Europe* (pp. 47–60). Oxford: Intellect.
Hoffmann, C. (1998) Luxembourg and the European Schools. In J. Cenoz and F. Genesee (eds) *Beyond Bilingualism: Multilingualism and Multilingual Education* (pp. 143–74). Clevedon: Multilingual Matters.
Kachru, B.B. (1992a) The other side of English and the 1990s. In B.B. Kachru (ed.) *The Other Tongue: English Across Cultures* (pp. 1–18). Urbana/Chicago: University of Illinois Press.
Kachru, B.B. (1992b) Models for non-native Englishes. In B.B. Kachru (ed.) *The Other Tongue: English Across Cultures* (pp. 48–74). Urbana/Chicago: University of Illinois Press.
Klapper, J. (1994) Germany's bilinguale Züge. *German Teaching* 10, 29–34.
Laver, J. and Roukens, J. (1996) The global information society and Europe's linguistic and cultural heritage. In C. Hoffmann (ed.) *Language, Culture and Communication in Contemporary Europe* (pp. 1–27). Clevedon: Multilingual Matters.
Lyon, J. (1996) *Becoming Bilingual: Language Acquisition in a Bilingual Community*. Clevedon: Multilingual Matters.
McArthur, T. (1996) English in the World and in Europe. In R. Hartmann (ed.) *The English Language in Europe* (pp. 3–12). Oxford: Intellect.
Viereck, W. (1996) English in Europe: its nativisation and use as a *lingua franca*, with special reference to German-speaking countries. In R. Hartmann (ed.) *The English Language in Europe* (pp. 16–23). Oxford: Intellect.
Wandruszka, M. (1979) *Die Mehrsprachigkeit des Menschen*. München: Deutscher Taschenbuch Verlag.
Wardhaugh, R. (1987) *Languages in Competition: Dominance, Diversity and Decline*. Oxford: Basil Blackwell.

## Chapter 2
# English as a European Lingua Franca
## Current Realities and Existing Dichotomies

ALLAN R. JAMES

> 'I don wanna drink alcohol.'
> 'Me too.'
> 'I also not.'
>
> (snippet of an Austrian/Italian/Slovenian
> conversation overheard in Central Europe)
>
> MENJALNICA – CAMBIO – WECHSEL – CHANGE
>
> (frequently observable bank sign in the Alpine–Adriatic region)

This chapter aims to address the issue of English as a European *lingua franca* in the particular context of its occurrence in natural face-to-face (or, strictly, voice-to-voice) interactions and transactions in everyday situations of life, as used by speakers of first languages (L1s) other than English. It will be argued that this locus of English use in Europe today provides a fertile starting-point for a new assessment and understanding of the place of English within bi/multilingualism in general. One such everyday situation (or function: perhaps 'negotiating social activity'?) is illustrated minimally by the above snippet of conversation among a group of young adults. The bank sign above represents a commercial–institutional realisation of the range of languages available for Slovenian/Italian/Austrian verbal exchange in the region where the three countries meet.

Returning to the 'conversation', such and similar uses of English may be recorded countless times daily throughout Europe. It shows English being created 'on-line' for immediate communication purposes in a relatively *ad hoc* way by speakers who have no doubt had at least four years of formal training in the language in their respective school systems. The use of the language in such contexts is as a *lingua franca*, and in this particular case in fact as a regional language, i.e. as a linguistic code available for trinational communication at the intersections of Austria, Italy and Slovenia. English here is a third language in two senses: it is available in addition to the *societal* bilingualism historically present in the region (German–Slovene in Austria; Italian–Friulian and Italian–Slovene in Italy; Slovene–Italian in Slovenia); and it is also available as an option in addition to the *individual* bilingualism found in the region (predominantly German–Italian and German–Slovene in Austria; Italian–Friulian and Italian–German in Italy; and Slovene–German and Slovene–Italian in Slovenia). It can equally be a special purpose language, used here for the regulation of communal leisure activity.

In the relatively short history of systematic research into English as a European *lingua franca*, however, the kind of locus for the activation and spread of English just outlined has scarcely, if at all, been given consideration. Attention has instead been drawn to the position and development of English as a national, rather than regional *lingua franca* in multilingual countries such as Switzerland (Durmüller, 1992) and to its developing function as a second, rather than foreign language in countries such as Denmark, Norway, Sweden and the Netherlands (see, for example, McArthur, 1998). Other research has addressed the growing spread of English in the educational systems of Europe (Hoffmann, 1996 and Chapter 1, this volume; Ammon, 1996), in the supranational bodies of Europe such as the EU (Dollerup, 1996) and in various cross-border regional organisations (Gellert-Novak, 1994). English as a third language has been investigated mainly in the context of its acquisition and learning in areas which are societally bilingual and/or by individuals who are by family upbringing bilingual in languages other than English (see Parts 2 and 4 of this volume). With regard to special purpose English, research has concentrated on the European and generally international domains of its use in the professional fields of business, science and technology, law and academic exchange (for recent discussion see Graddol, 1997).

In sum, research has focused generally on macro-levels of the occurrence of the language within well-circumscribed and quasi-institutionalised ecologies, in which the form of English employed will be subject to externally imposed norms of use and usage. By contrast, the kind of transnational polylogue illustrated above, but also the transnational social dialogue between a French and a Hungarian businessman in the framework of a negotiation, or equally the transnational conference small talk between Spanish, Croatian and Finnish academics, all constitute micro-levels of the occurrence of English in ecologies which are less well circumscribed, less institutionalised, and where the language itself is emergent and shifting in nature and hence far less subject to any externally imposed norms of use and usage.

In the remainder of this chapter I will argue that the analysis of such ubiquitous micro-level manifestations of English as a *lingua franca* in Europe forces a serious reassessment of some of the more macro-level categorisations and typologies relating to 'bilingualism with English' developed hitherto. It will also require a shift in the practice of (socio)linguistic research in this area from the quantitative to the qualitative.

## Further Considerations

It requires little linguistic sensitivity to note the omnipresence of English in Europe today – both in the national domains of the educational systems, and in the international specialist domains of supra-governmental, business, scientific, technological, legal and general academic communication. However, the most obvious impact that English makes on European life is undoubtedly via its presence in the public domains of the media, including the Internet, advertising, many forms of popular youth culture and popular entertainment. In the national and international domains, linguistic research has investigated the characteristics of special-purpose varieties such as 'Eurospeak' within the institutions of the EU (Dollerup, 1996), 'business English', 'English for science and technology' (EST), 'legal English' and 'English for academic purposes' (EAP). In the media domains there is a lively current linguistic interest in the language used, including that of the Internet (e.g. Goodman & Graddol, 1996), advertising (e.g. Cook, 1992) and most recently e-mail communication (Barron, 1998). However, much of this research is restricted to the various forms and effects of English in these domains within indigenously English-speaking communities, and less is known thus far on these forms and effects within indigenously non-English-speaking communities (although for initial discussion of the effects of English in advertising in Switzerland, see Cheshire & Moser, 1994). It should perhaps also be remembered that linguistic analysis of these public manifestations of English is of the product itself, and that the ultimate effects of exposure on the passive or active command of English of the non-L1 consumer are at present largely a matter of conjecture.

Moreover, these studies remain at a macro-level of analysis, in which the significances of the 'Englishes in Europe' are interpreted with reference to major recognised ecologies of language occurrence – 'The EU', 'The Professions', 'The Media', 'The World of Advertising', 'Popular Culture'. Each of these ecologies requires the use of a formally recognised variety of English appropriate for the particular context, with the linguistic point of reference being in the first instance native English norms. By contrast, the starting-point for our present discussion of English as a *lingua franca* in Europe is the examination at a micro-level of analysis of the language essentially as employed in the *ad hoc* ecologies of spontaneously created natural conversation, those which do not require a formally recognised appropriate variety of English and where the linguistic point of reference is not in the first instance native English norms.

Significantly in this respect, Fishman (1996), summarising the results of a number of studies examining the extent of 'Anglification' in a variety of countries world-wide – including countries within the EU – distinguishes seven relevant ecologies or 'socio-functional dimensions': elementary education, tertiary education, print media, non-print media, science/technology/commerce/industry, government services and operations (i.e. all those ecologies addressed in the works referred to above), *and* 'extensive informal usage'. With regard to the significance of 'extensive informal usage', he observes (1996: 630f.):

> A good barometer of the internalization of English, whereby it is no longer considered a foreign (let alone colonial) imposition is its entry and adoption into the informal sphere ...Unfortunately, language use in this sphere is still far less researched.

In a related context Fishman notes that 'a good deal of the spread of English in Europe is far from formalized' (1994: 69) and adds in passing that the use of English within the structures of the EU or the Council of Europe represents only 'a dot on the map' in the actual use of English in Europe. In a similar vein, Labrie and Quell (1997), in a study of potential language choice for conversation among EU nationals, refer to increasing European integration creating informal communication networks and contact situations among 'ordinary Europeans' (1997: 23).

However, as indicated in the previous comments, research into the actual occurrence of English in Europe in such 'informal' micro-contexts remains sparse. In Labrie and Quell's 1997 study, use was made of questionnaires sent out in the 'Eurobarometer' survey to some 13,000 nationals of twelve EU countries, one question in which pertained to the languages in which the respondents could carry out a conversation (excluding their mother tongue). On the basis of the responses, the authors calculated the probabilites of language use (English, French or German) in contacts of pairs of nationals from six EU countries (UK, France, Germany, Italy, Denmark, Greece) for two age groups (55+ and 15–24 years). As was to be expected, English dominated overall as the preferred *lingua franca* with the younger group, but especially with the nationality pairs Danish–Greek, Danish–Italian and Greek–Italian. Ammon (1991), using the results of a questionnaire sent to 17 academics in Eastern Europe to ascertain preferred language choice (German, Russian or English) between nationals of paired countries there, concludes that English is more strongly represented with the younger generation than with the older generation, but that German is still the overall preferred choice. The language contact situations given as the basis for language choice were 'tourists asking for directions in the street', 'informal conversation between scientists at the occasion of a conference', 'commercial or diplomatic contacts without the press being present', and 'written contact through letters'. However, in a more recent paper, Ammon (1994) himself points out that the preferred language choice might have changed since 1988 when these data were gathered.

These studies all belong to Fishman's seventh 'social-functional dimension' above, and do indeed investigate micro-contexts of informal language use and the present *ad hoc* ecologies of naturally created and occurring verbal interaction. However, by virtue of their methodologies they remain probabilistic in their findings, which are at least one step removed from the actual practice of language use, and they are of course exclusively quantitative in orientation. They serve to signal overall macro-level trends and patterns of language choice. Significantly, Labrie and Quell stress the necessity for much further empirical fieldwork in this area (1997: 23); this clearly means that qualitative analysis of the actual language used is imperative.

Returning to the trinational mini-conversation at the start of this chapter, it has already been claimed that this type and context of English in use constitute the actual locus of the position and spread of English as a *lingua franca* in Europe, an argument supported by the studies just reviewed. Furthermore, it has been suggested that linguistic analysis of a qualitative rather than a quantitative nature is required to pinpoint the nature of the language thus developing. It is also noted that such qualitative linguistic analysis will itself offer a challenge to both description and interpretation of 'English in use', given the fact that most descriptive and interpretative categories and frameworks of linguistic analysis have hitherto been premised on the existence of stable, endonormative codes, as exemplified in their standard written varieties. Finally, acceptance of the above type of micro-context as also the actual locus of widespread 'multilingualism with English' will force the serious reconsideration of a number of well-established analytical and conceptual dichotomies pertaining to 'the state of being bi/multilingual' as presently found in much bilingualism research. It is to this latter issue that the following section is devoted. The issue of linguistic analysis will be taken up in the fourth section below.

## Some Dichotomies in Bilingualism Research

### Bilingual competence and bilingual use/function/context

It is probably fair to say that in the systematic study of bilingualism from a linguistic, psycholinguistic or sociolinguistic point of view, the majority of research interest has been in the nature, development and occurrence of linguistic codes in well-defined, relatively stable macro-contexts. Inevitably, where research focuses on linguistic aspects of bilingualism the contextual dimension is secondary, and vice versa.

Within work relating to individual bilingualism, most attention has been paid to the age issue in bilingual development, the psycholinguistic/mental storage issue (including code-switching and interference), the order and sequence of bilingual acquisition, the bilingual competence issue itself and the attitude to bilingualism issue (see, e.g. Hoffmann, 1991: chap. 1). Reference to context in such work is largely limited to the macro-ecologies of the family, the educational system or immigration situations. This limited view of 'use' or 'function' has been seen as a matter of regret (Hoffmann, 1991: 23). It has also been seen as a matter of regret that much linguistic research on bilingual competence has implicitly, if not explicitly, taken native-speaker monolingual norms as a yardstick (see, e.g. Grosjean, 1985). Within work relating to societal bilingualism, considerable research has been devoted to territorial and/or national aspects of the presence of more than one language – as in studies on minority languages, language planning and policy (see, e.g. Hoffmann, 1991: chaps 10, 11). Here, too, reference to context is largely to the same macro-ecologies of family, school and immigration, often complemented by the ecologies of 'local community' and 'in-migration'.

With regard to the present concerns, it will be clear that the essence of English as a European *lingua franca* ties in poorly with these foci of research and moreover poses challenges to a number of established categorisations. For example, it is a matter for future investigation how, if at all, the effects of age influence the adoption and realisation of English as a *lingua franca* (ELF): is the greater propensity of younger speakers to adopt and realise ELF merely sociolinguistically or also psycholinguistically determined? How is ELF mentally stored? Does it involve a different type of storage from 'classic' bilingualism? Is the order in which ELF is acquired relative to the other languages of a bilingual in any way significant? What kind of bi/multingual competence defines ELF? Or may it be technically a kind of 'performance' without 'competence'? What attitudes remain to bi/multilingualism including ELF? Is ELF to be considered a minority or majority language and by which criteria? Is language policy and/or planning at all applicable to ELF? These and many other serious questions arise and need to be addressed in interpreting the significance of the new *lingua franca* within an understanding of bilingualism. What of the macro-ecologies referred to? Again, in the light of the previous discussion it is obvious that ELF does not square at all. At this point one might resort to earlier work on societal bilingualism by Fishman (1972), in which he introduces the technical concept of 'domains' as 'institutional contexts or socio-ecological co-occurrences' and 'major clusters of interaction situations that occur in particular multilingual settings' (1972: 19). At first glance, a domain may constitute the interface between the macro-ecology of 'informal usage' as proposed in Fishman (1996), and discussed in my second section above, and the micro-ecologies which are said to contextualise English as a *lingua franca* in the present argument. Hoffmann (1991: 178–9) observes that domains constitute the configuration of 'participants', 'place' and 'topic'. However, Fishman's domains and 'sociofunctional dimensions' (i.e. macro-ecologies) are proposed as analytical categories for societal bilingualism in the context of intra-societal bilingualism, whereas ecological categories relevant to 'bilingualism with ELF' must be defined in the first place with reference to individual bilingualism in the context of inter-societal bilingualism. It remains to be seen whether the modifications to the conceptualisation of domains suggested by Hoffmann (1991: 179), after Parasher (1980), in which they are bundled into 'situations' such as 'conversing with friends and acquaintances' or 'talking to people at social gatherings' (equally with reference to intra-societal bilingualism) may be transferrable to the ELF situation as interface contexts between macro- and micro-ecologies. The locus of ELF as a myriad of shifting micro-contexts may not permit these relatively stable formulations. A criterial issue in the adoption or formulation of such contextual categories is in any case that qualitative (socio)linguistic analysis must show that it is the context and form of the linguistic code, not which linguistic code, that are mutually defining. Indeed, English as a *lingua franca* in Europe represents a prime example of language in emergence, the essence of which is fundamentally defined by a close interaction of function and form (as with pidgins).

### (Bi)lingualism and (di)glossia

Traditional accounts of bilingualism and diglossia (Ferguson, 1959; Fishman, 1967) pertain to the presence of sociolinguistically high (H) and low (L) functions of lects or codes within particular societies or communities; they establish whether such H or L functions are fulfilled by, for example, different varieties of the same language (diglossia without bilingualism) or different languages (diglossia with bilingualism). However, while (bi)lingualism is premised on the existence of two or more linguistic codes, i.e. languages distinguished according to their linguistic *form or substance*, (di)glossia is premised on the existence of two or more linguistic varieties, i.e. languages distinguished according to their (socio)linguistic *function* (Fishman, 1967). And while Denison (1981) refers to a 'diglossic situation' being rapidly approached in German-speaking societies via the availability of English for a multiplicity of daily communicative needs, it is important to note that in this scenario English is just seen as an available parallel code for intra-societal use. By implication, if one shifts the focus of categorisation to individual bilingualism and individual diglossia in an inter-societal context, then English as used for a *lingua franca* (in Europe) – as code and as function – would qualify for both (multi)lingual and (poly)glossic status.

The lingualism/glossia distinction now becomes opaque. First and foremost, in macro terms, English in general can fulfil H as well as L functions in (poly)glossia. It can equally well be used for society-external, or even - internal, communication in science and technology, for instance, which is presumably an H function, as for informal communication, both society-externally and even society-internally (allowing for 'passive' communication), which is presumably an L function. Secondly, the code aspect of language realisation represented by 'lingualism' cannot necessarily have reference to a full command or full range of uses of English, contrary to the assumption that lingualism (better 'linguality'?) implies complete proficiency in the languages as used in the particular society. Thus, as with the discussion in the previous sub-section, an established form–function dichotomy in bilingual research may be seen as inappropriate for the characterisation of English as a *lingua franca* in Europe today.

### Second language (L2) and third language (L3)

Reference has already been made in the Introduction and in Chapter 1 to the position of ELF as a second language in certain European countries, and as a third language. It is an L2 also in the sense that it is, Europe-wide, the preferred first foreign language to be learned in the educational system. It is an L3 where societal or individual bilingualism exists involving languages other than English. Studies of the acquisition of English as an L3 in this sense (see for example Hufeisen & Lindemann 1997; Cenoz, Chapter 3) trace the learning and linguistic effects of bilingualism on the additional language. However, in the absence of societal or individual bilingualism, in a very special sense English as a *lingua franca* might be regarded as an L3 in a sequence:

- L1 non-English;
- L2 school/formally learned English;
- L3 non-institutional/informally acquired English, i.e. as a third variety/second code.

This situation presents partly the reverse case of contexts in which English is learned or acquired as a foreign language by speakers of an L1 dialect (not necessarily in a diglossic relation to an L1 standard) where chronologically, at least, the sequence is often:

- L1 non-English dialect;
- L1 non-English standard (= L2);
- L2 school/formally learned English (= L3), i.e., formal English is a third variety/second code (non-institutionally/informally acquired English might subsequently qualify as L4).

Interestingly, the linguistic and learning effects of the first and second lects on the third may in both scenarios be quite similar. For the latter scenario, research has established that the presence of the standard variety of the L1 inhibits positive transfer from the dialect L1 into the L2 (James & Kettemann, 1983). It is equally likely that in the former scenario, the presence of a formally learned standard variety of the L2, defined with reference to written norms, and however adequately learned, might equally inhibit positive transfer from the L1, this having presumably been acquired in all its register variations.

In the light of considerations such as these, it becomes clear that the classification of languages acquired or learned as L1, L2, L3, L4 or Lx, whether on chronological, linguistic–typological (code) or functional (variety) grounds, is only relevant to the analysis of English as a *lingua franca* to the extent that the previous (or even concurrent!) learning/acquisition of standard varieties may inhibit transfer from previously acquired informal varieties.

### Individual and societal bilingualism

Reference has been made to individual and societal bilingualism in all the above sections so far. However, English as an emerging European *lingua franca* has been largely interpreted as a component instance of individual, rather than societal bilingualism. As with other conceptualisations of 'lingualism' and 'glossia', societal bilingualism is premised on the existence of a relatively fixed, intranational set of macro-ecologies (see the discussion in my second section above), although certain commentators (e.g. Hoffmann, 1991: 173–4) also point to the changes brought about here by the effects of immigration and in-migration – if only in terms of the actual languages present in societies. Indeed, to the extent that English is present in European societies, not only within defined ecologies such as the educational system and popular culture, but also within the ecology of inter-society communication (where it is said to be becoming a second language or even one of intra-society communication, as in Switzerland), then it can be accorded a place as a component of societal bilingualism. Historically, English has moved from being a component of 'élite' bilingualism through 'cultural' bilingualism (Hoffmann, 1991: 173) to 'popular' bilingualism. Nevertheless, a move from the macro-level of analysis of the societal presence of English in European countries to a micro-analysis of its presence shows that beyond these ecologies it is the single speaker, with his or her potential for using English inter-societally with other single speakers in multifarious emerging and shifting micro-contexts, who forms the locus for the popular use and spread of English as a *lingua franca* today. In sum, ELF constitutes an aspect of both societal and individual bilingualism, its potential ubiquity in Europe forcing a serious reconsideration of the intertwining of both.

### Ascribed and achieved bilingualism

The significance in bilingualism research of the well-established distinction between 'ascribed' and 'achieved' bilingualism (Adler, 1977), reflecting the distinction between, respectively, additional languages naturally acquired and additional languages institutionally learned, dissipates in the light of the realities of English in use in the Europe of today. For example, the English of the young Austrian, Italian and Slovenian speakers exemplified at the outset of this chapter is in these terms both ascribed and achieved. The English as used in such encounters is achieved bilingualism in the sense that there is doubtless an underlay of school English as an exonormative factor controlling the actual language used. School or 'learned' English provides a basic reference point for sentence construction, vocabulary and pronunciation. However, the situational/contextual demands favour an ascribed English bilingualism, which is created and recreated endonormatively according to how the pragmatic and social conditions of the site of use occur and change. This ascribed bilingualism is a product of the successful linguistic solving of a 'need for communication' situation. Ascribed bilingualism in English also manifests itself in the ability – however 'incomplete' in exonormative terms – to organise and realise the language in its pragmatic and discoursal aspects. In other words, the realities of English as a naturally occurring *lingua franca* in Europe show abilities ('competencies'?) in language which are associated both with the ascribed types of linguistic skill supposed to exist in the natural bilingual and with the achieved types of the school bilingual.

## Basic Interpersonal Communication Skills (BICS) and Cognitive Academic Language Proficiency (CALP)

In the light of the discussion in the previous sub-section one might immediately equate BICS with what has been said on ascribed bilingualism and CALP with achieved bilingualism. However, while on initial observation the relevance of BICS and CALP to a characterisation of the competencies underlying the use of English as a *lingua franca* would seem to be obvious (i.e. both are present), it must be remembered that in the original conceptualisation of BICS and CALP (Cummins, 1981, 1984), these skill categories are embedded in a model which claims that it is their *interaction* that determines the success of bilingual achievement in a school immersion environment (for a clear statement, see Cummins, Chapter 4). The model, the 'developmental interdependence hypothesis', is premised on the existence of societal bilingualism, for example English and French in Canada, as this influences the individual's linguistic and cognitive make-up. It has been suggested above, however, that English as a *lingua franca* in Europe qualifies as societal bilingualism of a particular, restricted kind, and that its basic site is within individual bilingualism. Furthermore, the level of achievement or proficiency in this ELF is not so much a product of the influence of another language in a fixed societal ecology, but rather of the individual's bi/multilingual competency (BICS plus CALP plus other skills) as applied to English.

## Some Linguistic Aspects of English as a *Lingua Franca*

In the previous section it has been suggested how the essence of English as a *lingua franca* in Europe today poses serious challenges to established dichotomous conceptualisations of different aspects of 'the state of being bilingual'. This section will now offer some linguistic reflections of a typological and qualitative nature on the kind of emerging English discussed so far.

### A variety: dialect or register?

A very illuminating starting-point for a typological discussion of this language variety is the traditional distinction between dialect and register as explicitly formulated by Halliday (1978). *Dialect* is defined as 'a variety according to the user', *register* as 'a variety according to the use'. A dialect is 'what you speak (habitually), determined by who you are', whereas a register is 'what you are speaking (at the time), determined by what you are doing'. In principle, dialects are 'different ways of saying the same thing and tend to differ in phonetics, phonology, lexicogrammar (but not in semantics)', whereas registers are 'ways of saying different things and tend to differ in semantics (and hence in lexicogrammar, and sometimes phonology as a realization of this)' (1978: 35). Already, in terms of this typology, it should be becoming clear that the kind of English as a *lingua franca* under discussion has the characteristics of a register, rather than a dialect. This is confirmed by Halliday's further observations, for example that the 'extreme cases' of registers are constituted by 'restricted languages' and 'languages for special purposes' (those of dialects by 'antilanguages, mother-in-law languages'!); that register is characterised by 'major distinctions of spoken/written, language in action/language in reflection', and, above all, that the 'principal controlling variables' for register are *field* (type of social interaction), *tenor* (role relationships) and *mode* (symbolic organisation). By these criteria, then, English as an emerging *lingua franca* may be termed a register.

Summarising, it is certainly a form of language which:

- is characterised as that which the user is speaking at the time (not habitually);
- is determined by the nature of the social activity;
- is semantically flexible and diverse;
- has a restricted (special purpose) function;
- will show typical features of spoken (as opposed to written) varieties and 'language in action' (as opposed to 'language [in] reflection'); and
- will be controlled by the on-line variables of field, tenor and mode.

Concerning these variables, Halliday goes on to give examples of which particular lexicogrammatical patterns they typically control: field, for example controls transitivity and choice of basic vocabulary, as belonging to the *ideational* component of the semantic system; tenor controls mood and modality (plus intonation), as belonging to the *interpersonal* component; while mode controls cohesion, including ellipsis, and deixis, as belonging to the *textual* component (1978: 64). If we return to the original mini-conversation as an instance of register, (subject) 'drink alcohol' constitutes the common transitivity pattern and 'drink' and 'alcohol' individually constitute basic lexical choices, i.e. manifest field/the ideational component; 'wanna' constitutes one form of modality, i.e. manifests tenor/the interpersonal component; and 'me too' and 'I also not' constitute ellipsis (a form of cohesion), i.e. manifest mode/the textual component.

Of course, any naturally occurring instance of *any* register may be linguistically analysed in these terms and with these categories and shown in the choice of structures used to be co-determined by the social context. However, regarding this *particular* variety of English as a register permits a consistent linguistic analysis which particularly captures the essence of this particularly *ad hoc* and emergent form of everyday communication. Importantly, it allows a view of this variety which emphatically does not consider it as a kind of aberrant or defective (dia)lect of English. While it might be claimed that the linguistic substance of this variety may be derived from a dialect of English (standard English?), the *choice* of substance used is directly determined by the social situation of its use and not by the social situation of its users.

Directly relevant to the present interpretation are also Widdowson's (1997) reflections on the spread of English as a *lingua franca* world-wide. Adopting, as here, the general distinction between register and dialect in Halliday's formulation, he argues that English spreads as a 'virtual' language, which is in the process variously 'actualised' (1997: 139–40). This actualisation may take the form of dialects (i.e. regional forms of English) or of registers, where it is the special-purpose registers that hold English as an international language 'in place' and serve to maintain its global intelligibility. Indeed, Widdowson concludes that 'English as an international language is English for special purposes' (1997: 144). Although with 'English for special purposes' he primarily has in mind the quasi-institutionalised registers of medical, scientific and technological communication, his arguments equally apply to the types of register under discussion in this chapter. These *ad hoc* registers for informal international communication will equally regulate themselves in the interests of intelligibility and as actualisations of the virtual language thus serve as a brake on excessive diversity in the linguistic code. In summary, then, the interpretation of English as a *lingua franca* in Europe as a register (of the virtual language) would seem to provide the appropriate framework for a linguistic analysis and understanding of this emergent variety.

### Further linguistic aspects

Reference has already been made in the previous sub-section to certain linguistic features of this form of English, arguing that in Halliday's terms, this type of register shows characteristic lexicogrammatical choices relating to the local 'controlling variables' of field, tenor and mode, which in turn relate respectively to the ideational, interpersonal, and textual components of the semantic system. Indeed, syntactically one would generally expect a predominance of locative/circumstantial types of transitivity in the verb system (on the ideational level), of modality markers (on the interpersonal level), and of ellipsis and local deixis (on the textual level).The choice of main lexical items will reflect largely reference to the here and now (ideational); intonational choices will be mainly in terms of tonal rise vs. fall (interpersonal).

Over and above this, are there other elements in the code which might serve to characterise this type of language use? In the most general terms, one would expect degrees of syntactic regularisation not found in the standard written lect, as in the case of negation/negative orientation in the data above – 'me too', 'I also not'. Other cases might include a conflation of simple past and present perfect tense forms (with a possible use of adverbs as tense-markers), a conflation of continuous and non-continuous verb forms, a relative absence of prepositional and phrasal verbs, and an absence of morphological marking of adverbs. Further features might include the absence of clause subordination and, in general, a predominance of parataxis over hypotaxis. If these expectations are borne out, and of course much empirical research is required in any case, then ELF would seem to show a general reduction in structural redundancy relative to standard written English. However, it does not show significant structural 'reduction' relative to other forms of naturally occurring informal *spoken* English, as a glance at any analysis of the latter will confirm (for spoken British English, see, e.g., Carter & McCarthy 1997) – not surprisingly, since English as a *lingua franca* constitutes itself one of these forms. Nevertheless, one area stands out in which ELF might generally differ from 'native' forms of spoken English, namely the relative absence of figurative or idiomatic use (of which the surmised absence of prepositional and phrasal verbs is an indication). Indeed, one may conclude that ELF relies particularly heavily on the negotiated, local, here-and-now semantic reference of its linguistic structures for successful communication.

## Summary and Prospect

The main argument of this chapter has been that the true site of the spread of English as a *lingua franca* in Europe is the micro-context of naturally arising informal oral conversations between speakers who in their daily lives otherwise use a language or languages other than English. It has been suggested that a consideration of the realities of this *lingua franca* forces a reassessment of our understanding of what it is to be bilingual, and opens up new avenues of exploration for linguistic interpretation.

However, while data are abundant, analysis has so far been minimal, and it is imperative that this situation is soon corrected.

As a first step in this direction, the pilot phase of a project ('English as a lingua franca in the Alpine-Adriatic region') has now started to gather and analyse evidence of ELF in the form and use as discussed in this chapter and exemplified by the mini-conversation given at the outset. While this is not the appropriate place for an extensive description of the project (James, 1998), a few relevant background details may be given nonetheless: The geographical focus of the study is on the area described at the start of the chapter, specifically the province of Carinthia (southern Austria), the region of Friuli–Venezia Giulia (north-eastern Italy) and the districts of western Slovenia. Historically four languages are present in the region, contributing to various patterns of indigenous societal and individual bilingualism. To these may be added, as a fifth language, English, which with the gradual intensification of cross-border contacts of all kinds is both available and increasingly used as a general *lingua franca*. The linguistic focus of the pilot project is on the micro-level of English use as understood in this chapter, with the aim of ultimately producing a corpus of Alpine-Adriatic English. It will be obvious that this locus in two senses promises a particularly fertile ground for exploration of the issues addressed in this chapter.

## References

Adler, M. (1977) *Collective and Individual Bilingualism: A Sociolinguistic Study*. Hamburg: Helmut Buske.

Ammon, U. (1991) *Die internationale Stellung der deutschen Sprache*. Berlin/New York: Mouton de Gruyter.

Ammon, U. (1994) The present dominance of English in Europe. With an outlook on possible solutions to the European language problem. *Sociolinguistica* 8, 1–14.

Ammon, U. (1996) The European Union (EU – formerly European Community): Status change of English during the last fifty years. In J.A. Fishman, A.W. Conrad and A. Rubal-Lopez (eds) *Post-imperial English. Status Change in Former British and American Colonies, 1940–1990* (pp. 241–67). Berlin/New York: Mouton de Gruyter.

Barron, N.S. (1998) Letters by phone or speech by other means: The linguistics of email. *Language and Communication* 18, 133–70.

Carter, R. and McCarthy, M. (1997) *Exploring Spoken English*. Cambridge: Cambridge University Press.

Cheshire, J. and Moser, L.-M. (1994) English as a cultural system: The case of advertisements in French-speaking Switzerland. *Journal of Multilingual and Multicultural Development* 15, 451–67.

Cook, G. (1992) *The Discourse of Advertising*. London: Routledge.

Cummins, J. (1981) *Bilingualism and Minority Language Children*. Toronto: OISE Press.

Cummins, J. (1984) Bilingualism and cognitive functioning. In S. Shapston and D. Oyley (eds) *Bilingual and Multicultural Education: Canadian Perspectives* (pp. 55–67). Clevedon: Multilingual Matters.
Denison, N. (1981) English in Europe, with particular reference to the German-speaking areas. In W. Pöckl (ed.) *Europäische Mehrsprachigkeit. Festschrift zum 70. Geburtstag von Mario Wandruszka* (pp. 5–18). Tübingen: Niemeyer.
Dollerup, C. (1996) English in the European Union. In R. Hartmann (ed.) *The English Language in Europe* (pp. 24–36). Oxford: Intellect.
Durmüller, U. (1992) The changing status of English in Switzerland. In U. Ammon and M. Hellinger (eds) *Status Change in Languages* (pp. 355–70). Berlin/New York: Mouton de Gruyter.
Ferguson, C. (1959) Diglossia. *Word* 15, 325–40.
Fishman, J.A. (1967) Bilingualism with and without diglossia: Diglossia with and without bilingualism. *Journal of Social Issues* 23, 29–37.
Fishman, J.A. (1972) The relationship between micro- and macro-sociolinguistics in the study of who speaks what language to whom and when. In J.B. Pride and J. Holmes (eds) *Sociolinguistics* (pp. 15–32). Harmondsworth: Penguin.
Fishman, J.A. (1994) 'English Only' in Europe? Some suggestions from an American perspective. *Sociolinguistica* 8, 65–72.
Fishman, J.A. (1996) Summary and interpretation: Post-imperial English 1940–1990. In: J.A. Fishman, A.W. Conrad and A. Rubal-Lopez (eds) *Post-Imperial English. Status Change in Former British and American Colonies, 1940–1990* (pp. 623–41). Berlin/New York: Mouton de Gruyter.
Gellert-Novak, A. (1994) Die Rolle der englischen Sprache in Euroregionen. *Sociolinguistica* 8, 123–35.
Goodman, S. and Graddol, D. (1996) *Redesigning English. New Texts, New Identities.* London/New York: Routledge and Open University.
Graddol, D. (1997) *The Future of English?* London: British Council.
Grosjean, F. (1985) The bilingual as a competent but specific speaker–hearer. *Journal of Multilingual and Multicultural Development* 6, 467–77.
Halliday, M.A.K. (1978) *Language as Social Semiotic.* London: Edward Arnold.
Hoffmann, C. (1991) *An Introduction to Bilingualism.* London: Longman.
Hoffmann, C. (1996) Societal and individual bilingualism with English in Europe. In R. Hartmann (ed.) *The English Language in Europe* (pp. 51–60). Oxford: Intellect.
Hufeisen, B. and Lindemann, B. (eds) (1997) *Tertiärsprachen. Theorien, Methoden, Modelle.* Tübingen: Stauffenburg.
James, A.R. and Kettemann, B. (eds) (1983) *Dialektphonologie und Fremdsprachenerwerb* [*Dialect Phonology and Foreign Language Acquisition*]. Tübingen: Gunter Narr.
James, A.R. (1998) Englisch als *Lingua franca* im Alpen-Adria-Raum. In P.V. Zima (ed.) *Dynamik interkultureller Prozesse am Beispiel der Alpen-Adria-Region* (Interdisziplinäres SFB-Projekt der Universität Klagenfurt). University of Klagenfurt (mimeo).
Labrie, N. and Quell, C. (1997) Your language, my language or English? The potential language choice in communication among nationals of the European Union. *World Englishes* 16, 3–26.
McArthur, T. (1998) *The English Languages.* Cambridge: Cambridge University Press.

Parasher, S.N. (1980) Mother-tongue English diglossia: A case study of educated Indian bilinguals' language use. *Anthropological Linguistics* 22, 151–68.
Widdowson, H.G. (1997) EIL, ESL, EFL: Global and local interests. *World Englishes* 16, 135–46.

## Chapter 3
# Research on Multilingual Acquisition

JASONE CENOZ

As we have already seen in the Introduction to this volume, multilingual acquisition is a very common phenomenon. The aim of this chapter is to examine the differences between second language acquisition and multilingual acquisition and to review the research agenda in the field of multilingual acquisition.

Even though in a wide sense 'second language acquisition' is a variety of multilingual acquisition, we define the latter as 'the process of acquiring more than two languages'. It thus comprises the consecutive and simultaneous acquisition of three or more languages. As a process it is to be distinguished from its final product, multilingualism (see Table 3.1).

**Table 3.1** Multilingual acquisition and multilingualism

| Process | Product |
|---|---|
| Multilingual acquisition → | Multilingualism |
| Third language acquisition → | Trilingualism |
| Fourth language acquisition → | Quadrilingualism |

Multilingual acquisition is linked to multilingualism because to acquire a third or additional language is to acquire some type of multilingual competence and therefore some type of multilingualism (see Jessner & Herdina, Chapter 5).

## The Study of Multilingual Acquisition

Multilingualism and multilingual acquisition are often considered as simply variations on bilingualism and second language acquisition; as Sharwood Smith (1994:7) says:

> second language acquisition (SLA) will normally stand as a cover term to refer to any language other than the first language learned by a given learner or group of learners, (a) irrespective of the type of learning

environment and (b) irrespective of the number of other non-native languages known by the learner.

Second language acquisition has a lot in common with multilingual acquisition, but there are some differences regarding complexity and diversity. Multilingual acquisition presents more diversity than second language acquisition and its study presents greater complexity.

Second language acquisition can refer to the process of acquiring a second language after the first language has been acquired, but it can also refer to the acquisition of a second language *while* the first is being acquired ('early second language acquisition'). When two languages are involved in the acquisition process we only have two possible acquisition orders: the second language can be acquired either after the L1 (L1→L2), or at the same time as the L1 (Lx + Ly) (see Table 3.2).

**Table 3.2** Second language acquisition vs. multilingual acquisition

| Second language acquisition | Multilingual acquisition |
|---|---|
| 1  L1→L2<br>2  Lx + Ly | 1  L1→L2→L3<br>2  L1→Lx/Ly<br>3  Lx/Ly→L3<br>4  Lx/Ly/Lz<br>5  L1→L2→L3→L4<br>6  L1→Lx/Ly→L4<br>7  L1→L2→Lx/Ly<br>8  L1→Lx/Ly/Lz<br>9  Lx/Ly→L3→L4<br>10  Lx/Ly→Lz/Lz$_1$<br>11  Lx/Ly/Lz→L4<br>12  Lx/Ly/Lz/Lz$_1$ |

In the case of third language acquisition there is greater diversity and, as Table 3.2 shows, there are at least four possible acquisition orders. The three languages can be acquired consecutively (L1→L2→L3). Other possibilities include the simultaneous acquisition of two languages (Lx/Ly) that could take place after the L1 has been acquired (L1→Lx/Ly) or before the L3 is acquired (Lx/Ly→L3). Another possibility involves simultaneous contact with three languages (Lx/Ly/Lz). The formulae 5 to 12 in Table 3.2 can give us an idea of the way the diversity of the possible acquisition orders can increase when the acquisition of four languages is considered. These formulae reflect the different situations of second and multilingual acquisition (that is, third and fourth language acquisition) taking into account the simultaneous or consecutive acquisition of the different languages. The number of languages involved in multilingual acquisition multiplies their possible acquisition orders and this diversity complicates the study of the relationships among the languages involved in multilingual acquisition. This diversity is increased if we consider that the acquisition process can be interrupted by the process of acquiring an additional language and then restarted again (L1→L2→L3→L2).

Second language acquisition is usually regarded as a complex process (Larsen-Freeman & Long, 1991; Ellis, 1994) because of the large number of factors associated with it. The acquisition of additional languages increases this complexity, as noted by Cenoz and Genesee (1998: 16):

> Multilingual acquisition and multilingualism are complex phenomena. They implicate all the factors and processes associated with second language acquisition and bilingualism as well as unique and potentially more complex factors and effects associated with the interactions that are possible among the multiple languages being learned and the processes of learning them.

Second language acquisition can take place formally (through instruction), naturally (outside school) or by a combination of instruction and natural acquisition. In multilingual acquisition the *context* of acquisition is likely to present more complex patterns, because of the number of language acquisition situations involved. For example, when Welsh learners with English as their first language learn Welsh as a second language and French as a third language they can learn their second language through formal instruction, or they can combine formal instruction with natural acquisition in a Welsh-medium school or in a Welsh-speaking enviroment; but they are more likely to learn French, the foreign language, formally through instruction. In this specific case of multilingual acquisition the second language is acquired by a combination of instruction and natural interaction and the third language is acquired through instruction. This situation is quite different from that prevailing in for example Luxembourg, where Luxembourgish is the L1 for most speakers, but the L2 (German) and the L3 (French) are also used in some domains at the community level, and all three languages are used as languages of instruction (Hoffmann, 1998).

The languages involved in multilingual acquisition can also present important variation regarding *linguistic typology*. The L2 can be typologically related to the L3, as in Finland's immersion programmes in Swedish with English as a third language (see Björklund & Suni, Chapter 11), or as in the case of native speakers of Asian and African languages who acquire a second and a third Indo-European language (Ahukanna *et al.*, 1981; Singh & Carroll, 1979). Alternatively there can be more typological similarity between the L1 and the L3, as in the Basque Country's Basque immersion programmes for Spanish L1 learners with English as a third language (see Lasagabaster, Chapter 10).

Other variables such as the sociocultural status of the languages or their ethnolinguistic vitality (Bourhis *et al.*, 1981) also present greater diversity when more than two languages are involved. For example, when multilingual acquisition is studied in Canadian double immersion programmes in Quebec (see Genesee, 1998), where learners with English as their first language have French and Hebrew as languages of instruction, a factor that must be taken into account is the relative ethnolinguistic vitality of English as compared to French and Hebrew. This situation differs from that of some minority L1 children in Ontario who are bilingual in Italian and English and learn French as a third language (Bild & Swain, 1989).

Apart from the great diversity of situations and factors that can potentially influence multilingual acquisition, the study of multilingual acquisition also considers the cognitive and linguistic processes involved in the consecutive or simultaneous acquisition of more than two languages. The processes used in third language acquisition may be very similar to those used by L2 learners but, as Clyne (1997: 113) points out, 'the additional language complicates the operations of the processes'. The diversity and complexity of multilingual acquisition give rise to situations which are unique in language acquisition and which justify the need to conduct research in order to identify the characteristics of multilingual acquisition and the specific operations that affect this process.

In the following sections we try to identify the main research areas in multilingual acquisition and we describe the findings of research studies in these areas. Specifically we try to answer the following questions: How do children acquire more than two languages simultaneously? Does bilingualism influence third language acquisition? How do individual factors affect multilingual development? How does proficiency in L1 and L2 affect the acquisition of a third language? How is cross-linguistic influence reflected in third language acquisition?

## Early Multilingualism

Even though early trilingual (or even quadrilingual) acquisition is not a common phenomenon, the mobility of the population and the important increase of intra-European and international communications make early trilingualism less exceptional nowadays, both here and elsewhere. 'Early trilingualism' refers to situations in which the child is exposed to three languages from birth. It corresponds to the formula Lx + Ly + Lz and includes different situations. For example, two languages can be used at home, following the principle 'one parent/one language', and a different one at the community level, as in the study conducted by Hoffmann (1985) which looks at early multilingualism in a situation in which German and Spanish are spoken at home and English in the community. Similar situations involving different languages are described in Harding and Riley (1986) and Arnbert (1987).

In other situations there may be two languages at the community level; one of them is used at home by one of the parents, while the other speaks a language not used in the community. This is the case of some children in Ireland, whose parents speak Irish and French at home, but who are exposed to English and Irish at the community level (Helot, 1988). Early multilingualism can also take place when both parents speak the same language to the child but they live in a community where two additional languages are spoken, as could be the case for Moroccan children living in Barcelona (Spain) who speak Berber at home but who are exposed to Catalan and Spanish at the community level. In another situation a child may be exposed to three languages at home, where there are two or three adults using three different languages (see Baker & Jones, 1998: 45).

The examples given here cannot possibly include all the situations, but they help us to see different contexts in which early multilingualism can be developed. They also illustrate the diversity of the situations regarding the sociocultural status of the language and their presence at the community level. The variety of situations is still larger if we take into account other factors such as the complete fulfilment of the principle 'one person/one language', parents' proficiency in the language used to communicate with their children, their attitudes towards the different languages or the use of the languages in different contexts.

The fact that early trilingualism involves situations which are quite specific can explain the scarcity of research studies in this area by comparison with those on early bilingualism (De Houwer, 1995). The most important study on early trilingual acquisition is that conducted by Hoffmann (1985) on the acquisition of German, Spanish and English by two children. Her findings indicate that competence in the community language (English) increases as the children grow older, and also that the children are able to communicate fluently in all three languages, although with some stylistic problems in Spanish and German and some accuracy problems in German. Hoffmann (1985) and Mikes (1990) also describe cross-linguistic influence among three languages.

More research in early multilingualism is needed in order to analyse early trilingual development in different environments and to be able to identify the general characteristics of early multilingualism. Studies including typologically related and unrelated languages and differences in input (one person/one language vs. other possibilities) are necessary in order to identify the phonological, lexical, morphosyntactic, pragmatic and discourse characteristics of early multilingualism. An area of research that needs specific attention in multilingual acquisition is code-switching and cross-linguistic influence. More information on early multilingualism will help us to identify the differences between early bilingualism and early multilingualism and also to clarify controversial issues in bilingual acquisition such as separation of or interdependence among the different linguistic systems.

## The Influence of Bilingualism on Multilingual Acquisition

The situation in which bilinguals learn a third language is more common than early multilingualism. It is very common in bilingual communities with autochthonous languages, such as Friesland, the Basque Country, Wales, Catalonia or Brittany, where English is taught as a third language in bilingual programmes (see Muñoz, Ytsma, Lasagabaster, Chapters 9, 10 and 12). It also takes place when minority-language children attend immersion programmes as in the case of immigrant-speaking children living in Canada who learn French as a third language in immersion programmes (Bild & Swain, 1989; Swain et al., 1990). Third language acquisition can also take place when minority-language children attend regular programmes where a foreign language is included in the curriculum. This situation, which is very common all over the world, applies for example to Turkish children in the Netherlands or Germany who have Turkish as their first language, Dutch or German as a second language and English as a third language (Sanders & Meijers, 1995).

Most studies on bilingualism have shown that it presents positive cognitive effects (Baker, 1996) and that these effects are compatible with the possible beneficial effects of bilingualism on third language acquisition. In fact, most studies in which the proficiency of bilinguals and monolinguals in a third language has been compared prove that bilingualism favours the acquisition of third languages (see Bild & Swain, 1989; Cenoz & Valencia, 1994; Thomas, 1988; Lasagabaster, 1997). For example, research on the acquisition of French as a third language in Canadian immersion programmes has reported that bilingual children obtained higher scores than their monolingual counterparts in tests of French (see Bild & Swain, 1989; Hurd, 1993). Similar results where obtained by Thomas (1988), who compared the scores in French of English–Spanish bilinguals with those of English-speaking monolinguals. Cenoz and Valencia (1994) and Lasagabaster (1997) also proved that Basque–Spanish bilinguals obtained higher scores in English than Spanish monolinguals. The positive effects of bilingualism on third language acquisition are compatible, too, with the results of double immersion programmes (see Genesee, 1998).

However, not all research studies report positive effects for bilingualism on third language acquisition. Some studies comparing the degree of proficiency achieved in the third language acquisition by bilingual immigrant students and majority-language students have reported no differences. For example, in a study conducted in Sweden, Balke-Aurell and Linblad (1983) found no differences between bilinguals and monolinguals learning English as a foreign language. Jaspaert and Lemmens (1990) reported no significant differences between second and third language acquisition when they compared Italian immigrants learning Dutch as a third language in the trilingual Foyer project with native speakers of French learning Dutch as a second language. Similarly, Sanders and Meijers (1995) did not find any differences in English as a third language when they compared monolingual Dutch speakers and bilingual immigrant students who had Turkish or Moroccan Arabic as their first language.

Studies on specific areas of language proficiency tend to confirm the advantages of bilinguals over monolinguals. For example, studies on perceptual discrimination (Cohen et al., 1967; Davine et al., 1971; Enomoto, 1994) and listening comprehension in a third language (Edwards et al., 1977, Wightman, 1981) report advantages for bilinguals. Studies on the acquisition of grammar also associate previous language experience with advantages in multilingual acquisition. Klein (1995) found differences between monolingual and multilingual subjects in lexical and syntactic learning measured by means of grammaticality judgement and correction tasks. Even though Zobl (1993) found no significant differences between monolingual and multilingual subjects in the performance of a grammaticality judgement task, he noted that the multilingual subjects' responses suggested that they had formulated 'wider grammars' – arguably because they knew more languages. Both Klein (1995) and Zobl (1993) argued that these findings are compatible with the hypothesis that multilinguals are advantaged in learning additional languages.

In sum, studies on the effect of bilingualism on third language acquisition conducted in different contexts tend to associate bilingualism with advantages in third language acquisition. The findings of these studies on third language acquisition share some characteristics with the results of other studies on the effects of bilingualism, because those studies in which bilinguals present *no* advantages involve subtractive contexts (Lambert, 1974). However, the comparability of the results of these studies is severely limited by the diversity of the specific areas of language proficiency tested and by their differing research methodologies. Furthermore, given the diversity and complexity of third language acquisition these findings need to be confirmed by more studies involving a wider variety of acquisition contexts.

## Bilingual Competence and Multilingual Acquisition

According to the 'interdependence hypothesis' there is a positive and significant relationship between students' first language development, especially their development of literacy skills, and their second language development (Cummins, 1981). A similar relationship might be expected to hold good in the case of multilingual acquisition, so that different degrees of proficiency in the first and second languages would affect the acquisition of the third (or fourth) language. Specific research questions derived from the interdependence hypotheses could be the following: Does proficiency in L1 and L2 affect the acquisition of L3? Which are the specific conditions required for positive interdependence to take place? Is proficiency in other languages influential at all stages of second language acquisition? Do different areas of proficiency in L1 and L2 exert a specific effect on different areas of proficiency in the third language? Does acquiring an L3 or L4 affect competence in L1 or L2?

The studies on the effect of bilingualism on third language acquisition just described in the previous section provide evidence of the relationship of proficiency in the three languages, and the studies on linguistic interdependence presented in this volume also confirm this relationship (Muñoz, Lasagabaster, Chapters 9 and 10).

Some researchers have tried to identify the specific conditions needed for linguistic interdependence to take place. Research conducted with learners with a minority language as their first language tend to identify formal training in the minority language and literacy skills with advantages in third language acquisition. For example, Thomas (1988), in a study conducted in the US, found that those bilinguals who had received formal training in Spanish obtained higher scores on a grammar test in French as a third language than bilinguals who had had exposure to Spanish in natural settings. Swain *et al.* (1990) also found that bilingual students who were literate in their first and second languages were more proficient in the third language than those who were literate only in their second language. Nevertheless, the specific conditions for positive transfer to take place are still controversial and some researchers have reported opposite results to those of Thomas (1988) and Swain *et al.* (1990). For example, Wagner *et al.* (1989), in a study conducted in Morocco, found that instruction in a second language without literacy in the first does not hinder the acquisition of a third language. On the other hand, Balke-Aurell and Linblad (1983) reported that only a passive knowledge of the first language was positively associated with third language acquisition.

Evidence on the effects of multilingual acquisition on first and second language development is also very limited. Cenoz (1997) reports the results of a longitudinal study on the effects of the early introduction of a third language on proficiency in L1 and L2. The results indicate that after three years of instruction in English, children presented the same scores on the Basque and Spanish tests as children in the control group who had had no instruction in English. When focusing on a more specific aspect of language proficiency, however, Kecskés and Papp (Chapter 6, this volume) found that third language acquisition did have a positive effect on average metaphorical density.

In sum, even though research studies seem to confirm interdependence among the different languages involved in multilingual acquisition, more of them are needed in this area if we are to be able to specify the nature of the relationship between the languages and the way this might affect multilingual acquisition at different stages. More studies on multidirectional interdependence among the languages involved in multilingual acquisition and on specific areas of language proficiency (phonetics, lexis, grammar, pragmatics, discourse) will provide insights into the characteristics of multilingual acquisition.

## Individual and Contextual Factors in Multilingual Acquisition

Multilingual acquisition, a complex process influenced by a large number of individual and contextual factors, is potentially influenced by the same factors as affect second language acquisition, but also by those that have been identified as outcomes of bilingualism (see Table 3.3).

**Table 3.3** Factors affecting SLA and outcomes of bilingualism

| Second language acquisition | Individual | • IQ and aptitude<br>• Cognitive style<br>• Strategies<br>• Attitudes and motivation<br>• Personality<br>• Age |
|---|---|---|
| | Contextual | • Natural vs. formal settings<br>• Ethnolinguistic vitality<br>• Socioeconomic status<br>• Educational context |
| Bilingualism | | • Creativity<br>• Metalinguistic awareness<br>• Communicative sensitivity |

When comparing second language acquisition to multilingual acquisition we could hypothesise that these factors affect multilingual learners differently because they can benefit from their experience as language learners and therefore present specific abilities when learning another language. Regarding cognitive factors, we could consider whether multilingual learners are more intelligent or present a higher level of language aptitude, and also whether they have a specific cognitive style or different strategies for processing information. We might also analyse whether multilingual learners have better attitudes or are more motivated than learners acquiring a second language, or whether specific personality traits are associated with multilingualism. Another factor to be considered is the relationship between multilingual acquisition and age (see Muñoz, Chapter 9). Among contextual factors, we could investigate the effect of natural vs. formal contexts, of having a majority vs a minority language as L1, of socioeconomic status and of the education background on multilingual acquisition, as compared to the effect of such factors on second language acquisition. If we took into consideration the effects of bilingualism we could examine whether multilingual learners are more creative or present a more highly developed metalinguistic awareness and communicative sensitivity.

The number of studies on the effect of individual and contextual factors on multilingual acquisition is very limited. According to a single case study, an exceptionally talented multilingual speaker presented exceptional verbal memory and coding ability, but his IQ, musical and visual–spatial abilities were average (Obler, 1989). On the other hand, in a number of studies multilingual learners have been reported to use a wider variety of processing strategies than monolinguals. In a series of comparisons between monolinguals and multilinguals learning artificial linguistic systems, Nation and McLaughlin (1986), McLaughlin and Nayak (1989) and Nayak et al. (1990) all found that the multilingual subjects demonstrated greater flexibility in switching strategies according to the demand characteristics of the task – for example, they preferred mnemonic strategies for a memory task and linguistic strategies for a rule-discovery task; they were more likely to modify strategies that were not effective in language learning; and they were more effective at using implicit learning strategies (see also Hurd, 1993). Their superiority in these domains was attributed to their experience as language learners.

Bilingual subjects learning a third language have also been reported to present a more highly developed metalinguistic awareness than monolinguals, but similar levels of creativity (Lasagabaster, 1997). There are not many studies on the effect of motivation in multilingual acquisition, but bilinguals have also been reported to be more motivated than monolinguals when learning an additional language (see Gulutsan, 1976).

In sum, even though the number of studies on the role of individual and contextual factors in multilingual acquisition is still very limited, results indicate that multilingual learners may benefit from being more experienced language learners.

## Cross-linguistic Influence in Multilingual Acquisition

Another area of research in multilingual acquisition is the study of cross-linguistic influence, achieved by analysing the effect of L1, L2 (L3 or L4) on the acquisition of an additional language. Research in this area investigates the influence of linguistic distance on cross-linguistic influence and the specific role of the first language in cross-linguistic influence. Other areas of investigation could include the study of cross-linguistic influence at different stages of multilingual acquisition, or in formal and natural settings, or at different linguistic levels such as phonetics, lexis, grammar or discourse.

Although research in the area of cross-linguistic transfer in multilingual acquisition is still preliminary, some trends have been observed.

Cross-linguistic influence can be affected by the linguistic distance between the languages involved (Bild & Swain, 1989). There is evidence for cross-linguistic transfer in multilingual acquisition when the languages involved are similar with respect to phonetic structure, vocabulary and syntax (Möhle, 1989; Singleton, 1987; Cenoz, 1998). For example, learners of French and English who have a non-Indo-European language as their first language tend to transfer vocabulary and structures from other Indo-European languages they know rather than from their first language (Ahukanna *et al.*, 1981; Bartelt, 1989; Ringbom, 1987; Singh & Carroll, 1979).

Even though it has also been suggested that transfer is more likely from the first language than from those learned later on (Ringbom, 1987), such effects seem to be less potent than typological similarity between the languages. Most research studies on cross-linguistic acquisition have been conducted in school contexts, but there is evidence that similar patterns of cross-linguistic influence take place in natural acquisition (Hammarberg & Williams, 1993). Research on cross-linguistic influence in third language acquisition indicates that linguistic typology is an important factor, one that determines the choice of a specific language as the source language of influence. It also indicates that bi/multilingual learners could use one of the languages they know as the base language when acquiring an additional language (Clyne, 1997).

## Conclusion

Research on multilingual acquisition presents interesting findings regarding the relationship between bilingualism and third language acquisition, linguistic interdependence and cross-linguistic influence. Nevertheless, the limited number of studies in each of the areas discussed in this chapter, and the different aims of these studies and their different methodological approaches are not enough to identify the specific characteristics of third language acquisition. Research into second language acquisition and bilingualism can certainly benefit multilingual acquisition, which shares some characteristics with these phenomena. On the other hand, a thorough understanding of the diversity and complexity of multilingual acquisition itself is certain to provide insights that are relevant not just to the study of second language acquisition and of bilingualism, but to all researchers interested in language processing.

### References

Ahukanna, J.G.W., Lund, N.J. and Gentile, J.R. (1981) Inter- and intra-lingual interference effects in learning a third language. *Modern Language Journal* 65, 281–7.

Arnbert, L. (1987) *Raising Children Bilingually: The Pre-school Years*. Clevedon: Multi-

lingual Matters.
Baker, C. (1996) *Foundations of Bilingual Education and Bilingualism.* Clevedon: Multilingual Matters.
Baker, C. and Jones, S.P. (1998) *Encyclopedia of Bilingualism and Bilingual Education.* Clevedon: Multilingual Matters.
Balke-Aurell, G. and Linblad, T. (1983) *Immigrant Children and their Languages.* Molndal, Sweden: Department of Education Research, University of Gothenburg.
Bartelt, G. (1989) The interaction of multilingual constraints. In H.W. Dechert and M. Raupach (eds) *Interlingual Processes* (pp. 151–77). Tübingen: Gunter Narr.
Bild, E.R. and Swain, M. (1989) Minority language students in a French immersion programme: Their French proficiency. *Journal of Multilingual and Multicultural Development* 10, 255–74.
Bourhis, R.Y., Giles, H. and Rosenthal, D. (1981) Notes on the construction of a subjective vitality questionnaire for ethnolinguistic groups. *Journal of Multilingual and Multicultural Development* 2: 145–55.
Cenoz, J. (1997) L'acquisition de la troisième langue: Bilinguisme et plurilinguisme au Pays Basque. *AILE* 10: 159–80.
Cenoz, J. (1998) Linguistic distance and cross-linguistic influence in bilinguals' oral production in English as a third language. Paper presented at Eurosla, Paris, September 1998.
Cenoz, J. and Valencia, J.F. (1994) Additive trilingualism: Evidence from the Basque Country. *Applied Psycholinguistics* 15, 195–207.
Cenoz, J. and Genesee, F. (1998) Psycholinguistic perspectives on multilingualism and multilingual education. In J. Cenoz and F. Genesee (eds) *Beyond Bilingualism: Multilingualism and Multilingual Education* (pp. 16–32). Clevedon: Multilingual Matters.
Clyne, M. (1997) Some of the things trilinguals do. *International Journal of Bilingualism* 1, 95–116.
Cohen, S.P., Tucker, R. and Lambert, W.E. (1967) The comparative skills of monolinguals and bilinguals in perceiving phoneme sequences. *Language and Speech* 10, 159–68.
Cummins, J. (1981) The role of primary language development in promoting educational success for language minority children. In California State Department of Education (eds) *Schooling and Language Minority Students: A Theoretical Framework* (pp. 3–49). Los Angeles: Evaluation, Dissemination and Assessment Centre.
Davine, M., Tucker, R. and Lambert, W.E. (1971) The perception of phoneme sequences by monolingual and bilingual elementary school children. *Canadian Journal of Behavioural Science* 3, 72–6.
De Houwer, A. (1995) Bilingual language acquisition. In P. Fletcher and B. MacWhinney (eds) *The Handbook of Child Language* (pp. 219–50). Oxford: Blackwell.
Edwards, H.P., Doutriaux, C.W., McCarrey, H. and Fu, L. (1977) *Evaluation of the Federally and Provincially Funded Extensions of the Second Language Programmes in the Schools of the Ottawa Roman Catholic Separate School Board.* Ottawa: Ottawa Roman Catholic Separate School Board.
Ellis, R. (1994) *The Study of Second Language Acquisition.* Oxford: Oxford University Press.

Enomoto, K. (1994) L2 perceptual acquisition: The effect of multilingual linguistic experience on the perception of a 'less novel' contrast. *Edinburgh Working Papers in Applied Linguistics* 5, 15–29.

Genesee, F. (1998) A case study of multilingual education in Canada. In J. Cenoz and F. Genesee (eds) *Beyond Bilingualism: Multilingualism and Multilingual Education* (pp. 243–58). Clevedon: Multilingual Matters.

Gulutsan, M. (1976) Third language learning. *Canadian Modern Language Review* 32, 309–15.

Hammarberg, B. and Williams, S. (1993) A study of third language acquisition. In B. Hammarberg (ed.) *Problem, Process, Product in Language Learning* (pp. 60–70). Stockholm: Stockholm University.

Harding, E. and Riley, P. (1986) *The Bilingual Family*. Cambridge: Cambridge University Press.

Helot, C. (1988) Bringing up children in English, French and Irish: Two case studies. *Language, Culture and Curriculum* 1, 281–7.

Hoffmann, C. (1985) Language acquisition in two trilingual children. *Journal of Multilingual and Multicultural Development* 6, 479–95.

Hoffmann, C. (1998) Luxembourg and the European schools. In J. Cenoz and F. Genesee (eds) *Beyond Bilingualism: Multilingualism and Multilingual Education* (pp. 143–74). Clevedon: Multilingual Matters.

Hurd, M. (1993) Minority language children and French immersion: Additive multilingualism or subtractive semi-lingualism? *Canadian Modern Language Review* 49, 514–25.

Jaspaert, K. and Lemmens, G. (1990) Linguistic evaluation of Dutch as a third language. In M. Byram and J. Leman (eds) *Bicultural and Trilingual Education: The Foyer Model in Brussels* (pp. 30–56). Clevedon: Multilingual Matters.

Klein, E.C. (1995) Second versus third language acquisition: Is there a difference? *Language Learning* 45, 419–65.

Lambert, W.E. (1974) Culture and language as factors in learning and education. In F.E. Abour and R.D. Meade (eds) *Cultural Factors in Learning and Education* (pp. 91–122). Bellingham, Washington: 5th Western Washington Symposium on Learning.

Lasagabaster, D. (1997) *Creatividad y conciencia metalingüística: Incidencia en el aprendizaje del inglés como L3*. Leioa: University of the Basque Country.

Larsen-Freeman, D. and Long, M. (1991) *An Introduction to Second Language Acquisition Research*. London: Longman.

McLaughlin, B. and Nayak, N. (1989) Processing a new language: Does knowing other languages make a difference? In H.W. Dechert and M. Raupach (eds) *Interlingual Processes* (pp. 5–16). Tübingen: Gunter Narr.

Mikes, M. (1990) Some issues of lexical development in early bi- and trilinguals. In G. Conti-Ramsdem and C. Snow (eds) *Children's Language* (Vol. 7, pp. 103–20). Hillsdale, NJ: Erlbaum.

Möhle, D. (1989) Multilingual interaction in foreign language production. In H.W. Dechert and M. Raupach (eds) *Interlingual Processes* (pp. 179–94). Tübingen: Gunter Narr.

Nation, R. and McLaughlin, B. (1986) Novices and experts: An information-processing approach to the 'good language learner' problem. *Applied Psycholinguistics* 7, 41–56.

Nayak, N., Hansen, N., Krueger, N. and McLaughlin, B. (1990) Language-learning

strategies in monolingual and multilingual adults. *Language Learning* 40, 221–44.
Obler, L. (1989) Exceptional second language learners. In S. Gass, C. Madden, D. Preston and L. Selinker (eds) *Variation in Second language Acquisition: Psycholinguistic Issues* (pp. 141–59). Clevedon: Multilingual Matters.
Ringbom, H. (1987) *The Role of the First Language in Foreign Language Learning.* Clevedon: Multilingual Matters.
Sanders, M. and Meijers, G. (1995) English as L3 in the elementary school. *ITL Review for Applied Linguistics* 107–8, 59–78.
Sharwood Smith, M. (1994) *Second Language Learning: Theoretical Foundations.* London: Longman.
Singh, R. and Carroll, S. (1979) L1, L2 and L3. *Indian Journal of Applied Linguistics* 5, 51–63.
Singleton, D. (1987) Mother- and other-tongue influence on learner French. *Studies in Second Language Acquisition* 9, 327–46.
Swain, M., Lapkin, S., Rowen, N. and Hart, D. (1990) The role of mother-tongue literacy in third language learning. *Language, Culture and Curriculum* 3, 65–81.
Thomas, J. (1988) The role played by metalinguistic awareness in second and third language learning. *Journal of Multilingual and Multicultural Development* 9, 235–46.
Wagner, D.A., Spratt, J.E. and Ezzaki, A. (1989) Does learning to read in a second language always put the child at a disadvantage? Some counter-evidence from Morocco. *Applied Psycholinguistics* 10: 31–48.
Wightman, M. (1981) *The French Listening Comprehension Skills of Grade Six English Programme Students; Second Year of Testing.* Ottawa: Research Centre/Centre de Recherches, Ottawa Board of Education.
Zobl, H. (1993) Prior linguistic knowledge and the conservation of the learning procedure: Grammaticality judgements of unilingual and multilingual learners. In S.M. Gass and L. Selinker (eds) *Language Transfer in Language Learning* (pp. 176–96). Amsterdam: John Benjamins.

*Chapter 4*
# Putting Language Proficiency in its Place
## Responding to Critiques of the Conversational/ Academic Language Distinction

JIM CUMMINS

The issue of how language proficiency relates to academic achievement is clearly relevant to the educational development of bilingual and trilingual children. These children may be exposed to a wide variety of language interaction patterns in home and at school. In many contexts in Europe and elsewhere, it is increasingly common for schools to promote knowledge of three (or more) languages. A typical pattern is for primary schooling to be conducted bilingually through a minority language, which children speak at home, and the national language, with instruction in a language of wider communication – frequently English – introduced at a later stage (see Cummins & Corson, 1997, for numerous examples).

A number of issues arise for policy-makers contemplating the introduction of bilingual and trilingual education programmes. For example, if instruction is divided among two or three languages, will proficiency in each language develop adequately? When is it appropriate to compare bilingual children's proficiency in their two languages (L1 and L2) with that of monolingual children whose instruction has been totally through their L1? In other words, how long does it take children to attain grade expectations in their second (or third) language? In transitional bilingual programmes such as those implemented for minority students in the United States and parts of the Netherlands (e.g. Verhoeven, 1991), when should children be mainstreamed to classes taught predominantly or totally through their L2? If children experience academic difficulties (e.g. in reading) in a bilingual programme, should they be transferred to a monolingual programme where more intensive instruction can be given through just one language? How valid are tests administered through a bilingual child's second language, or even first language if that language is not being promoted strongly in school? Should the introduction of reading in a second language be delayed until a certain level of oral language proficiency in that language has been attained? If so, what level?

These issues have been debated in the context of bilingual education for linguistic minority students in the United States, for majority language students in Canadian French immersion programmes, and in a wide variety of bilingual and trilingual programmes in Europe. I have suggested that underlying many of these issues is the question of *language proficiency*: what does this actually mean? And how is it related to academic achievement? Two examples will illustrate the relevance of this underlying concern. In North America, minority children have frequently been tested on IQ tests through English (their L2) after two or three years in the country and assigned to special needs classes on the basis of these tests (usually a pattern of low verbal scores and higher non-verbal scores). In Texas in the early 1980s, for example, there were more than three times as many Latino/Latina students labelled as 'learning disabled' as would be expected from their proportion in the school population (Ortiz & Yates, 1983). This pattern raises obvious concerns, such as the validity of ability and achievement tests whose norms reflect the experiences of the dominant group in the society; but it also raises the issues of how conversational fluency in a second language may be related to academic development in that language and how long students might typically require to develop conversational and academic language skills in a second language.

A related example is the debate in the United States over how long bilingual students should remain in bilingual programmes before being transferred to all-English classrooms. Because of controversy over the desirability of permitting minority languages into the school system, there is considerable pressure on educators to limit the time that a student can spend in a bilingual programme to less than three years. Students who are transferred after this period of time to classrooms without additional support for learning English and catching up academically frequently experience academic failure. An obvious question that arises is 'How much proficiency in a language is required to follow instruction through that language?'

In short, the question of how we conceptualise language proficiency and its relationship to academic development is central to many volatile policy issues in the area of bilingual education. I have suggested that in order to address these issues we need to make a fundamental distinction between *conversational* and *academic* aspects of language proficiency, originally labelled (Cummins, 1979) 'basic interpersonal communicative skills' (BICS) and 'cognitive academic language proficiency' (CALP). In this chapter I use the terms 'conversational' and 'academic language proficiency' interchangeably with BICS/CALP.

This distinction has been influential in a number of contexts (e.g. Cline & Frederickson, 1996) but it has also been severely critiqued by a number of investigators (Edelsky *et al.*, 1983; Martin-Jones & Romaine, 1986; Romaine, 1989; Wiley, 1996). In this chapter, I shall try to clarify the rationale and nature of the distinction in light of research evidence from a number of contexts and respond to the critiques that have been addressed to the distinction. In the first section below I elaborate the rationale for the distinction and the evolution of the constructs over the past 20 years.

## Evolution of the Conversational/Academic Language Proficiency Distinction

Skutnabb-Kangas and Toukomaa (1976) had drawn attention to the fact that Finnish immigrant children in Sweden often appeared to educators to be fluent in both Finnish and Swedish but still showed levels of verbal academic performance in both languages considerably below grade and age expectations. Similarly, analysis of psychological assessments administered to minority students showed that teachers and psychologists often assumed that children who had attained fluency in English had overcome all difficulties with the language (Cummins, 1984). Yet these children frequently performed poorly on English academic tasks as well as in psychological assessment situations. The need to distinguish between conversational fluency and academic aspects of L2 performance was highlighted by the re-analysis of large-scale language acquisition data from the Toronto Board of Education (Cummins, 1981a). These data showed clearly that there was a gap of several years, on average, between the attainment of peer-appropriate fluency in L2 and the attainment of grade norms in academic aspects of L2. Conversational aspects of proficiency reached peer-appropriate levels usually within about two years of exposure to L2, but a period of between five and seven years was required, on average, for immigrant students to approach grade norms in academic aspects of English.

The distinction between BICS and CALP (Cummins, 1979) was intended to draw educators' attention to these data and to warn against the premature exit of minority students (in the United States) from bilingual to mainstream English-only programmes on the basis of their attainment of surface level fluency in English. In other words, the distinction highlighted the fact that educators' conflating of these aspects of proficiency was a major factor in the creation of academic difficulties for minority students.

The BICS/CALP distinction also served to qualify John Oller's (1979) claim that all individual differences in language proficiency could be accounted for by just one underlying factor, which he termed 'global language proficiency'. Oller synthesised a considerable amount of data showing strong correlations between performance on cloze tests of reading, standardised reading tests, and measures of oral verbal ability (e.g. vocabulary measures). I pointed out that not all aspects of language use or performance could be incorporated into one dimension of global language proficiency. For example, if we take two monolingual English-speaking siblings, a 12-year-old child and a 6-year-old, there are enormous differences in these children's ability to read and write English and in their knowledge of vocabulary, but minimal differences in their phonology or basic fluency. The 6-year-old can understand virtually everything that is likely to be said to her in everyday social contexts and she can use language very effectively in these contexts, just as the 12-year-old can. Similarly, as noted above, in second language acquisition contexts, immigrant children typically require very different time periods to catch up with their peers in everyday face-to-face aspects of proficiency, as compared to academic aspects.

This distinction was elaborated into two intersecting continua (Cummins, 1981b) which highlighted the range of cognitive demands and contextual support involved in particular language tasks or activities (context-embedded/context-reduced, cognitively undemanding/cognitively demanding; see Figure 4.1). The BICS/CALP distinction was maintained within this elaboration and related to the theoretical distinctions of several other theorists. The terms used by different investigators have varied, but the essential distinction refers to the extent to which the meaning being communicated is supported by contextual or interpersonal cues (such as gestures, facial expressions, and intonation present in face-to-face interaction) or is dependent on linguistic cues that are themselves largely independent of the immediate communicative context.

The framework elaborated in Figure 4.1 differs from distinctions made by theorists such as Bruner (1975; communicative/analytic competence), Donaldson (1978; embedded and disembedded thought and language), Olson (1977; utterance and text) and Snow *et al.* (1991; contextualised and decontextualised language) in that it goes beyond a simple dichotomy in mapping the underlying dimensions of linguistic performance in academic contexts. In these one-dimensional distinctions, as in distinctions between oral and literate forms of language, the degree of cognitive demand of particular tasks or activities is not represented. Thus there would be no way of highlighting the fact that an intense intellectual discussion with one or two

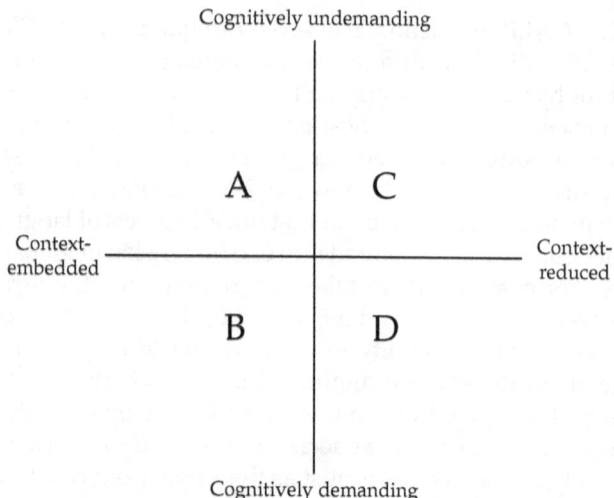

**Figure 4.1** Range of contextual support and degree of cognitive involvement in language tasks and activities

other people can be just as cognitively demanding as writing an academic paper, despite the fact that the former is contextualised while the latter is relatively decontextualised.

## Cognitive and contextual demands

The framework outlined in Figure 4.1 is designed to identify the extent to which students are able to cope successfully with the cognitive and linguistic demands made on them by the social and educational environment in which they are obliged to function. These demands are conceptualised within a framework made up of the intersection of two continua, one relating to the range of contextual support available for expressing or receiving meaning and the other to the amount of information that must be processed simultaneously or in close succession by the student in order to carry out the activity.

The extremes of the context-embedded/context-reduced continuum are distinguished by the fact that in *context-embedded* communication the participants can actively negotiate meaning (e.g. by providing feedback that the message has not been understood) and the language is supported by a wide range of meaningful interpersonal and situational cues. *Context-reduced* communication, on the other hand, relies primarily (or, at the extreme of the continuum, exclusively) on linguistic cues to meaning, and thus successful interpretation of the message depends heavily on knowledge of the language itself. In general, context-embedded communication is more typical of the everyday world outside the classroom, whereas many of the linguistic demands of the classroom (e.g. manipulating text) reflect communicative activities that are close to the context-reduced end of the continuum.

The upper parts of the vertical continuum consist of communicative tasks and activities in which the linguistic tools have become largely automatised and thus require little active cognitive involvement for appropriate performance. At the lower end of the continuum are tasks and activities in which the linguistic tools have not become automatised and thus require active cognitive involvement. Persuading another individual that your point of view is correct, and writing an essay, are examples of Quadrant B and D skills respectively. Casual conversation is a typical Quadrant A activity; examples of Quadrant C are copying notes from the blackboard or filling in worksheets.

The framework elaborates on the conversational/academic distinction by highlighting important underlying dimensions of conversational and academic communication. Thus, conversational abilities (Quadrant A) often develop relatively quickly among immigrant second language learners because these forms of communication are supported by interpersonal and contextual cues and make relatively few cognitive demands on the individual. Mastery of the academic functions of language (Quadrant D), on the other hand, is a more formidable task because such uses require high levels of cognitive involvement and are only minimally supported by contextual or interpersonal cues. Under conditions of high cognitive demand, it is necessary for students to stretch their linguistic resources to the limit to function successfully. In short, the essential aspect of academic language proficiency is the ability to make complex meanings explicit in either oral or written modalities by means of language itself rather than by means of contextual or paralinguistic cues such as gestures and intonation.

As students progress through the grades, they are increasingly required to manipulate language in cognitively demanding and context-reduced situations that differ significantly from everyday conversational interactions. In writing, for example, they must learn to continue to produce language without the prompting that comes from a conversational partner and they must plan large units of discourse, and organise them coherently, rather than planning only what will be said next. The difference between the everyday language of face-to-face interaction and the language of schooling is clearly expressed by Pauline Gibbons (1991) in outlining the differences between what she terms 'playground language' and 'classroom language':

> This playground language includes the language which enables children to make friends, join in games and take part in a variety of day-to-day activities that develop and maintain social contacts. It usually occurs in face-to-face contact, and is thus highly dependent on the physical and visual context, and on gesture and body language. Fluency with this kind of language is an important part of language development; without it a child is isolated from the normal social life of the playground ...
>
> But playground language is very different from the language that teachers use in the classroom, and from the language that we expect children to learn to use. The language of the playground is not the language associated with learning in mathematics, or social studies, or science. The playground situation does not normally offer children the opportunity to use such language as: *if we increase the angle by 5 degrees, we could cut the circumference into equal parts*. Nor does it normally require the language associated with the higher order thinking skills, such as hypothesizing, evaluating, inferring, generalizing, predicting or classifying. Yet these are the language functions which are related to learning and the development of cognition; they occur in all areas of the curriculum, and without them a child's potential in academic areas cannot be realized. (Gibbons, 1991: 3)

Thus the context-embedded/context-reduced distinction is not one between oral and written language. Within the framework, the dimensions of contextual embeddedness and cognitive demand are distinguished because some context-embedded activities are clearly just as cognitively demanding as context-reduced activities. For example, an intense intellectual discussion with one or two other people is likely to require at least as much cognitive processing as writing an essay on the same topic. Similarly, writing an e-mail message to a close friend is, in many respects, more context-embedded than giving a lecture to a large group of people.

Contextual support involves both internal and external dimensions. Internal factors are *attributes of the individual* that make a task more familiar or easier in some respect, such as prior experience, motivation, cultural relevance, interests and so on. External factors refer to *aspects of the input* that facilitate or impede comprehension; for example, language input that is spoken clearly and contains a considerable amount of syntactic and semantic redundancy is easier to understand than input that lacks these features.

A central implication of any framework for the instruction of second and third language learners is that language and content will be acquired most successfully when students are challenged cognitively but also provided with the contextual and linguistic supports or scaffolds required for successful task completion. In other words, optimal instruction for linguistic, cognitive and academic growth will tend to fall into Quadrant B.

## Clarifications of the conversational/academic (BICS/CALP) distinction

The distinction between BICS and CALP has sometimes been misunderstood or misrepresented. For example, the distinction was criticised on the grounds that a simple dichotomy does not account for many dimensions of language use and competence such as sociolinguistic aspects of language (see for example Wald, 1984). However, the distinction was not proposed as an overall theory of language but as a very specific conceptual distinction addressed to specific issues related to the education of second language learners. As outlined above, the distinction entails important implications for policy and practice. The fact that the distinction does not address issues of sociolinguistics or discourse styles or any number of other linguistic issues is irrelevant. The usefulness of any theoretical construct should be assessed in relation to the issues that it attempts to address, not in relation to issues that it makes no claim to address. To suggest that the BICS/CALP distinction is invalid because it does not account for subtleties of sociolinguistic interaction or discourse styles is like saying 'this apple is no good because it doesn't taste like an orange'.

Another point concerns the sequence of acquisition between BICS and CALP. August and Hakuta (1997), for example, suggest that the distinction specifies that BICS must precede CALP in development. This is not at all the case. The sequential nature of BICS/CALP acquisition was suggested as typical in the specific situation of immigrant children learning a second language. It was not suggested as an absolute order that applies in every, or even the majority of situations. Thus attainment of high levels of L2 CALP can precede attainment of fluent L2 BICS in certain situations, such as that of a scientist who can read a language for research purposes but who can't speak it.

Another misunderstanding is to interpret the distinction as dimensions of language that are autonomous or independent of their contexts of acquisition (Romaine, 1989: 240). To say that BICS and CALP are conceptually distinct is not the same as saying that they are separate or acquired in different ways. Developmentally they are not necessarily separate; all children acquire their initial conceptual foundation (their knowledge of the world) largely through conversational interactions in the home. Both BICS and

CALP are shaped by their contexts of acquisition and use. Consistent with a Vygotskian perspective on cognitive and language development, BICS and CALP both develop within a matrix of social interaction. However, they follow different developmental patterns: phonological skills in our native language and our basic fluency reach a plateau in the first six or so years; in other words, the rate of subsequent development is very much reduced in comparison to previous development. This is not the case for literacy-related knowledge such as range of vocabulary which continues to develop at least throughout our schooling and usually throughout our lifetimes.

It is also important to point out that cognitive skills are involved, to a greater or lesser extent, in most forms of social interaction. For example, cognitive skills are undoubtedly involved in one's ability to tell jokes effectively, and if we worked at it we might improve our joke-telling ability throughout our lifetimes. But our joke-telling ability is largely unrelated to our academic performance. This intersection of the cognitive and social aspects of language proficiency does not mean that they are identical or reducible one to the other. The implicit assumption that conversational fluency in English is a good indicator of 'English proficiency' has resulted in countless bilingual children being 'diagnosed' as learning-disabled or retarded. Despite their developmental intersections, BICS and CALP are conceptually distinct and follow different developmental patterns.

An additional misconception is that the distinction characterises CALP (academic language) as a 'superior' form of language proficiency to BICS (conversational language). This interpretation was never intended, although it is easy to see how the use of the term 'basic' in BICS might appear to devalue conversational language as compared to the perceived higher status of 'cognitive academic' language proficiency. Clearly, various forms of oral language performance are highly complex and sophisticated both linguistically and cognitively. However, these forms of language performance are not necessarily strongly related to the linguistic demands of schooling. As outlined above, access to very specific forms of language are required to continue to progress academically, and a major goal of schooling for all students is to expand students' registers and repertoires of language into these academic domains. However, the greater relevance of academic language proficiency for success in schooling, as compared to conversational proficiency, does not mean that it is intrinsically superior in any way or that the language proficiency of non-literate or non-schooled communities is in any way deficient.

A final point of clarification concerns the relationship of language proficiency to social determinants of minority students' academic development (e.g. Troike, 1984). The conversational/academic language proficiency theoretical construct is psychoeducational in nature in so far as it focuses primarily on the cognitive and linguistic dimensions of proficiency in a language. The role of social factors in minority students' academic success or failure was acknowledged in early work but not elaborated in detail. In 1986 I proposed a framework within which the intersecting roles of sociopolitical and psychoeducational factors could be conceptualised (Cummins, 1986). Specifically, the framework highlighted the ways in which the interactions between educators and minority students reflected particular role definitions on the part of educators in relation to students' language and culture, community participation, pedagogy, and assessment. It hypothesised that minority students are educationally disabled in school in much the same way that their communities have historically been disabled in the wider society and pointed to directions for reversing this process. The framework argues that educational interventions will be successful only to the extent that they constitute a challenge to the broader societal power structure (Cummins, 1986, 1996).

## Linguistic Evidence for the Conversational/Academic Language Distinction

Up till now, two major sets of evidence have been advanced to support the conversational/academic language distinction:

- In monolingual contexts, the distinction reflects the difference between the language proficiency acquired through interpersonal interaction by virtually all 6-year-old children and the proficiency developed through schooling and literacy which continues to expand throughout our lifetimes. For most children, the basic structure of their native language is in place by the age of 6 or so but their language continues to expand with respect to the range of vocabulary and grammatical constructions they can understand and use and the linguistic contexts within which they can function successfully. A typical 16-year-old student has considerably greater knowledge of language and options for language use (reading novels, encyclopedias and so on) than a typical 6-year old, despite the fact that both are fluent native speakers of their L1.
- Research studies since the early 1980s have shown that immigrant students can quickly acquire considerable fluency in the target language when they are exposed to it in the environment and at school, but also that despite this rapid growth in conversational fluency, it generally takes a minimum of about five years (and

frequently much longer) for them to catch up with native speakers in academic aspects of the language (Collier, 1987; Cummins, 1979, 1981a; Klesmer, 1994), as assessed by measures of literacy and formal language knowledge.

In addition to the evidence noted above, the distinction receives strong support from two other sources: (1) Douglas Biber's (1986) analysis of a corpus of authentic discourse gathered from a wide range of communicative situations, both written and oral, and (2) David Corson's (1995) documentation of the lexical differences between English everyday conversational language and textual language, the former deriving predominantly from Anglo-Saxon sources and the latter from Graeco-Latin sources.

## Biber's analysis of textual variation

Biber used psychometric analysis of an extremely large corpus of spoken and written textual material in order to uncover the basic dimensions underlying textual variation. Among the 16 text types included in Biber's analysis were broadcasts, spontaneous speeches, telephone conversation, face-to-face conversation, professional letters, academic prose and press reports. Forty-one linguistic features were counted in 545 text samples, totaling more than one million words.

Three major dimensions emerged from the factor analysis of this corpus. These were labelled by Biber as *interactive vs. edited text, abstract vs. situated content*, and *reported vs. immediate style*. The first dimension is described as follows:

> Thus, Factor 1 identifies a dimension which characterizes texts produced under conditions of high personal involvement and real-time constraints (marked by low explicitness in the expression of meaning, high subordination and interactive features) – as opposed to texts produced under conditions permitting considerable editing and high explicitness of lexical content, but little interaction or personal involvement. ... This dimension combines both situational and cognitive parameters; in particular it combines interactional features with those reflecting production constraints (or the lack of them). (1986: 385)

The second factor has positive weights from linguistic features such as nominalisations, prepositions and passives and, according to Biber, reflects a 'detached formal style vs. a concrete colloquial one' (1986: 396). Although this factor is correlated with the first, it can be empirically distinguished from it; this is illustrated by professional letters, which, according to Biber's analysis, represent highly abstract texts that have a high level of personal involvement.

The third factor has positive weights from linguistic features such as past tense, perfect aspect and third person pronouns which can all refer to a removed narrative context. According to Biber this dimension

> distinguishes texts with a primary narrative emphasis, marked by considerable reference to a removed situation, from those with non-narrative emphases (descriptive, expository, or other) marked by little reference to a removed situation but a high occurrence of present tense forms. (1986: 396)

Although Biber's three dimensions provide a more detailed analysis of the nature of language proficiency and use than the conversational/academic distinction (as is to be expected in view of the very extensive range of spoken and written texts analysed), it is clear that the distinctions highlighted in his dimensions are consistent with the broad distinction between conversational and academic aspects of proficiency. For example, when factor scores were calculated for the different text types on each factor, telephone and face-to-face conversation were at opposite extremes from official documents and academic prose on Textual Dimensions 1 and 2 (interactive vs. edited text, and abstract vs. situated content). In short, Biber's research shows clearly that the general distinction that has been proposed between conversational and academic aspects of language has linguistic reality that can be identified empirically.

Consistent with Biber's distinctions is work carried out recently in Australia by Gibbons and Lascar, who point to the fact that Biber's descriptions of different registers of language are consistent with the characteristics that Michael Halliday (e.g. Halliday & Hasan, 1985) assigns to the concept of *mode*. This 'examines the linguistic effects produced by the distance (in terms of time, space and abstractness) between a text and the context to which it refers, and also the distance between listener/reader and speaker/writer' (Gibbons & Lascar, 1998: 41). They note that degree of context-embeddedness is a defining feature of this register parameter 'mode' and refer to it as the *literate register* on the grounds that it 'constitutes an important element of literacy'. They also point out that many minority language speakers often have a well-developed domestic or everyday register but have not had opportunities to acquire many others, in particular the academic or literate register. Their research used multiple choice cloze procedures as a way of operationalising cognitive academic language proficiency.

## Corson's analysis of the English language lexicon

Corson (1993, 1995) has pointed out that the academic language of texts in English depends heavily on Graeco-Latin words whereas everyday conversation relies more on an Anglo-Saxon-based lexicon: 'most of the specialist and high status terminology of English is Graeco-Latin in origin, and most of its more everyday terminology is Anglo-Saxon in origin' (1993: 13). He cites data suggesting that approximately 60% of all the words in written English text are of Graeco-Latin origin. These words tend to be three or four syllables long, whereas the everyday high-frequency words of the Anglo-Saxon lexicon tend to be just one or two syllables in length.

Corson (1997: 677) points out that:

> printed texts provided much more exposure to [Graeco-Latin] words than oral ones. For example, even children's books contained 50% more rare words than either adult prime-time television or the conversations of university graduates; popular magazines had three times as many rare words as television and informal conversation.

An obvious implication of these data is that if second language learners are to catch up academically to native speakers they must engage in extensive reading of written text, because academic language is reliably to be found only in written text. The research on reading achievement also suggests, however, that in addition to large amounts of time for actual text reading, it is important for students to have ample opportunities to talk to each other and to a teacher about their responses to reading (see Fielding & Pearson, 1994, for a review). Talking about the text in a collaborative context ensures that higher-order thinking processes such as analysis, evaluation and synthesis engage with academic language in deepening students' comprehension of the text.

To better illustrate the centrality of the Graeco-Latin lexicon to the comprehension of academic language, consider the following passage from Edgar Allan Poe's nineteenth-century story 'The pit and the pendulum' which appeared in a high school literature compendium:

> My outstretched hands at length encountered some solid obstruction. It was a wall, seemingly of stone masonry – very smooth, slimy, and cold. I followed it up; stepping with all the careful distrust with which certain antique narratives had inspired me. (Poe, 1997: 256)

Among the more difficult words in this passage are the following: outstretched, encountered, solid, obstruction, masonry, slimy, distrust, antique, narratives, inspired. With the exception of 'slimy' and 'outstretched', all of these words are Graeco-Latin in origin and have semantic relationships across the Romance languages. Thus, at least in English, the lexicon used in conversational interactions is dramatically different from that used in more literate and academic contexts.

In summary, there is solid linguistic evidence for the reality of the conversational/academic language distinction in addition to the evidence of different time periods required to develop peer-appropriate levels of each dimension of language proficiency among second language learners. In the North American context, failure to take account of this distinction has led to inappropriate psychological testing of bilingual students and premature exit from bilingual or ESL support programmes into 'mainstream' classes where students have received minimal support for continued academic language development. In other words, the conceptual distinction between conversational and academic language proficiency has highlighted misconceptions about the nature of language proficiency that have contributed directly to the creation of academic failure among bilingual students.

## Critiques of the Conversational/Academic Language Distinction

Early critiques of the conversational/academic distinction were advanced by Carole Edelsky and her colleagues (Edelsky *et al.*, 1983) and in a volume edited by Charlene Rivera (1984). These critiques were responded to and will not be discussed in depth in this chapter (see Cummins & Swain, 1983). Edelsky (1990) later reiterated and reformulated her critique, and others were advanced by Martin-Jones and Romaine (1986) and Romaine (1989). More recently, Terrence Wiley (1996) has provided a detailed review and critique.

The major criticisms in these and other critiques are as follows:

- The conversational/academic language distinction reflects an autonomous perspective on language that ignores its location in social practices and power relations (Edelsky *et al.*, 1983; Romaine, 1989; Troike, 1984; Wald, 1984; Wiley, 1996).
- CALP or academic language proficiency represents little more than 'test-wiseness' – it is an artefact of the inappropriate way in which it has been measured (Edelsky *et al.*, 1983).
- The notion of CALP promotes a 'deficit theory' in so far as it attributes the academic failure of bilingual/minority students to low cognitive/academic proficiency rather than to inappropriate schooling; in this

respect it is no different from notions such as 'semilingualism' (Edelsky, 1990; Edelsky *et al.*, 1983; Martin-Jones & Romaine, 1986).

I will outline in more detail the points raised by Edelsky (1990) and Wiley (1996) as representative of the general orientation of these critiques.

### Edelsky's (1990) critique

Consistent with her previous critique (Edelsky *et al.*, 1983), Edelsky disputes the legitimacy of the constructs of cognitive academic language proficiency (CALP) and basic interpersonal communicative skills (BICS). She argues that CALP consists of little more than test-taking skills and that the construct encourages skills-oriented instruction, thereby impeding the literacy development of bilingual students who will thrive only in meaning-oriented whole-language instructional contexts. The tone and substance of her critique can be gauged from the following extracts:

> The fundamental problem with all versions of Cummins' *theory* is that it is premised on an erroneous, psychologically derived 'theory' of the nature of reading – a conception of reading as consisting of separate skills with discrete components of language. What counts as either reading-in-action or as evidence of reading ability is 'reading skills'. These are demonstrated by performance in miscontextualized tasks (performed for the sole purpose of either demonstrating proficiency or complying with the assignment) or on tests whose scores are presumed to represent some supposedly context-free reading ability. (Edelsky, 1990: 60–1)

> Despite Cummins' occasional use of 'whole language' terminology (e.g. 'inferring', 'predicting' 'large chunks of discourse'), his underlying skills orientation shows through ... he uses a discourse of empowerment and puts forward a set of suggestions that implicitly contradict his 'theory' of reading as consisting of separate skills (Cummins, 1986) ...And Cummins uses the right rhetoric. He talks of students setting their own goals and generating their own knowledge and he mentions congruent educational practice ...Even so, the separate skills 'theory' slips out and he contradicts his own message. For example, for empirical support, he relies heavily on test score data that can only provide evidence of how well students perform on skill exercises. He applauds and describes at length programs that operate according to a skills 'theory'. For instance, he talks of two programs that make language or cultural accommodations which benefit minority language children by helping them attain readiness or success.

Readiness for what? For the academic tasks of the traditional kindergartens the children will enter in California. Success at what? Success in doing reading exercises in tests and basal reading lessons in Hawaii. (pp. 61–2)

What Edelsky is referring to here is reference to two programmes which incorporated many of the characteristics that I postulated were necessary to challenge coercive power structures in school. One was a bilingual preschool programme in Carpinteria that used Spanish as the predominant language of instruction and attempted to incorporate children's cultural background experience into its design, which was strongly child-centered (Campos & Keatinge, 1988). The other was the Kamehameha programme in Hawaii, which dramatically improved native Hawaiian children's reading performance by incorporating culturally familiar communal story-construction patterns into reading instruction (Au & Jordan, 1981).

According to Edelsky, the theoretical construct 'gained popularity so fast and was so effective in influencing policy' because it reinforced ideas that 'undergird predominant thinking about education in North America', namely that 'written language consists of separate skills, that curriculum should teach those skills, that tests can assess them' (1990: 63).

Edelsky points out that in disputing the constructs of CALP and BICS, she is not claiming that all children are equally competent. She also points out that she does not believe that proficiency with any language variety, in either oral or written modes, enables one to do everything humanly possible with language (1990: 65):

> Though *potentially* equal, at any given historical moment different language repertoires (including literate repertoires) of particular speech communities are unequally efficient for all purposes and even then, unequally assigned to members .. However, the nature of those repertoires, their functions, their meanings, and their inequalities must be determined by ethnographies of speaking and of literacy, not by differential performance in one (testing) context that is subject to criticism on multiple grounds.

She is explicit about how she views the construct of cognitive academic language proficiency: it is nothing more than 'test-wiseness' (p. 65) or what she terms 'skill in instructional nonsense' (SIN). Any research that has used any form of 'test', whether standardised reading measures or non-standardised measures of any kind of cognitive performance, is dismissed. For example, in referring to Gordon Wells' (1986) documentation of the relation between exposure to literacy at home and subsequent literacy performance in school she notes: 'In fact, from the use he makes of Wells' research, Cummins seems to interpret the social grounding of CALP to mean no more than a correlation between test scores and certain kinds of home interactions' (p. 68). It is not surprising to her that support for the theoretical constructs of CALP and BICS would come

> almost entirely from studies using tests of separate so-called reading skills. No wonder. His small parts, psychometric orientation that views all human activity as first divisible into atomized skills and then measurable would certainly lead him to prefer such evidence. (1990: 61)

Edelsky concludes her critique by rejecting theories that locate 'failure in children's heads (in their IQ, their language deficits, their cognitive deficits, their learning styles, their underdeveloped CALP)'.

## Response to Edelsky's critique

A first point to note is that there is nothing new in the Edelsky (1990) critique that was not already in the Edelsky et al. (1983) one. The only difference is that any elaboration of the sociopolitical determinants of students' academic difficulties is dismissed as suffering from 'internal contradictions'. The same charge is levelled against any explication of the pedagogical implications of the theoretical framework which attempt to go beyond apolitical, one-size-fits-all, whole-language approaches towards transformative or critical pedagogy (Cummins, 1986, 1996; see also Delpit, 1988, and Reyes, 1992, for critiques of whole language from progressive educators).

To set the record straight, the sociopolitical and instructional implications of the theoretical framework which Edelsky dismisses as internally contradictory were expressed in 1986 as follows:

### Sociopolitical perspective

> Minority students are disabled or empowered in schools in very much the same way that their communities are disempowered in interactions with societal institutions ...This analysis implies that minority students will succeed educationally to the extent that the patterns of interaction in school reverse those that prevail in the society at large. (Cummins, 1986: 24)

> Given the societal commitment to maintaining the dominant/dominated power relationships, we can predict that educational changes threatening this structure will be fiercely resisted. (p. 34)

### Instructional perspective

A central tenet of the reciprocal interaction model is that 'talking and writing are means to learning' (Bullock Report, 1975: 50) ...This model emphasizes the development of higher-level cognitive skills rather than just factual recall, and meaningful language use by students rather than correction of surface forms. Language use and development are consciously integrated with all curricular content rather than taught as isolated subjects, and tasks are presented to students in ways that generate intrinsic rather than extrinsic motivation. In short, pedagogical approaches that empower students encourage them to assume greater control over setting their own learning goals and to collaborate actively with each other in achieving these goals (Cummins, 1986: 29)

In terms of the quadrants outlined in Figure 4.1, these approaches fall into Quadrant B (cognitively demanding, context-embedded). In later work I have emphasised the importance of going beyond whole-language or 'progressive' pedagogy, as illustrated in the quotation below:

> Transformative pedagogy uses collaborative critical inquiry to enable students to relate curriculum content to their individual and collective experience and to analyze broader social issues relevant to their lives. It also encourages students to discuss ways in which social realities might be transformed through various forms of democratic participation and social action.
>
> Thus, transformative pedagogy will aim to go beyond the sanitized curriculum that is still the norm in many schools. It will attempt to promote students' ability to analyze and understand the social realities of their own lives and of their communities. It will strive to develop a critical literacy. (Cummins, 1996: 157)

So how are these perspectives 'internally contradictory' with the conversational/academic language distinction and with the dimensions outlined in Figure 4.1? *They are not in any way contradictory*. The construct of academic language proficiency does not in any way depend on test scores as support, either for its construct validity or for its relevance to education. Three out of four sources of evidence cited above make no mention of test scores. The obvious differences between 6-year-old and 16-year-old monolingual students in multiple aspects of literacy-related knowledge (assessed by any criterion) illustrate this reality, as does Corson's analysis of the lexicon of English and Biber's analysis of more than one million words of English speech and written text (although Biber's work might be suspect to Edelsky, since he did use psychometric tools to analyse relationships among words and their linguistic and social contexts of use).

Edelsky's vehement dismissal of any test used for any purpose in any context and her adamant endorsement of one single way of collecting data on language proficiency (through ethnographies of speaking and literacy) might appear to some researchers extreme. To others it might appear as a fundamentalist approach which recognises only one truth and adopts an 'off with their heads' attitude to other perspectives. There are very few researchers in the area of bilingual education (or indeed any other area of educational research) who, on ideological grounds, have refused to even cite research that used statistics or that involved formal testing of academic progress.

A characteristic of fundamentalist approaches to any topic or belief system is that attempts at dialogue tend not to progress very far. This is illustrated in the fact that Edelsky (1990) makes no attempt to respond to the rebuttals of the Edelsky *et al.* (1983) position advanced by Cummins and Swain (1983). In response to the arguments that the CALP/BICS distinction entailed a 'deficit position' that blamed the victim by attributing school failure to 'low CALP', and furthermore that it promoted a 'skills' approach to pedagogy that would further victimise minority group students, we made three basic points. We suggested:

- That rational discussion of which theories constitute 'deficit theories' requires explicit criteria of what constitutes a 'deficit theory'; does it, for example, constitute a 'deficit theory' to note, as many researchers and theorists have done (e.g. Wells, 1981), that middle-class children tend to have more experience of books than low-income students when they come to school and that this gives them access to a greater range of language functions and registers that are relevant to the ways schools tend to teach initial literacy? In this case, children's linguistic experience and their consequent earlier access to certain registers of language is seen as an intervening variable that interacts with patterns of instruction at school. Is *any* positing of learner attributes and linguistic experience as an intervening variable a 'deficit theory'?

- That universal condemnation of all formal test situations is simplistic and fails to account for considerable data documenting strong positive relationships between reading test scores and 'authentic' assessment measures such as miscue analysis and cloze procedures. We pointed out that 'if cloze tests are to be dismissed as "irrelevant nonsense" then this surely merits some comment in view of their

widespread use and acceptance among applied linguists' (Cummins & Swain, 1983: 28) – including Sarah Hudelson, one of Edelsky's co-authors.
- That when language proficiency or CALP 'is discussed as part of a causal chain, it is never discussed as an isolated causal factor (as Edelsky *et al.* consistently depict it) but rather as one of a number of individual learner attributes which are determined by societal influences and which interact with educational treatment factors in affecting academic progress' (p. 31). In other words, language proficiency is always seen as an *intervening variable* rather than as an autonomous causal variable; it develops through social interaction in home and school.

To deny this essentially Vygotskian perspective on language and academic development, one must either adopt an extreme Chomskian perspective that identifies 'language proficiency' as a Universal Grammar immune from virtually all social interactional and environmental influence, or claim that a student's language proficiency in a particular language bears no relationship to that student's ability to benefit from instruction in that language.

Edelsky's (1990) failure to define what she means by a 'deficit position', explain how 'authentic' measures of reading can be so closely related to 'skill in instructional nonsense', and discuss the extent to which, within her belief system, there is a place for any construct of 'language proficiency' and if so how this relates to academic progress (intervening variable, 'causal' variable, totally unrelated?) suggests that she is more interested in rhetoric than dialogue.

A more open approach would admit that there is no contradiction between the concept of 'language proficiency' outlined in the early part of this chapter and a theoretical framework that

- identifies coercive power relations as the causal factors in the underachievement of subordinated group students; and
- promotes transformative pedagogy as a central component in challenging these coercive relations of power in the classroom.

In fact, the distinction between conversational and academic dimensions of proficiency has been instrumental in highlighting how both standardised tests (such as the IQ tests used in psychological assessment) and premature exit from bilingual programmes on the basis of conversational rather than academic development in English have contributed to the perpetuation of coercive power relations in the educational system. A balanced critique would have acknowledged the impact of the conversational/academic distinction in highlighting these realities.

A final issue concerns Edelsky's dismissal of the efforts of dedicated educators in Carpinteria and Hawaii (and countless other programmes that have used standardised tests as one way of documenting student progress and establishing credibility to sceptical policy-makers and the general public). While the offensive tone of this dismissal is probably unintended, it illustrates the consequences of adopting a one-dimensional perspective on the contradictions encountered by educators attempting to create contexts of empowerment in the real world of classrooms and schools.

### Wiley's (1996) critique

Wiley's critique forms a chapter in his useful volume *Literacy and Language Diversity in the United States*. The critique derives from a basic distinction he makes between different orientations to literacy. Specifically, he contrasts the 'autonomous' approach with the 'ideological' approach. The former is described as follows:

> The autonomous approach to literacy tends to focus on formal mental properties of decoding and encoding text, excluding analyses of how these processes are used within social contexts. The success of the learner in acquiring literacy is seen as correlating with individual psychological processes ... Those operating within the autonomous approach see literacy as having 'cognitive consequences' at both the individual and societal level ... An autonomous perspective largely ignores the historical and sociopolitical contexts in which individuals live and differences in power and resources between groups. (Wiley, 1996: 31)

By contrast, in the ideological approach advanced by Street (1993) and critical pedagogy theorists such as Freire (1970), 'literacy is viewed as a set of practices that are inextricably linked to cultural and power structures in the society' (Wiley, 1996: 32). From this perspective, literacy problems are seen as related to social stratification and to gaps in power and resources between groups. The role of schools in reinforcing this stratification is expressed as follows (p. 33):

> Because schools are the principal institutions responsible for developing literacy, they are seen as embedded within larger sociopolitical contexts. Because some groups succeed in school while others fail, the ideological approach scrutinizes the way in which literacy development is carried out. It looks at the implicit biases in schools that can

privilege some groups to the exclusion of others. Finally, the social practices approach values literacy programs and policies that are built on the knowledge and resources people already have.

Wiley's major concern is that constructs such as BICS/CALP or the conversational/academic language and the contextual and cognitive dimensions outlined in Figure 4.1 appear to invoke an autonomous orientation to language and literacy that isolates language and literacy practices from their sociocultural and sociopolitical context. He concurs with the critiques of Edelsky *et al.* (1983) that the construct of CALP relies on inauthentic test data, and cites Martin-Jones and Romaine (1986: 30) to reinforce his view that the distinction between CALP and BICS is suspect 'if both are seen as independent of rather than shaped by the language context in which they are acquired and used ...The type of literacy-related skills described by Cummins are, in fact, quite culture-specific: that is, they are specific to the cultural setting of the school.'

Wiley is also concerned about the higher status supposedly assigned to academic as compared to conversational language:

> Notions of academic language proficiency and decontextualization, as they are often used, are particularly problematic because they confound language with schooling and equate a higher cognitive status to the language and literacy practices of school. Academic language proficiency seems to equate broadly with schooling. Schooling is not a neutral process. It involves class and culturally specific forms of socialization. (1996: 183)

Finally, Wiley criticises the 'simplistic' but 'well-intentioned' ways in which practitioners have attempted to operationalise the kinds of language tasks/activities that would fall into the four quadrants of Figure 4.1. He gives one set of examples of such tasks/activities used for professional development in California which he describes as 'value laden and arbitrary', with categorisation of tasks which is 'confused and inaccurate'. He points out that 'professional development materials such as these illustrate the limitations of applying constructs in practice that have not been fully elaborated at the theoretical level'. In conclusion he says that it is:

> necessary to rid the framework of those constructs that are compatible with an autonomous view of language use .. It would require focusing more on social than on cognitive factors affecting language development (Troike, 1984) and on the cultural factors that affect language and literacy practices in the schools. (1996: 178)

## Response to Wiley's critique

Wiley's analysis suffers from a rigid 'either/or' perspective on what forms of inquiry are appropriate in the area of literacy and schooling. Either an approach is autonomous, or it is ideological, but it can't be both, or draw from each tradition in order to address different kinds of question. Linked to this is a prescriptivism which, although much less strident than Edelsky's (1990), suggests that only questions deriving from an ideological perspective can and should be asked.

This rigid dichotomy leads Wiley largely to ignore the fact that the theoretical constructs associated with the notion of language proficiency (e.g. as outlined in Figure 4.1) have been integrated since 1986 with a detailed sociopolitical analysis of how schools construct academic failure among subordinated groups. This framework (Cummins, 1986, 1989, 1996) analyses how coercive relations of power in the wider society ('macro-interactions') affect both educator role definitions and educational structures which, in turn, result in patterns of 'micro-interactions' between educators and subordinated group students that have constricted students' academic language development and identity formation. The framework documents educational approaches that challenge this pattern of coercive power relations and promote the generation of power in the micro-interactions between educators and students.

This framework, however, does not regard 'language proficiency' as irrelevant to the schooling of subordinated group students. I believe that, in order to analyse how power relations operate in the real world of schooling, it is crucial to ask questions such as 'How long does it take second language learners to catch up with native speakers in English academic development?' The data showing that five years are minimally required to bridge this gap continue to provide bilingual educators with a powerful rebuttal to efforts to deny students access to bilingual programmes or exit them rapidly from support services, whether bilingual or English-only. Yet Wiley would presumably classify this question as deriving from an 'autonomous' perspective.

I also believe that it is legitimate to ask 'What forms of proficiency in English do bilingual students need to survive academically in all-English classrooms after they have been transitioned out of bilingual programmes?' This question would also fall into the 'autonomous' category of the artificial either/or dichotomy that Wiley constructs. The conversational/academic language proficiency distinction has been instrumental in helping educators understand why students who have been transitioned on the basis of conversational fluency in English frequently experience severe academic difficulties in all-English mainstream classrooms.

The same issue surfaces with respect to the assessment of bilingual children for special education purposes. The BICS/CALP distinction highlighted the fact that psychological assessment in English was considered appropriate by psychologists and teachers when students had gained conversational fluency in English but frequently were far from their native English-speaking peers in academic English development (Cummins, 1984).

Wiley's dichotomy would also consign any question regarding how language and cognition intersect (in either monolingual or multilingual individuals) to the garbage heap of scientific inquiry. All of the research studies documenting that the acquisition of bilingualism in childhood entails no adverse cognitive consequences for children, and is in fact associated with more advanced awareness of language and ability to analyse language, would also be castigated as reflecting an 'autonomous' perspective.

It is also legitimate, I believe, to ask how linguistic interactions in home and school, and interactions related to print, affect children's linguistic, cognitive, and academic development. These interactions take place within a sociocultural and sociopolitical context, but their effects are still linguistic, academic, and cognitive. A student from a bilingual background who does not understand the language of instruction in school and receives no support to enable him or her to do so is unlikely to develop high levels of academic or literacy skills in either first or second language.

The list of questions could go on. The point I want to make is that within the framework I have proposed, 'language proficiency' is seen as an *intervening variable* that mediates children's academic development. It is not in any sense 'autonomous' or independent of the sociocultural context. I fully agree with Martin-Jones and Romaine's point that the development of conversational and academic aspects of proficiency are 'shaped by the language context in which they are acquired and used', and that academic language is 'specific to the cultural setting of the school'. Their claim that the BICS/CALP distinction proposes otherwise is without foundation. A central aspect of the framework is, in fact, that language proficiency is shaped by the patterns and contexts of educator–student interaction in the school and will, in turn, mediate the further outcomes of schooling.

The claim that the BICS/CALP distinction ascribes a superior status to academic language as compared to conversational has already been addressed above. No form of language is cognitively or linguistically superior to any other in any absolute sense outside of particular contexts.

However, within the context of school, knowledge of academic language (such as the Graeco-Latin lexicon of written English text) is clearly relevant to educational success and adds a crucial dimension to conversational fluency in understanding how 'language proficiency' relates to academic achievement. Wiley, like Martin-Jones and Romaine, takes a conceptual distinction that was addressed only to issues of schooling and criticises it on the grounds that this distinction is 'specific only to the cultural setting of the school'. These writers seriously misrepresent the distinction when they label it 'autonomous' or 'independent' of particular contexts.

An inconsistency in Wiley's attitude to 'inauthentic test data' should be noted. He suggests (1996: 167) that there is a major concern regarding the authenticity of using school-test data as a means of determining language proficiencies. I would agree. School-test data attempt to assess certain kinds of language proficiencies but often do it very inadequately, without regard to cultural and linguistic biases in the test instruments, as the study of psychological test data has demonstrated (Cummins, 1984). However, in view of Wiley's dismissal of school-test data as even a partial basis for constructing theory, it is surprising to see him invoke exactly this type of data to assert that there is 'an ever-growing body of evidence that bilingual education is effective in promoting literacy and academic achievement among children when adequate resources are provided' (1996: 153). Virtually all of this evidence derives from 'inauthentic' standardised test data. For example, among the references cited to back up this claim are Ramirez (1992) and Krashen and Biber (1988), who all relied almost exclusively on standardised test data to support their claims for the effectiveness of bilingual education.

A final point concerns Wiley's unease with the 'simplistic', 'confused and inaccurate' interpretations by some practitioners of what kinds of language task or activities would fall into the four quadrants of Figure 4.1. He fails to appreciate that the quadrants represent a visual metaphor that incorporates hypotheses about the dimensions underlying various kinds of language performance. It makes linkages between the theoretical literature on the nature of proficiency in a language and those specific instructional and policy issues faced on a daily basis by educators working with bilingual learners (for instance, how much 'English proficiency' do children need to participate effectively in an all-English classroom?). It attempts to provide tentative answers to certain questions such as why certain kinds of 'English proficiency' are acquired to peer-appropriate levels relatively quickly while a longer period is required for other aspects of proficiency. However, it was also intended as a heuristic tool to stimulate discussion regarding the linguistic and cognitive challenges posed by different academic tasks and subject-matter content, and in both the British and North American context it has been effective in this regard (e.g. Cline & Frederickson, 1996). Thus to dismiss as 'simplistic' the efforts of educators to use the framework as a tool to discuss, and attempt to better understand, the linguistic challenges their students face risks appearing condescending.

In summary, Wiley's basic point is that the theoretical construction of language and literacy and prescriptions regarding how they should be taught are never neutral in the context of societal power relations. An 'ideological' approach is fundamental to understanding literacy development, particularly in linguistically and culturally diverse settings. I am in full agreement with this perspective and have attempted to highlight how coercive power relations affect the development of language and literacy among bilingual students. However, there are also many important and legitimate questions regarding the nature of language proficiency, the developmental patterns of its various components, and the relationships among language proficiency, cognitive development and academic progress, that cannot be totally reduced to the status of 'ideological' or sociopolitical questions. To dismiss these issues as reflecting an 'autonomous' orientation and to demand that any traces of such an orientation be purged from theoretical approaches to literacy is not only to dismiss much of the entire combined disciplines of psychology and applied linguistics but also to demonstrate a misunderstanding of the nature of intervening or mediating variables. There is absolutely no internal inconsistency in asking questions about the nature of the relationships between language, bilingualism, cognition, and academic achievement within the broader context of a sociopolitical causal model.

## Conclusion

Although much of the discussion in this chapter has revolved around theoretical issues relating to language proficiency and how this relates to academic development, my primary goal has been to clarify misconceptions regarding these issues so that policy-makers and educators can refocus on the issue of how to promote academic language development effectively among bilingual children. If academic language proficiency or CALP is accepted as a valid construct, then certain instructional implications follow. In the first place, as Stephen Krashen (1993) has repeatedly emphasised, extensive *reading* is crucial for academic development, since academic language is found primarily in written text. If bilingual students are not reading extensively, they are not getting access to the language of academic success. Opportunities for collaborative learning and talk about text are also relevant in helping students internalise and more fully comprehend the academic language they find in their extensive reading of text.

*Writing* is also crucial, because when bilingual students write about issues that matter to them they not only consolidate aspects of the academic language they have been reading, they also express their identities through language and (hopefully) receive feedback from teachers and others that will affirm and further develop their expression of self.

In general, the instructional implications of the framework within bilingual/multilingual programmes can be expressed in terms of the three components of the construct of CALP:

- *cognitive:* instruction should be cognitively challenging and require students to use higher-order thinking abilities rather than the low-level memorisation and application skills that are tapped by typical worksheets or drill-and-practice computer programs;
- *academic:* academic content (science, maths, social studies, art) should be integrated with language instruction so that students acquire the specific language of these academic registers; and
- *language:* the development of critical language awareness should be fostered throughout the programme by encouraging students to compare and contrast their languages (phonics conventions, grammar, cognates and so forth) and by providing them with extensive opportunities to carry out projects investigating their own and their community's language use, practices and assumptions – for example, in relation to the status of different varieties.

In short, instruction within a strong bilingual/multilingual programme should provide a *focus on message,* a *focus on language,* and a *focus on use* in both languages (Cummins, in press). If we can say with confidence that our students are generating new knowledge, creating literature and art, and acting on social realities that affect their lives, we know that our programme is effective and that it is developing CALP. These are the kinds of (Quadrant B) instructional activity that the conversational/academic language distinction is intended to foster.

## Acknowledgement

I should like to thank David Corson for helpful comments on an earlier version of this chapter.

## References

Au, K.H. and Jordan, C. (1981) Teaching reading to Hawaiian children: Finding a culturally appropriate solution. In H. Trueba, G.P. Guthrie and K.H. Au (eds) *Culture and the Bilingual Classroom: Studies in Classroom Ethnography* (pp. 139–52). Rowley, MA: Newbury House.

August, D. and Hakuta, K. (eds) (1997) *Improving Schooling for Language-minority Children: A Research Agenda*. Washington, DC: National Academy Press.

Biber, D. (1986) Spoken and written textual dimensions in English: Resolving the contradictory findings. *Language* 62, 384–414.

Bruner, J.S. (1975) Language as an instrument of thought. In A. Davies (ed.) *Problems of Language and Learning* (pp. 61–88). London: Heinemann.

Bullock Report (1975) *A Language for Life*. Report of the Committee of Inquiry appointed by the Secretary of State for Education and Science under the chairmanship of Sir Alan Bullock. London: HMSO.

Campos, J. and Keatinge, R. (1988) The Carpinteria language minority student experience: From theory, to practice, to success. In T. Skutnabb-Kangas and J. Cummins (eds) *Minority Education: From Shame to Struggle* (pp. 299–308). Clevedon: Multilingual Matters.

Cline, T. and Frederickson, N. (1996) *Curriculum-related Assessment, Cummins and Bilingual Children*. Clevedon: Multilingual Matters.

Collier, V.P. (1987) Age and rate of acquisition of second language for academic purposes. *TESOL Quarterly* 21, 617–41.

Corson, D. (1993) *Language, Minority Education and Gender: Linking Social Justice and Power*. Clevedon: Multilingual Matters.

Corson, D. (1995) *Using English Words*. New York: Kluwer.

Corson, D. (1997) The learning and use of academic English words. *Language Learning* 47, 671–718.

Cummins, J. (1979) Cognitive/academic language proficiency, linguistic interdependence, the optimum age question and some other matters. *Working Papers on Bilingualism* 19, 121–29.

Cummins, J. (1981a). Age on arrival and immigrant second language learning in Canada. A reassessment. *Applied Linguistics* 2, 132–49.

Cummins, J. (1981b) The role of primary language development in promoting educational success for language minority students. In California State Department of Education (ed.) *Schooling and Language Minority Students: A Theoretical Framework* (pp. 3–49). Los Angeles: Evaluation, Dissemination and Assessment Center, California State University.

Cummins, J. (1984) *Bilingualism and Special Education: Issues in Assessment and Pedagogy*. Clevedon: Multilingual Matters.

Cummins, J. (1986) Empowering minority students: A framework for intervention. *Harvard Educational Review* 56, 18–36.

Cummins, J. (1989) *Empowering Minority Students*. Sacramento: California Association for Bilingual Education.

Cummins, J. (1996) *Negotiating Identities: Education for Empowerment in a Diverse Society*. Los Angeles: California Association for Bilingual Education.

Cummins, J. (in press) *Teaching the Language of Academic Success*. Monograph to be published by New Jersey TESOL/Bilingual Education Association.

Cummins, J. and Corson, D. (eds) (1997) *Bilingual Education*. Dordrecht: Kluwer Academic.
Cummins, J. and Swain, M. (1983) Analysis-by-rhetoric: Reading the text or the reader's own projections? A reply to Edelsky et al. *Applied Linguistics* 4, 22–41.
Delpit, L.D. (1988) The silenced dialogue: Power and pedagogy in educating other people's children. *Harvard Educational Review* 58, 280–98.
Donaldson, M. (1978) *Children's Minds*. Glasgow: Collins.
Edelsky, C. (1990) *With Literacy and Justice for All: Rethinking the Social in Language and Education*. London: Falmer Press.
Edelsky, C, Hudelson, S., Altwerger, B., Flores, B., Barkin, F. and Jilbert, K. (1983) Semilingualism and language deficit. *Applied Linguistics* 4, 1–22.
Fielding, L.G. and Pearson, P.D. (1994) Reading comprehension: What works. *Educational Leadership* 51, 62–8.
Freire, P. (1970) *Pedagogy of the Oppressed*. New York: Herder & Herder.
Gibbons, J. and Lascar, E. (1998) Operationalizing academic language proficiency in bilingualism research. *Journal of Multilingual and Multicultural Development* 19, 40–50.
Gibbons, P. (1991) *Learning to Learn in a Second Language*. Newtown, Australia: Primary English Teaching Association.
Halliday, M.A.K. and Hasan, R. (1985) *Language, Context and Text: Aspects of Language in a Social-semiotic Perspective*. Geelong, Victoria: Deakin University Press.
Klesmer, H. (1994) Assessment and teacher perceptions of ESL student achievement. *English Quarterly* 26, 5–7.
Krashen, S. (1993) *The Power of Reading*. Englewood, CO: Libraries Unlimited.
Krashen, S. and Biber, D. (1988) *On Course: Bilingual Education's Success in California*. Sacramento: California Association for Bilingual Education.
Martin-Jones, M. and Romaine, S. (1986) Semilingualism: A half-baked theory of communicative competence. *Applied Linguistics* 7, 26–38.
Oller, J. (1979) *Language Tests at School: A Pragmatic Approach*. London: Longman.
Olson, D.R. (1977) From utterance to text: The bias of language in speech and writing. *Harvard Educational Review* 47, 257–81.
Ortiz, A.A. and Yates, J.R. (1983) Incidence of exceptionality among Hispanics: Implications for manpower planning. *NABE Journal* 7, 41–54.
Poe, E.A. (1997) The pit and the pendulum. In *Literature and Integrated Studies: American Literature* (pp. 253–264). Glenview, IL: Scott Foresman.
Ramirez, J.D. (1992) Executive summary. *Bilingual Research Journal* 16, 1–62.
Reyes, M.L. (1992) Challenging venerable assumptions: Literacy instruction for linguistically different students. *Harvard Educational Review* 62, 427–46.
Rivera, C. (ed.) (1984) *Language Proficiency and Academic Achievement*. Clevedon: Multilingual Matters.
Romaine, S. (1989) *Bilingualism*. Oxford: Blackwell.
Skutnabb-Kangas, T. and Toukomaa, P. (1976) *Teaching Migrant Children's Mother Tongue and Learning the Language of the Host Country in the Context of the Sociocultural Situation of the Migrant Family*. Helsinki: Finnish National Commission for UNESCO.
Snow, C.E., Cancino, H., De Temple, J. and Schley, S. (1991) Giving formal definitions: A linguistic or metalinguistic skill? In E. Bialystok (ed.) *Language Processing in Bilingual Children* (pp. 90–112). Cambridge: Cambridge University Press.

Street, B.V. (ed.) (1993) *Cross-Cultural Approaches to Literacy.* Cambridge: Cambridge University Press.

Troike, R. (1984) SCALP: Social and cultural aspects of language proficiency. In C. Rivera (ed.) *Language Proficiency and Academic Achievement* (pp. 44–54). Clevedon: Multilingual Matters.

Verhoeven, L. (1991) Acquisition of biliteracy. *AILA Review* 8, 61–74

Wald, B. (1984) A sociolinguistic perspective on Cummins' current framework for relating language proficiency to academic achievement. In C. Rivera (ed.) *Language Proficiency and Academic Achievement* (pp. 55–70). Clevedon: Multilingual Matters.

Wells, G. (1981) *Learning through Interaction: The Study of Language Development.* Cambridge: Cambridge University Press.

Wells, G. (1986) *The Meaning Makers.* Portsmouth, NH: Heinemann.

Wiley, T.G. (1996) *Literacy and Language Diversity in the United States.* Washington, DC: Center for Applied Linguistics and Delta Systems.

*Chapter 5*
# The Dynamics of Third Language Acquisition

PHILIP HERDINA AND ULRIKE JESSNER

This chapter focuses on research paradigms and their usefulness in third language acquisition (TLA). As already discussed by Jasone Cenoz in Chapter 3, the process of learning a third language is more complex than second language acquisition (SLA) and requires different skills of the learner. Research on TLA therefore implies specific challenges. In this chapter we intend to analyse the dynamic processes of third language learning and to explain the advantages a holistic view of multilingualism offers by comparison with other research models currently in use.

We propose to combine various fields of language acquisition research, transcending the distinctions made between first language acquisition (FLA) research, SLA research and research on multilingualism comprising more than two languages. Due to the limitations of a chapter of this kind we will not be able to give an overview of the current theories; the reader is therefore referred to, for example, Fletcher and MacWhinney (1995) for FLA, Ellis (1994), Ritchie and Bhatia (1996) for SLA and Baker (1996) for both SLA and bilingualism. Taking into consideration the degree of convergence in these theoretically divergent and multifaceted fields of research we suggest a paradigm shift in research on multilingualism (as seen in this volume), where the traditional borders between FLA, SLA and TLA might have to be redrawn. The approach described in this chapter is also intended to offer new perspectives on language learning for the field of applied linguistics, especially in questions on multilingual education.

## Clarification of Terms

As there seems to be some confusion concerning the terminology used to define our object of reference, trilingualism, we shall first specify those terms most frequently utilised to refer to multilingual phenomena from our perspective. Discussion of multilingualism is often equated with research on bilingualism. We should, however, bear in mind that bilingualism is only one possible form of multilingualism, albeit a common one, and that multilingualism is more challenging theoretically when it involves more than two languages. From our position it is therefore important to view multilingualism as a varied phenomenon ranging from monolingual acquisition (the acquisition of a foreign language based on the command of one language), through balanced bilingualism, to the command of three or more languages, to name but a few of the stages on the multilingual continuum.

Research on multilingualism, which can also cover learning a third, fourth or more languages, must therefore clearly go beyond bilingualism and SLA. We definitely do not wish to identify bilinguals with multilinguals, as has frequently been the case in research where the use of only two languages has been investigated; hence it is of interest to focus on trilingualism, meaning the use of three languages, and on TLA, meaning the process of learning a third language. In this context, therefore, trilingualism presents a significant specification of the term 'multilingualism'. As this discussion has already made clear, we regard SLA as linked to bilingualism – although most often the two have been discussed in different fields of research, we consider them, as do for example Baker (1996) and Bialystok (1991), to be similar processes, with a wide range of products dependent on the various factors involved in the language acquisition process.

## Some Features of Multilingual Development

### Non-linearity

One of the common denominators in current theories of language learning seems to be the idea of a gradual sequence of language improvement leading to an acceptable degree of mastery of a language system. Language acquisition has thus traditionally been considered a linear process (see Figure 5.1). This opinion is voiced both in cognitive psychology and in applied linguistics research:

> If developmental paths were always straight and always uphill, they would not be nearly as interesting as they are. One usually implicitly assumes a linear model of growth and change; we presuppose that, all things being equal, development will be gradual (no sudden accelerations or decelerations), monotonic (always move in the same upward direction), and continuous (reflecting quantitative changes in some constant measure or dimension). This is the 'garden variety' model of change. (Elman *et al.*, 1998: 42)

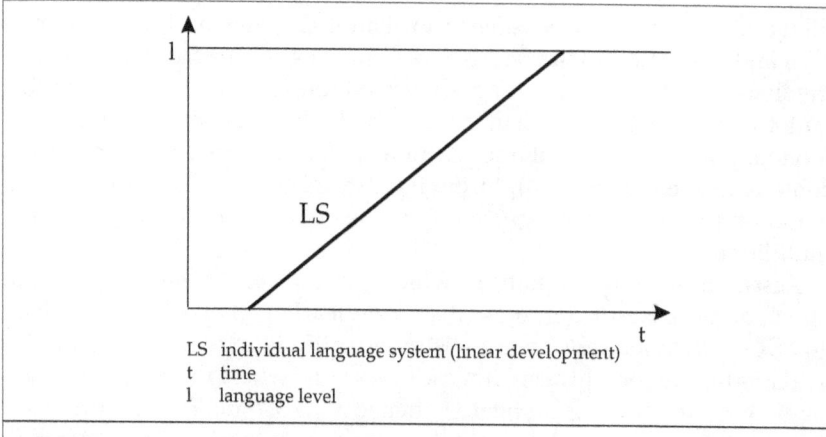

**Figure 5.1** Linear process
*Most theories of language learning presuppose an implicit linear model of acquisition. The graph is intended to express the assumption of monotonous or homogeneous growth.*

Much of the research to date has assumed that L2 acquisition is a linear process in which learners acquire one linguistic item perfectly, one item at a time. This is what I have called the 'building-block' metaphor. The learner puts down one linguistic block at a time, until the imposing edifice called an L2 is complete. (Nunan, 1996: 37)

We have been presented with a theory of language learning explaining the progress made in acquiring the command of a language, be it first, second or third, as an ordered sequence of individual steps. We thus obtain some kind of ladder, suggesting a steady upward motion where one step follows on the other (see Figure 5.2).

Biological growth processes are, however, known not to follow this model. As argued by Waddington (1977) and van Geert (1994), they are far more likely to develop non-linear patterns. We must assume that growth patterns in real life are non-linear; this means that under ideal circumstances we obtain a growth curve that shows some similarity to a sinus curve. Initially we observe slow growth which then increases its rate of acceleration before it finally slows down to achieve a state of equilibrium:

> If we look at the actual growth that one is likely to find in a real biological system ...there is often a short period at the beginning, known as a lag phase, in which the system is adapting itself to its surroundings. Then it may grow for a long time exponentially ...But eventually the

rate of growth begins to slacken, the curve of size begins to rise less steeply, and then turns over and becomes flat. (Waddington, 1977: 73)

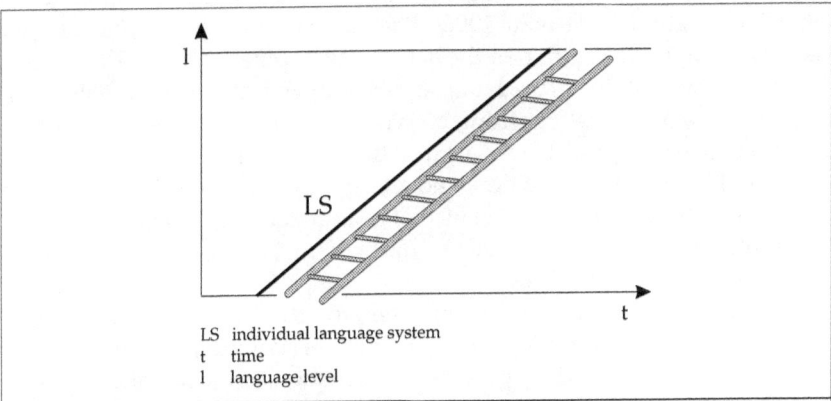

**Figure 5.2** Ladder
*The ladder illustration shows that the assumed stages of development do not change the underlying principle of homogeneous growth. The discovery of stages of development does not preclude the homogeneous linear growth assumption.*

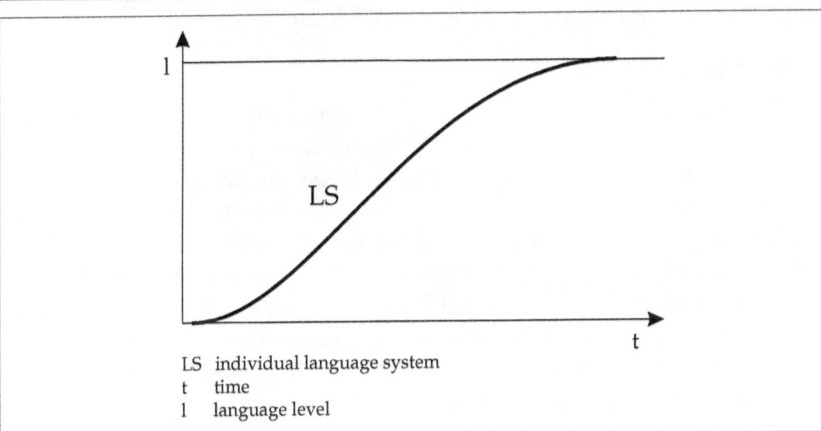

**Figure 5.3** Biological growth
*According to biological principles language development is seen as a dynamic process with phases of accelerated growth and retardation. The development is dependent on environmental factors and is indeterminate.*

This sine curve is obviously only an approximation of the effective development of the system as the learning process goes through individual stages of improvement and restructuring (see for example, McLaughlin, 1990; McLaughlin & Heredia, 1996). The curve we therefore obtain is to be seen as a rough idealisation of the actual development observed.

The reason why the growth curve slows down is because in real-world terms the learner is confronted with limited resources. Within a psycholinguistic context we argue that these limited resources are expressed in the amount of time and energy learners are able to spend on the acquisition and the maintenance of a language. If learners do not continue to refresh their knowledge of a particular L2 or L3, a gradual process of language attrition will set in.

The fact that finite resources limit the growth process is a well-known biological fact (Waddington, 1977: 74). From an evolutionary point of view this is obviously a necessary process of adaptation, as the retention of skills that have outlived their usefulness would unnecessarily increase the information load on a biological system.

We must therefore object that language learning has all too frequently been seen in excessively abstract terms; such terms fail to include a biological model of the language learner, who is seen as some kind of theoretical learning-machine with unlimited resources, whereas in fact any learner will have to apportion a certain amount of time to a learning process and that time will not then be available for other processes.

## Learner variation

Ellis (1994: 467–560), for instance, gives a very comprehensive overview of research on individual learner differences, which makes it clear that learners achieve significantly differing levels of competence (see also Skehan, 1989; Kuhs, 1989; Cenoz, Chapter 3 this volume). To our minds far too little attention has been paid to these sometimes very pronounced differences. Needless to say, the divergence can be so marked that it is difficult to believe that the learners started from the same initial conditions. If we assume that learner and speaker differences cannot be attributed to innate disposition alone, we must accept that environmental factors, both psychological and sociological, determine both the rate of growth and the rate of attrition of the command of a language.

We can therefore assume the existence of at least two types of factor determining the rate of language growth or language attrition. These are traditionally presented as psychological on the one hand and sociological on the other. They should not, however, be seen as two entirely separate categories. One should rather take it that the psychological factors are embedded in sociological factors, i.e. the psychological factors are at least in part to be seen as dependent on sociological ones.

Let us take one factor for the purpose of illustration. We can reasonably propose that individual motivation will have a significant effect on the amount of effort put into the maintenance of a specific language system, and therefore on language growth or language attrition (see Dörnyei, 1998). The factor 'motivation' will itself depend on the desirability of a certain language (which is determined by sociological parameters) and the competence the individual perceives herself or himself to have. Perceived language competence is, however, not identical to language competence as attributed or measured by others, although these two factors are likely to be related.

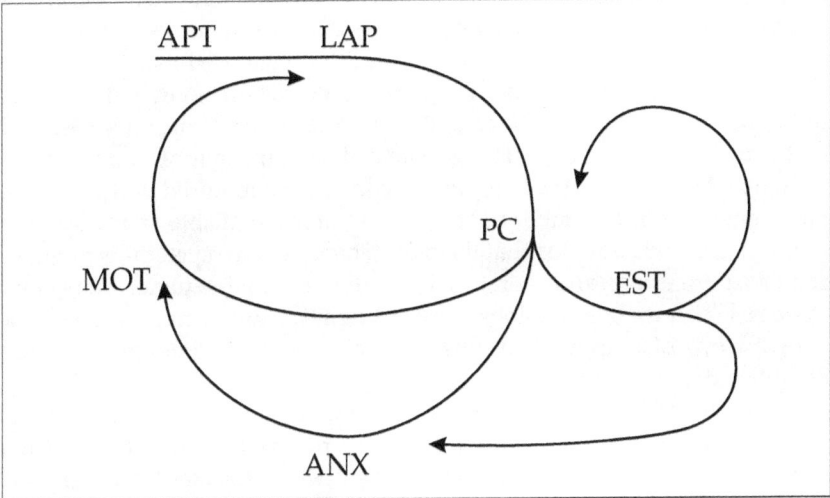

**Figure 5.4** Complex relations between factors

APT     aptitude
LAP     language acquisition progress
PC      perceived language competence
ANX    anxiety
MOT    motivation
EST     esteem

*The relationship between the exemplary factors (aptitude, perceived language competence, anxiety, motivation, esteem) determine the rate and direction of the development of the new language system. The presentation is intended to show the autodynamic behaviour of the system.*

It is furthermore important to note that these factors not only relate to language growth, but also relate to each other in more than merely unidirectional relationships. As soon as the system contains feedback loops, it obviously has the ability to determine its own conditions of growth. The input provided by the individual factors will determine the direction of growth and the size of the input will determine the rate of growth. This behaviour can be termed 'autodynamic' or in Maturana's terms, 'autopoetic'(Maturana & Varela, 1980; 1987).

### Maintenance, reversibility and stability

The theoretical progress we would thus expect in learning is countered by the requirements made by language maintenance (see Herdina & Jessner, 1998). A language system needs obviously not only to be learned; it has also to be maintained. At some stage in the learning process, therefore, the effort required for the maintenance of the system will start to exceed that available for learning and the growth process will begin to decelerate, until growth as such comes to an end because all available input is required for the maintenance of the existing system at a certain level of competence.

It must be clear that the amount of maintenance required will at least in part depend on the number of language systems available at any specific point in time. It is obvious that the maintenance of two systems is going to require more effort (and therefore time) than the maintenance of just one system. When we begin to look at multilingual systems that exceed established forms of bilingualism, this issue obviously becomes rather more complicated.

As discussed in Jessner and Herdina (1996), acquired language systems do not exist side by side in 'mutual harmony' but start to interfere with each other (see also Cenoz, Bouvy, Chapters 3 and 8). As the language learner is forced to deploy identical language resources for more than one language system, competition for shared resources essentially also means not only that we can observe learning processes, but that these learning processes are necessarily reversible.

Language requirements (for example a redefinition of language needs due to emigration) force language users to divert their attention from the maintenance of a certain language system. As a consequence that language system will not be fully active and will inevitably begin to decay. As we still only have a very rough or rudimentary idea of the variety of factors influencing language development, we can only hint at a few of the influences to be considered relevant within a dynamic model. The rate of decay will depend on:

- the limitations of available resources;
- the pressure created by competing language systems;
- the duration of language maintenance (how long the language has been used for will determine the rate of decay); and
- the age of language acquisition, which due to neurophysiological maturation processes (see for instance Obler, 1993) will determine the susceptibility of language systems to processes of decay – which does not necessarily correspond to age (Harley & Hart, 1997; Muñoz, Lasagabaster, Chapters 9 and 10).

The process of language acquisition can therefore be mirrored in the process of language attrition, where the idealised sinus curve is inverted, lack of maintenance leading to the gradual onset of language attrition and on to a phase of steep decline which finally evens out when maintenance is reduced to a minimum (see Figure 5.5).

An interesting factor to be determined is therefore the relative stability of a language system. We can assume that stability will depend on the degree of flexibility present in the maintenance effort that the learner of a specific language has to put in. If the learner can freely vary the amount of effort, this process of adaptation to environmental pressure will obviously

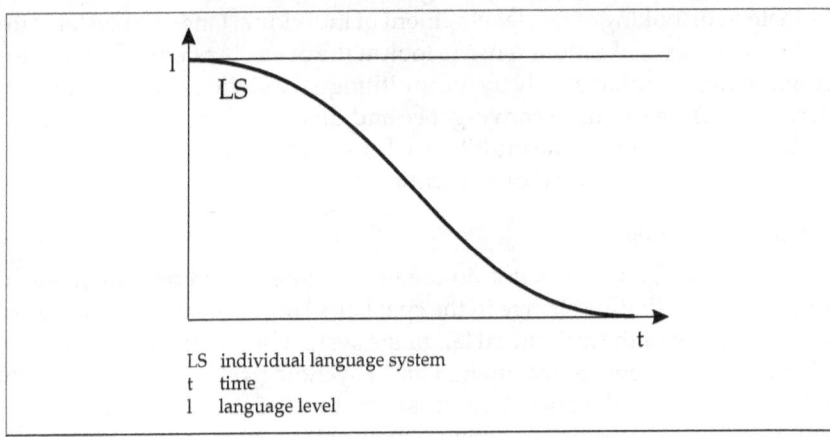

**Figure 5.5** Language attrition
*Gradual language attrition is an inversion of language growth. Lack of maintenance of a language system results in an adaptive process by which language competence is adjusted to meet the perceived communicative needs of the individual speaker.*

increase system stability as a desired effect. System stability will also depend on the number of languages involved – the greater the number of languages available, the greater the amount of maintenance required and the more difficult it will be for the speaker to find the necessary resources.

As suggested above, other factors relevant to individual language stability are the maturational age at which the language concerned is acquired and a relative systems stability is established, and the duration of time over which the language system is maintained, as well as the level of competence at which this takes place.

### Interdependence

If the rate of growth or the rate of attrition of one language system is dependent on the development or behaviour of other language systems used by the multilingual speaker – and/or other interdependent factors – then it does not make sense to look at language acquisition or language growth in terms of isolated language development. The development of each individual language within one multilingual speaker largely depends on the behaviour of previous and subsequent systems. The number and developmental age of preceding language systems or language acquisition processes will determine the rate of growth and rate of attrition of the specific language system under investigation.

Instead of looking at the development of individual language systems in isolation it may make more sense to look at the overall system of languages commanded simultaneously by the multilingual individual and then try to determine the patterns of convergence and divergence of the multilingual system, rather than see the multilingual system as a mere accumulation of the effects of concatenated or sequential individual systems.

### Change of quality

Multilingualism that is not automatically interpreted as bilingualism results in a qualitative change in the speaker's language system. It leads to an enrichment of the individual language system but, as the whole system adapts to meet new environmental and psychological requirements, also changes its nature. We can therefore assume that the acquisition of a further language leads to the development of new skills which begin to form part of the multilingual repertoire. These fall into three main categories.

*Language learning skills*

The cognitive aspect of language learning, i.e. how to learn to learn a language or how to acquire the skills needed for the development of another language system, is one of the factors which due to prior experience with the second language learning process must be considered as developed at a higher level in third language learners than in second language learners (Hufeisen, 1998; Jessner, 1999). Differing language learning strategies in multilinguals are thus also assumed to be connected to an enhanced progress in learning additional languages (Naiman et al., 1995).

*Language management skills*

Depending on the perceived communicative needs of the speaker a certain language from her/his repertoire is chosen as the medium in a communicative act (cf. James, Chapter 3). Yet this repertoire includes not only more than one language but also the means of both integrating different language resources and at the same time keeping them apart. Language management can therefore be defined as the multilingual art of balancing communicative requirements with language resources. The reader can relate this statement to Cummins' extension of language skills (Chapter 4) to include cognitive academic language proficiency created by specific educational environments.

*Language maintenance skills*

Language maintenance has been very little researched so far, but deserves much more attention in future linguistic investigations, since it appears to be the most crucial aspect of the language acquisition process. As we have already noted (Herdina & Jessner, 1998), a lack of effort is more apparent in multilinguals than in mono- or bilingual speakers, because learning becomes much more difficult when the learner is having to not only maintain a certain level of competence in three languages but actually increase the level of all three competences in order to progress. Neither the need to maintain a language at a particular level of competence nor the degree of effort put into its acquisition have so far been brought into discussions of failure to achieve native-like competence, because none of the dominant theories has seen language attrition as a key factor in SLA.

All the above-mentioned skills could be seen as contributing to 'language awareness' or 'metalinguistic awareness' which has been identified as one of the cognitive advantages bilinguals develop due to contact with two language cultures (see for example Baker, 1996; also Cenoz, Lasagabaster, Chapters 3 and 10). To find out about the exact nature of language awareness in multilinguals presents a most challenging issue that needs further research (Jessner, 1999; Kecskés & Papp, Chapter 6). We can, however, assume that the conditions of language acquisition undergo a change of quality in the multilingual speaker, in so far as the acquisition of more than one language encourages the development of a metasystem which is then used in subsequent processes of language learning. It is indeed no longer a question of learning a language, rather one of learning to learn a language. Furthermore, while SLA is always precisely that, i.e. learning a second language in contrast to a first, learning a third language must then relate to a system of two languages (a bilingual norm) rather than just the first language (a monolingual norm).

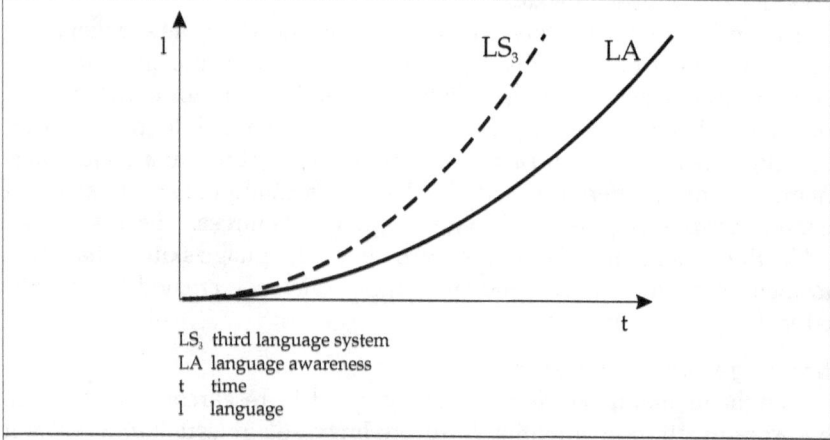

**Figure 5.6** Change of quality
*The acquisition of a third language system leads to the development of new skills in the language learner which necessarily result in a change in the quality of the language system of the multilingual speaker.*

## A Dynamic Model of Multilingualism

### Investigating the complexity of language systems

All the skills mentioned above contribute to the complex psycholinguistic system to be found in a multilingual, a system which not only exhibits its own kind of behaviour but, due to certain parameter changes, is also subject to change over time. In order to describe the nature of multilingualism in its various patterns (cf. Cenoz, Chapter 3) and to be able to explain the changing nature of the linguistic phenomena linked with multilingualism we have developed a dynamic model of multilingualism or DMM (Herdina & Jessner, forthcoming).

As we have tried to make clear in the preceding discussion, the process involved in the learning of a third language is characterised by its complexity, which is a characteristic property of an autodynamic system (cf. van Geert, 1994, on autocatalysis). This complexity is the result of interaction between various factors, linguistic, social and individual. The relationship between some of the variables that play an important role in the SLA process was shown in a study by Gardner, Tremblay and Margoret (1997), the first to examine how language anxiety, self-confidence, attitudes and motivation, language aptitude, learning strategies and field independence interrelated and complemented one another in a single sample of L2 learners. In SLA research investigating the nature of these various factors and the relationship between them have presented a challenge. And more research will be needed if we are to get closer to a clarification of these issues. The development of a third language necessarily makes the picture even more complex.

The claim that a multilingual system is a complex system should not be equated with the claim that multilingual systems are complicated ones. *Complicatedness* must be taken to refer simply to the number of factors involved which will make the system more difficult to understand from a reductionist position. The *complexity* of a system, however, should be taken to imply that – due to the recursive relations between the factors contained in it – the system develops its own dynamism or, in other words, becomes autodynamic.

## Holism

The top-down procedure applied in this chapter, expressed in the assumption that theoretically the understanding of multilingualism has to precede the understanding of monolingualism, is probably most aptly identified with the philosophical tradition of holism. As is well known, the essential tenet of holism is that the whole is more than the sum of its parts. Psycholinguistic holism must therefore assume that a multilingual system is not to be considered as no more than an accumulation of the effects of individual language systems and their acquisition, and that it cannot be adequately understood by adopting this approach.

## Connectionism

We might ask whether, if DMM is a holistic approach, it is at the same time a connectionist one. A connectionist position can be contrasted with a cognitivist one where the principle of symbolic representation of knowledge is replaced by the idea of knowledge or rule-governed behaviour as the result of learning. According to connectionist principles, knowledge as a command of a language is seen as the emergent property of a system of atomic relationships between decision nodes (Varela, 1990; Elman *et al.*, 1998).

Whilst on the one hand DMM does not make specific claims as to which neurophysiological model of learning it rests upon, it does specify an approach which can best be described as analytical holism. This must be taken to mean that although the approach is essentially holistic, DMM will not fail to specify individual subcomponents such as language systems, or purely psychological factors such as self-esteem, as factors identifiably involved with the causal determinants of language development.

## Conclusion

The main arguments of this chapter can be summed up as follows:

- Whilst it would initially appear plausible to assume that the acquisition of a third language just means another language acquired and that the same principles can be applied to TLA as to SLA, we believe that learning a third language differs essentially from learning a second – something third language learners themselves intuitively perceive.

- It must also be argued that a trilingual system differs essentially from a bilingual system, as different competences have resulted from the previous language-related cognitive processes.

- Finally this also implies that multilingual language acquisition research based exclusively on research into bilingualism and SLA will be unable to deal with and explain the phenomena occurring in trilingualism.

The need to develop a new understanding of multilingualism that breaks with the traditions of interpreting language acquisition as a linear process, and to formulate new applications of multilingual theories such as the investigation and encouragement of trilingualism as a linguistic and sociocultural phenomenon, present new challenges to theoretical and applied linguistics.

### References

Baker, C. (1996) *Foundations of Bilingualism and Bilingual Education*. Clevedon: Multilingual Matters.
Bialystok, E. (1991) Introduction. In E. Bialystok (ed.) *Language Processing in Bilingual Children* (pp. 1–9). Cambridge: Cambridge University Press.
Dörnyei, Z. (1998) Motivation in second and foreign language learning. *Language Teaching* 31, 117–85.
Ellis, R. (1994) *The Study of Second Language Acquisition*. Oxford: Oxford University Press.
Elman, J., Bates, E., Johnson, M., Karmiloff-Smith, A., Parisi, D. and Plunkett, K. (1998) *Rethinking Innateness. A Connectionist Perspective on Development*. Cambridge, MA: MIT Press.

Fletcher, P. and MacWhinney, B. (eds) (1995) *Handbook of Child Language*. London: Blackwell.

Gardner, R., Tremblay, P. and Margoret, A. (1997) Towards a full model of second language learning: an empirical investigation. *Modern Language Journal* 8, 344–62.

Harley, B. and Hart, D. (1997) Language aptitude and second language proficiency in classroom learners of different ages. *Studies in Second Language Acquisition* 19, 379–400.

Herdina, P. and Jessner, U. (1998) Language maintenance in multilinguals. A psycholinguistic perspective. In J. Leather and A. James (eds) *New Sounds 97: Proceedings of the Third International Symposium on the Acquisition of Second Language Speech* (pp.135–43). Klagenfurt: University of Klagenfurt.

Herdina, P. and Jessner, U. (forthcoming) *A Dynamic Model of Multilingualism. Changing the Psycholinguistic Perspective*. Clevedon: Multilingual Matters.

Hufeisen, B. (1998) L3 – Stand der Forschung – Was bleibt zu tun? In B. Hufeisen and B. Lindemann (eds) *Tertiärsprachen. Theorien, Modelle, Methoden* (pp. 169–83). Tübingen: Stauffenburg.

Jessner, U. and Herdina, P. (1996) Interaktionsphänomene in multilingualen Menschen: Erklärungsmöglichkeiten durch einen systemtheoretischen Ansatz. In A. Fill (ed.) *Sprachökologie und Ökolinguistik* (pp. 217–30). Tübingen: Stauffenburg.

Jessner, U. (1999) Metalinguistic awareness in multilinguals: Cognitive aspects of third language acquisition. *Language Awareness* 8 (3&4), 201–9.

Kuhs, K. (1989) *Sozialpsychologische Faktoren im Zweitspracherwerb. Eine Untersuchung bei griechischen Migrantenkindern in der Bundesrepublik Deutschland*. Tübingen: Narr.

Maturana, H. and Varela, F. (1980) *Autopoiesis and Cognition. The Realization of the Living*. Dordrecht: Riedel.

Maturana, H. and Varela, F. (1987) *Der Baum der Erkenntnis. Die biologischen Wurzeln menschlichen Erkennens*. Bern: Scherz.

McLaughlin, B. (1990) Restructuring. *Applied Linguistics* 11, 113–28.

McLaughlin, B. and Heredia, R. (1996) Information-processing approaches to research on second language acquisition and use. In W. Ritchie and T.K. Bhatia (eds) *Handbook of Second Language Acquisition* (pp. 213–28). San Diego: Academic Press.

Naiman, N., Fröhlich, M., Stern, H. and Todesco, A. (1995). *The Good Language Learner*. Clevedon: Multilingual Matters.

Nunan, D. (1996) Issues in second language acquisition research: Examining substance and procedure. In W. Ritchie and T.K. Bhatia (eds) *Handbook of Second Language Acquisition* (pp. 349–74). San Diego: Academic Press.

Obler, L. (1993) Neurolinguistic aspects of second language development and attrition. In K. Hyltenstam and Å. Viberg (eds) *Progression and Regression in Language* (pp. 178–95). Cambridge: Cambridge University Press.

Ritchie, W. and Bhatia, T.K. (eds) (1996) *Handbook of Second Language Acquisition*. San Diego: Academic Press.

Skehan, P. (1989) *Individual Differences in Second Language Learning*. London: Edward Arnold.

van Geert, P. (1994) *Dynamic Systems of Development. Change between Complexity and Chaos*. New York: Harvester Wheatsheaf.

Varela, F. (1990) *Kognitionswissenschaft – Kognitionstechnik. Eine Skizze aktueller Perspektiven.* Frankfurt: Suhrkamp.
Waddington, C.H. (1977) *Tools for Thought.* Paladin: Frogmore.

## Chapter 6
# Metaphorical Competence in Trilingual Language Production

ISTVAN KECSKÉS AND TUNDE PAPP

Relying on data collected in a longitudinal experiment, the study described in this chapter examines metaphorical density in written productions of trilingual (Hungarian, Russian, English/French) and bilingual students (Hungarian and Russian) in order to investigate conceptual fluency in multilinguals from a cognitive–pragmatic perspective. Although the focus of attention is on students studying English as a third language, their production will be compared with that of students who have studied either French or Russian as their second or third language.

## Multicompetence

Knowledge of more than one language can result in 'multicompetence', defined by Cook as 'the compound state of a mind with two grammars' (1991: 112). We have argued, however, that what makes a speaker multicompetent is the common underlying conceptual base (CUCB), rather than the existence of two grammars in the mind, and have postulated a multilingual language processing device (LPD) which consists of two or more constantly available interacting systems (CAIS) and a CUCB (Kecskés & Papp, 2000). But multicompetence does not develop in every multilingual. A proficiency threshold has to be passed if the CUCB is to develop (Kecskés & Papp, 2000). If this threshold has not been reached, the learning of subsequent languages is merely an educational enhancement since, as De Bot (1992) has claimed, the L1 is usually flexible enough to add the emerging foreign language as an additional register to those already in existence. The trilingual situation constitutes an interesting case of multicompetence because very often multicompetence is already established in the process of the acquisition of the second language, and the third language can either become an incorporated part of the CUCB (if the proficiency threshold has been reached), or just another register of the bilingual LPD. A possible third case is where a speaker is learning two foreign languages but will not achieve multicompetence because proficiency in neither of them is strong enough for a CUCB to develop.

## Language specificity of the CUCB

The CUCB is a single store for multi-modal mental representations which are acquired through experience in discourse (Paradis, 1995; Kecskés & Papp, 2000). Consequently, these representations are linguistically and culturally grounded. Based on her findings Pavlenko (1996: 68) concluded that 'bilingual cognition is not code-dependent but rather concept-dependent, with the language of origin of the bilingual's concepts related to the learner's history'. She suggested that cultural exposure is crucial in the development of concepts. The full acquisition and proper use of a concept requires the learner to know not only its lexical–semantic counterpart and the associated declarative knowledge, but also the multi-modal mental representation and culturally based behavioural scripts and schemata which are acquired through genuine communication. Learners need direct experience with concepts in the target language because the conceptual system of each language operates differently. Lakoff and Johnson (1980: 3) argued that 'our ordinary conceptual system in terms of which we both think and act is fundamentally metaphorical in nature'. Metaphor is not just a matter of language, that is, of mere words. Human thought processes are largely metaphorical because a considerable part of the human conceptual system is metaphorically structured and defined. There is psychological evidence to support the cognitive reality of metaphorical structuring (for example Gentner & Gentner, 1982; Hunt & Agnoli, 1991; Sweetser, 1990).

The language and culture dependency of the CUCB leads us to the issue of linguistic relativism, basically a rejection of the monolingual view which goes back to great philosophers such as Locke and Leibniz as well as to great linguists like von Humboldt and Sapir. Locke (1690/1959), for instance, was convinced that lexical variation reflects cultural differences among different speech communities. He argued:

> If we look a little more nearly into this matter, and exactly compare different languages, we shall find that, though they have words which in translations and dictionaries are supposed to answer one another, yet there is scarce one of ten amongst the names of complex ideas, especially of mixed modes, that stands for the same precise idea which the word does that in dictionaries it is rendered by. (vol. 2: 49)

Wilhelm von Humboldt (1903/1936, vol. 4:2) expressed similar ideas, saying 'thinking is not merely dependent on language in general but, up to a certain degree, on each specific language'. He considered different languages as bearers of different cognitive perspectives and different world views. These ideas were further developed by Sapir and Whorf. *Linguistic relativism,* known as the Sapir–Whorf theory (Sapir, 1921; Whorf, 1956a, 1956b) and emphasising the bidirectional relationship between language and cultural or cognitive structure, has been rejected from a monolingual, universalist perspective which has made the 'intertranslatability postulate' one of the basic maxims of modern linguistics. This maxim claims that anything can be expressed in any language (Lenneberg, 1953; Searle, 1969).

A multilingual approach requires that the Sapir–Whorf theory be re-examined from the perspective of a possible CUCB. The acknowledgment of a bidirectional or multidirectional influence between the L1 and Lx in multilinguals, together with Vygotsky's (1962) claim of cognitive–linguistic interdependency through thought and word, must urge us to rethink the theory. Sweetser (1990: 7) argued that 'few linguists or anthropologists would be upset by the hypothesis that learning a word for a culturally important category could linguistically reinforce the learning of the category itself'. Her conclusion is that there seem to be areas of interdependence between cognition and language. This is basically what we emphasised earlier about the CUCB. The main criticism against the Sapir– Whorf theory is true: a considerable part of the basic cognitive apparatus is *not* dependent on language and culture. That makes it possible for human beings to share a lot of prelinguistic and extralinguistic experience that is likely to shape language rather than to be shaped by it (Sweetser, 1990). Consequently, the 'strong' version of linguistic relativism has to be rejected.

The 'weak' version of the theory, however, does seem to be supported by the multicompetence approach. It can hardly be denied that language has some kind of a limited role in shaping cognition. We must return to Humboldt's argument which postulated that thinking depends on a specific language up to a certain degree. So the real issue here is not dependency, but the *degree* of dependency. This concurs with Wierzbicka's (1993: 7) view that the real question is 'to what extent languages are shaped by "human nature" and to what extent they are shaped by culture'. The multilingual CUCB contains concepts which are language-specific because they represent a unique part of the culture associated with that language (Kecskés & Papp, 2000).

A cross-linguistic study by Osgood *et al.* (1975) of universals and language-specific elements in the lexicon also supported a limited form of linguistic relativism. They found that connotations associated with certain words are quite similar across languages, but that a number of words have special emotional significance which vary in different languages. One difficulty with multilingual development is that each language has its own metaphorical and figurative system which is not compatible with the metaphorical system of another language: Americans 'make money', Russians 'work for money' ('зарабатывать'), Hungarians 'look for money' (*pénzt keres*).

Taylor argued (1993: 212) that:

> if the meanings of linguistic forms are equated with conceptualizations, and these conceptualizations are conventionalized in a language, then the conceptualizations are made available to speakers of a language by the language system that they have learned.

This has a very important consequence for multilingualism. Formal differences between languages are reflections of differences in conceptualisation. When acquiring a non-primary language, learners have to learn not only the forms of that particular language but also *the conceptual structures that are associated with those forms*. Here is the main difference between second language acquisition and foreign language learning. Whereas in the second language environment there exists the possibility of learning forms and conceptual structures represented by those forms simultaneously, in the foreign language environment learners are usually expected to focus on forms while learning little or nothing about the conceptual structures those forms represent. This often results in a non-native-like production which is usually good and understandable but lacks the idiomaticity of native-speaker speech.

Lack of knowledge of underlying conceptual structures in the target language does not mean, however, that foreign language learners use target language forms without conceptual structures; it means that, not having full access to Taylor's 'conventionalised conceptualisations' of the target language, they usually rely on the conceptual base of their mother tongue and map target language forms on L1 conceptualisations (Kecskés, 1995). Consequently, their problem is primarily not grammatical but conceptual. Grammatical and lexical problems usually derive from conceptual failures. Acquiring a second or foreign language requires reconceptualisation (changing at least a part of the existing L1-based conceptual base) which involves not only lexical and cultural concepts but also grammatical categories.[1] The main problems in multilingual development do not necessarily lie in grammatical knowledge and communicative skills. The grammar of a non-primary language is completely learnable and communicative skills can be acquired. We have hundreds of years of experience of how to learn and/or teach them. *The real problem lies in conceptualisation*. This is why there is nothing like full mastery of a second or foreign language, and this is where multicompetence should be distinguished from monocompetence. Foreign language learners have not only to master the grammatical structures and communicative peculiarities of the new language but also, in order to sound native-like, they have to learn to think as native speakers do, perceive the world the way native speakers do, and use the language metaphorically as native speakers do. Since this conceptual fluency (Danesi, 1992) is the basis of all linguistic acts in a language, problems occurring in grammar and in the use of communicative skills are also, quite frequently, the result of inadequate conceptual fluency. Danesi (1992) argued that students typically use target language words and structures as 'carriers' of their own native language concepts.

## Conceptual fluency

Among foreign language learners there is an assumption that no real fluency is possible in a foreign language unless the learner spends some time in the target language country. Every language learner travelling in the target language country has experienced a certain kind of frustration which is the result of not conveying meaning the same way as native speakers do, i.e. using wrong or non-native-like constructions, phrases, and words. What these learners lack most is *conceptual fluency* which means knowing how the target language reflects or encodes its concepts on the basis of metaphorical structuring (Danesi 1992: 490) and other cognitive mechanisms (Kövecses & Szabó, 1996). This kind of knowledge is as important as grammatical and communicative knowledge. We think that it is even more important than the other two because conceptual knowledge *serves as a basis* for grammatical and communicative knowledge. For example, in order to be able to use conditional sentences in English properly, one must understand how the conditional is conceptualised in English. Or when a native speaker says 'I don't get your *point'*, he scans the conceptual domain in his mind that has the form 'Ideas are geometrical objects' (Danesi 1992: 490). What happens in the foreign language environment is that learners acquire grammatical knowledge and communicative knowledge without firm conceptual knowledge in the target language. That makes their language use significantly different from that of native speakers. One would think conceptual fluency is important only for advanced language proficiency, but that is only partly true. Language learners can achieve fairly good fluency in the target language without conceptual fluency in the Lx mainly because there are many aspects of language learning that are not conceptual. These aspects may be perceptual, indexical, iconic, or denotative, which can be obtained by the foreign language learners without much difficulty. But speakers with low levels of conceptual fluency will never sound native-like.

## Metaphorical competence

Research suggests that at least a certain portion of the human mind is 'programmed' to think metaphorically (cf. Lakoff & Johnson, 1980; Lakoff, 1987; Johnson, 1987; Danesi, 1992). Metaphor probably underlies the representation of a considerable part of our common concepts. Coining an analogous term to grammatical competence and communicative competence Danesi (1992) suggested that metaphorical competence (MC) is as important as the other two because it is closely linked to the ways in which a culture organises its world conceptually. Not only are thinking and acting based on this conceptual system but in large part communication as well. Therefore, language is an important source of evidence of what that system is like. MC is a basic feature of native-speaker speech production because native speakers usually programme discourse in metaphorical ways. According to Winner (1982: 253), recent experimental literature has made it clear that 'if people were limited to strictly literal language, communication would be severely curtailed, if not terminated'. One of the reasons why foreign language learners' speech does not sound native-like is that they use literal rather than metaphorical or figurative language.

At this point, however, Valeva's criticism (1996) of Danesi's approach appears to be correct. She argued against the reduction of conceptual fluency to metaphorical competence. There are many 'literal' concepts, in the sense of being directly understood, without any metaphorical processes. This is absolutely true: metaphorical competence is a very important part of conceptual fluency but it would be a mistake to equate MC with conceptual fluency. Consequently, the real question from our perspective is to what extent can conceptual fluency (rather than metaphorical competence!) be developed in a foreign language environment?

To answer this question we will have to review research on MC as well as other constituents of conceptual fluency. As the result of a pilot study Danesi (1992: 495) suggested that metaphorical competence, even at the level of comprehension, is inadequate in typical classroom learners. In his opinion the reason for this is not that students are incapable of learning metaphors, but most likely that they have never been exposed in formal ways to the conceptual system of the target language. Another study by Danesi (1992) that focused on 'metaphorical density' in non-native speakers' essays found that student compositions showed a high degree of 'literalness' and contained conceptual metaphors that were alike in both languages (Spanish and English). Danesi concluded that after three or four years of study in a classroom those students had learned virtually no 'new way' of thinking conceptually but were still relying mainly on their L1 conceptual base. There are no studies yet that compare the metaphorical competence of second language learners and foreign language learners. But there is little doubt that second language learners would do better.

Danesi argued that grammatical, communicative and metaphorical competence constitute overlapping layers in discourse programming, and that MC is teachable in classroom situations just like grammatical and communicative competence. He urged educators to develop instructional techniques and materials to acquire MC. In fact, as we have said, the focus of attention should be on conceptual fluency rather than on metaphorical competence. The importance of developing conceptual fluency has been emphasised in other contexts in a number of research reports. Discussing the production of idioms Irujo (1993) suggested that students should be taught strategies to deal with figurative language, and those strategies would help them take advantage of the semantic transparency of some idioms. Kövecses and Szabó (1996) argued that teaching about "orientational" metaphors underlying phrasal verbs will result in better acquisition of this difficult type of idiom. Bouton (1994) reported that formal instruction designed to develop pragmatic skills seemed to be highly effective when it was focused on formulaic implicatures. These studies suggest that conceptual fluency (including metaphorical competence) can be developed in the classroom if students are taught about the underlying cognitive mechanisms. Valeva (1996), however, thinks that the issue of learnability should be investigated before facing the question of teachability, and it is still an open question whether or not the conceptual system of a foreign language is learnable or not in a classroom setting.

## The Experiment

As mentioned above, Danesi (1992) found that even after three or four years of foreign languages studies students demonstrate low levels of metaphorical density in their target language productions.

In order to verify the validity of Danesi's assumption we analysed the written production of tri- and bilingual students who had taken part in an experiment conducted in Hungary with the aim of measuring the effect of foreign language learning on the development and use of mother-tongue skills (see reports on the experiment in Papp, 1991; Kecskés & Papp, 1995; Kecskés, 1998; Kecskés & Papp, 2000). We thought that the data collected during the experiment would serve our purposes very well, for three reasons:

(1) We would be able to investigate metaphorical density in data collected earlier for other purposes. This should mean avoiding any kind of bias in data collection procedures, since these had been designed with a research addendum in mind that differed significantly from our own.
(2) On one occasion during the longitudinal experiment data were collected in both the L1 and the target language simultaneously. Students were expected to write a story about a picture-series, first in the L3, and then in their L1. These data would give us the chance to compare metaphorical density (MD) in the L1 texts with MD in the foreign language texts.
(3) As English was to be the main focus of attention in our study, it was important that we have data from students who had studied English in a specialised class or in a normal class. We would have the opportunity to compare their results with those of trilingual students studying French in a dual language school and bilingual students studying Russian in a specialised class or in a normal class.

The primary goal of the longitudinal experiment conducted in Hungary in 1988–90 was to find out how foreign language learning influences mother-tongue development and use at a decisive period (age 14–16) when acquisition of the mother tongue is intensive, and individual writing, learning, and problem-solving strategies and styles are being developed (Papp, 1991; Kecskés & Papp, 1995; Kecskés & Papp, 2000). The participants in the experiment were Hungarian high school students aged 14, all of whom had studied Russian for at least four years, usually in three classes a week, before entering high school because Russian was compulsory from Grade 4 of elementary school at that time in Hungary.[2] Consequently English or French was the third language for the majority of the participants, with the exception of the specialised class where half the students studied English and the other half studied Russian for between seven and eight hours a week. Some of the students had already learned some English in the elementary school as well, but French was entirely new to the immersion class. The three types of class involved in the experiment were as follows:

*Immersion class*
Some school subjects such as maths, biology, chemistry were taught in

the foreign language: there were 36 students in the immersion class, whose target language was French.

*Specialised class*

Students in the specialised class studied either English or Russian. They had seven or eight foreign language classes a week, but the target language was not the medium of instruction in any content area class. All the school subjects were taught in Hungarian and there were 35 students.

*Control (normal) class*

Students had two or three hours of foreign language instruction a week in either English or Russian. All the school subjects were taught in Hungarian and there were 33 students.

As the description of the classes shows, all students had three languages with the exception of the second half of the specialised and control classes where students continued their Russian studies. The students' social background and education was approximately the same in each of the three classes. Most of them came from middle-class families, and all of them had good grades in elementary school. The selected high schools were well-known and prestigious institutions. On entering high school all participants in the experiment were aged 14.

## Data Collection

Although data collection methods were developed with respect to the primary goal of the longitudinal experiment, a considerable part of the data thus collected can also be used for the purposes of our own study, in which we will be relying on the results of two tests out of the three conducted during the earlier experiment. The first test in the original experiment was given in Hungarian only and aimed at measuring the state of L1 knowledge in the participants; therefore we shall not describe that survey here. The other two tests, however, are relevant to our subject matter.

The second test was conducted at the end of the first year in high school, when the students were 15. Their task was to write a story based on a picture-series, first in the target language, and then in their mother tongue. The picture-series was slightly modified when students were required to write their story in the L1, but this modification was required by the original goals of the experiment and has nothing to do with our own subject matter.

The third test was administered a year later. Students were given several classified newspaper advertisements in their mother tongue and in the foreign language. They had to choose to respond to one advertisement in their L1, and to respond to a different one in the foreign language they were studying.

## Analysis of data

Data were analysed with the aim of answering the following research questions:

(1) How does the average metaphorical density (AMD) of English texts relate to the AMD of texts written in the other two languages?
(2) How do the results in the foreign language relate to the scores in the mother tongue in the first test?
(3) How do trilingual productions relate to bilingual ones?
(4) Are there any differences between genders in the use of metaphorical language?
(5) How does metaphorical density relate to structural well-formedness? (the latter was discussed in Papp, 1991; Kecskés & Papp, 1995; and Kecskés, 2000.)

An index of metaphorical density (MD) was computed for each written production in the foreign language. This simply measured the number of metaphorical expressions in the writings of the students as a percentage of the total number of sentences written. If, for instance, a text consisting of nine sentences contained three metaphorical expressions the MD index was 3/9 = 0.33 = 33%. It was irrelevant for this count whether metaphorical expressions occurred in one sentence only or in several sentences. We did not count repeated instances of a conceptual metaphor because these can be considered simply as elaborations. An average metaphorical density (AMD) was then computed for each group and test. The two surveys gave the results presented in Tables 6.1, 6.2 and 6.3.

### Metaphorical density (MD)

Number of metaphorical expressions = ME
Total number of sentences = TS

**Table 6.1** AMD index (average metaphorical density): immersion class

| Students | First test | Second test | |
|---|---|---|---|
| | L3 (French) | L1 (Hungarian) | L3 (French) |
| Boys | 20% | 56% | 26% |
| Girls | 17% | 42% | 30% |

**Table 6.2** AMD index: specialised class

| Students | First test | Second test | | | |
|---|---|---|---|---|---|
| | L3 (English) | L2 (Russian) | L1 (Hungarian) | L3 (English) | L2 (Russian) |
| Boys | 20% | 13% | 35% | 24% | 11% |
| Girls | 16% | 5% | 32% | 23% | 14% |

**Table 6.3** AMD index: control class

| Students | First test | | Second test | |
|---|---|---|---|---|
| | L3 and L2 (English/ Russian) | L1 | L3 (English) | L2 (Russian) |
| Boys | no minimum data | 38% | 16% | 0% |
| Girls | no minimum data | 30% | 7% | 8% |

## Discussion

### Data analysis

This clearly demonstrated two important things, the first of which was that *metaphorical competence significantly depends upon the intensiveness of language learning and the quality of input.* The results of the class specialised in English (SEC) were basically almost the same as the results of the French immersion class (FIC) in the first test. After a year the French class was slightly ahead of the English class.

This slight difference is a bit surprising. After two years of immersion in French one would expect the FIC group to do much better than the specialised English class, where students did not have English as a medium of instruction and studied the language for no more than seven to eight hours a week. We think this can be explained by two facts. First, the majority of the trilingual SEC had studied English before they were accepted into the high school. Consequently they had had a relatively longer exposure to English than the students in the French immersion class had had to French, which was new to all of them when they started high school two years before. Second, exposure to Anglophone culture (music, books, magazines,

TV, films and so following) in Hungary has always been more intensive than to Francophone culture. All this has some kind of an indirect influence on the conceptual fluency of students studying English as their third language in a foreign language setting. The difference is greater between the specialised English class (SEC) and the normal English class (NEC) than between the FIC and the SEC. In the second test the SEC boys produced 8% better than the NEC boys, and the SEC girls' results were 16% (!) better than that of the NEC girls. These numbers clearly demonstrate how important the intensiveness of learning can be in the development of conceptual fluency in a foreign language.

Analysis also demonstrated that even if language learning is intensive and successful, *the development of conceptual fluency may be a very slow process because language learners have little access to the conceptual system of the target language when language learning takes place in a classroom setting.* These findings concur with those of Danesi, who claimed that non-native speakers learned virtually no 'new ways' of thinking conceptually after three or four years of study in a classroom (Danesi, 1992: 497). The percentages in our survey are quite low, with 30% being the highest in the production of FIC girls in the second test. The numbers are between 10% and 20% which is somewhat similar to Danesi's data (Danesi, 1992: 496). Lower numbers in his data can be explained by the length of texts produced by the students. In our surveys students were expected to produce shorter texts than in Danesi's experiment.

*The sociopolitical dimension*

Comparison between English (L3) and Russian (L2) in the specialised class demonstrated that students of English did much better in both tests than students of Russian in spite of the fact that the former had studied English for a shorter time than the latter had studied Russian. Because of the unique educational situation[2] prevailing in Hungary at that time, however, we think it would be a mistake to make any generalisations on the basis of these results. The fact that English students had a higher command of language although they had been exposed to their target language for a relatively shorter time than the Russian students had been to theirs proves very well how important extralinguistic factors can be in foreign language learning. The reasons for this significant difference in the command of the two languages must be sought in the sociopolitical situation that existed in Hungary before 1990. Students were required to study Russian, but most of them did not like it because it was the language of intruders. Besides, Russian language teaching methodology was way behind English and French language teaching methodology. Russian textbook materials were politically manipulated, and far from telling the truth or showing real lifelike situations. Classroom work was mainly based on the grammar–translation method, with little communication. By contrast, English, French or German teachers emphasised communicative methodology and encouraged lifelike classroom activities which resulted in more insight in the conceptual system of the target language than readings about how Lenin went sledging with children or how pioneer comrade Abrosimov saved a train and the like. Another important factor was that many more teachers were involved in teaching Russian than in teaching Western languages, and their methodological preparation was significantly different from that of the relatively small group of English or French teachers, who took special pride in teaching these languages. In the case of many Russian teachers it was just another job.[3] All these factors had a serious influence on the quality of teaching and learning process. In sum, we do not think that the comparison of trilinguals with bilinguals in these circumstances would give us any real insight into the differences between the two types of multicompetence.

## Conceptual fluency

A comparison of AMD indices in the L3 and L1 highlights some important facts. After one year of studies in the immersion, specialised and normal classes, students were expected to write a story based on a series of pictures, first in the target language and then in their native tongue. These stories provide especially good material for analysing conceptual fluency in the multicompetent mind because they are capable of demonstrating how much students rely on their L1-dominated conceptual base.

Our findings showed, first, that there were *high AMD numbers in the L1 in the immersion class*: boys 56%, girls 42%. This gave us the chance to argue elsewhere that these excellent results may be due to the influence of the intensive foreign language learning (Kecskés & Papp, 1995; Kecskés & Papp, 2000). Our claim was based on the comparison of AMD indices in this test with the AMD results of the survey which was administered to all students in the L1 at the beginning of the longitudinal experiment. The AMD indices in the L1 in the primary survey compare with the results of the picture-series test as set out in Table 6.4 (Kecskés & Papp, 2000).

These numbers clearly demonstrate that there is a notable increase in the AMD indices in the L1 in the immersion class. This is how one year of intensive language learning can influence the development and use of the common underlying conceptual base or CUCB of multilinguals.[4] There is no sign of this development, however, in the case of the specialised and normal classes; the use of the foreign language was much more restricted

**Table 6.4** AMD indices in L1 and results of picture-series test

| Class | | Survey | Test |
|---|---|---|---|
| Immersion | Boys | 48% | 56% |
| | Girls | 36% | 42% |
| Specialised | Boys | 40% | 35% |
| | Girls | 30% | 32% |
| Normal | Boys | 34% | 38% |
| | Girls | 35% | 30% |

here than in the immersion class, where French was the medium of instruction in several content area subjects.

Our second conclusion was that *there does not seem to be any important connection between the numbers in the Lx and the L1*. High AMD indices in the L1 do not necessarily mean high AMD indices in the L3 or L2. The high level of metaphorical thinking in one language hardly results in better metaphorical competence in the other, according to this data. Conceptual fluency is dominated by the L1, but proficiency in the L2 and/or the L3 usually has a positive influence on the monolithic conceptual base, and this can result in the language learners' better understanding of conceptual thinking in the target language. From this perspective it is interesting to examine some samples of what our students wrote about the series of pictures, first in the target language and then in their native tongue. We have chosen three types as illustration:

(1) The influence of L1 metaphorical thinking is obvious when students use target-language words and phrases as 'carriers' of their native-language concepts. In our data there is a clear connection between proficiency in the target language and the effect of L1 conceptual thinking. The less proficient students are in the target language the more they rely on L1-dominated metaphorical thinking. This is very common in the Russian productions of the specialised class, and not unusual in English and French trilingual production either. Here are some examples:[5]

- (L1 *Pénzt keresett*: he was making money.) Он искал деньги.
- (L1 *Szeretnék megismerkedni veled*.) I would like know with you.
- (L1 *Pierro nagyon könnyednek tünik*: Pierro seemed to be very

relaxed.) *Pierro semble trés léger.*

(2) However, there are some counter-examples where students like the L3 phrase so much that they try to use an equivalent in the L1 even if this is non-existent, or sounds a bit strange in Hungarian. This occurs in the French texts only. For instance:

*invitálom (j'ai invité*: I have invited)
*kis barátnöjét (petite amie*: girlfriend)

In the SEC productions there are some cases where students clearly try to use an equivalent of the L3 metaphor in the L1. In the example below the student first comes up with a non-metaphorical expression in Hungarian: *meglátott*. But she crosses it out, probably because she does not find it as expressive as the English. So she tries to use another expression in Hungarian as metaphorical and expressive as the English one:

*A beautiful girl with long fair hair caught his eyes*: (*Meglátott*) *Szembe jött vele egy csinos szöke lány.*

(3) Here are some instances of concept mediation when there is a metaphor in the L3 text and the student looks for an equivalent in the L1. Several times students use conceptual metaphors that are alike in both languages, for example:

*Je suis tombé sur une ancienne amie*: *Belebotlottam egy rég nem látott barátnömbe.* (I came across an old friend of mine.)

Real concept mediation, however, occurs when metaphors that are differently lexicalised are used in both languages, for instance:

*..and his eyes caught on a very pretty girl*: *..észrevett egy feltünöen csinos lányt.*

### Gender variations

The tables also give results by gender. The numbers demonstrate better results for the boys than for the girls both in the L3 and L1 with the exception of the second survey in the French immersion class, where the boys achieved 26% while the girls' production was 30% in the target language. We could not find any explanation for this phenomenon until we compared the AMD results in the foreign languages with the structural well-formedness test results in the L1 which are reported in Kecskés and Papp (2000). We have no room here to describe that part of the experiment, but some comment seems necessary, because a comparison of the results of the two different approaches demonstrates something very interesting. Table

6.5 presents the structural well-formedness results from the picture-series test in the L1 (Kecskés, 1998; Kecskés & Papp, 2000):

**Table 6.5** Structural well-formedness in L1

| Indices | | FI | US | LI | LN |
|---|---|---|---|---|---|
| Immersion class | Boys | 0.53 | 0.285 | 0.268 | 10.66 |
| | Girls | 0.481 | 0.276 | 0.233 | 14.58 |
| Intensive class | Boys | 0.308 | 0.115 | 0.28 | 5.33 |
| | Girls | 0.384 | 0.213 | 0.252 | 11.86 |
| Control class | Boys | 0.412 | 0.197 | 0.138 | 5.25 |
| | Girls | 0.386 | 0.199 | 0.195 | 7.00 |

FI = *Frequency Index*: total of subordinations (total of finite verbs)
US = *Unusual Subordinations*: total of unusual subordinations (total of finite verbs)
LI = *Loban Index*: total number of B, C, D (total number of A, B, C, D)
LN = *Loban Number*: total point value of A, B, C, D

The third of these, Loban's *Weighted Index of Subordination* (LI), is based on four categories of subordinate clause:

A   (1 point): a subordinate clause that is directly dependent upon a main clause;
B   (2 points): a dependent clause modifying or placed within another dependent clause;
C   (2 points): a dependent clause containing a verbal construction (e.g. infinitive, gerund, participle); and
D   (3 points): a dependent clause modifying or placed within another dependent clause, which in turn is within or modifying another dependent clause.

As any of these four indices can be misleading if used separately, the evaluation of structural well-formedness has always been based on an analysis of the numerical data from all four. Since our focus here is not on structural well-formedness we will discuss only one, the Loban Number (LN). This refers to the complexity of sentence structures. The higher the number, the more complex and embedded the sentences used by the students. It is therefore not the number of subordinate clauses that counts but their complexity. A text can have numerous simple subordinations but still have a relatively low LN. It is surprising how high the girls' LN is in their L1 by comparison with the boys' results in each class type. In sum, the boys' production demonstrated a higher level of AMD in both their L3 and their L1, and a lower level of structural well-formedness in their L1. Girls' production is the other way round: low AMD indices and high LNs.

What do these numbers demonstrate? Girls seem to be more careful in their language use: they try to apply what they have already acquired and take less risk than boys. Structural well-formedness is a good sign of this approach. This, however, does not in any way mean that girls are not creative enough in their language use. If we compare their numbers in the two

**Table 6.6** Boys' and girls' improvement

| Class | | Improvement |
|---|---|---|
| Immersion | Boys | 20% → 26% |
| | Girls | 17% → 30% |
| Specialised | Boys | 20% → 24% |
| | Girls | 16% → 23% |
| Normal | Boys | n/a → 16% |
| | Girls | n/a → 7% |

tests (Table 6.6) we can see that there is a notable improvement in their results, whereas the boys' improvement is insignificant.

The increase is especially significant in the case of the FIC girls: 13%! We can think of two reasons for this change: on the one hand intensiveness of learning, and on the other the thoroughness characteristic of girls' learning style. These numbers may basically lead us to a generalisation that concurs with popular opinion on the foreign language learning strategies of boys and girls: girls prefer to use what they know for sure, whereas boys seem to be willing to take more risks and make errors. In order to confirm the

**Table 6.7** AMD in L1

| Immersion Class | Boys | 56% |
|---|---|---|
| | Girls | 42% |
| Intensive Class | Boys | 35% |
| | Girls | 32% |
| Control Class | Boys | 38% |
| | Girls | 30% |

validity of this statement we calculated the AMD on the picture-series stories in the L1 and the results are presented in Table 6.7.

In each class the girls' numbers are lower than the boys', just as for the foreign language stories. But as demonstrated above, the structural well-formedness results of the girls are better than those of the boys. This tends to prove that our assumption is valid for the L1: girls seem to use language more carefully and consciously, taking less risk and paying more attention to well-formedness than boys. Although we have not analysed the foreign language texts for structural well-formedness, this gender difference in use of the first language may well be true for foreign languages too. These assumptions, however, require further research. Gender difference may be an important factor in language acquisition and needs further investigation.

## Conclusion

### CUCB in the Hungarian context

The Hungarian trilingual situation (Hungarian, Russian and English or French) is unique in several respects. Russian represented our students' first encounter with a foreign language in elementary school. But because of social, political and methodological reasons the majority of them never achieved high proficiency in the language, and Russian language learning rarely resulted in multicompetence with a common underlying conceptual base (CUCB). Motivation was higher when students studied Western languages such as English or French. Trilingual students in the class specialising in English could even compete with French trilingual students in the immersion class who were experiencing the third language as their medium of instruction. This demonstrates very well how important extralinguistic factors such as motivation and exposure to music, media, films and the like can be in the development of a CUCB, which is itself crucial for native-like language acquisition because metaphorical thinking is a dominant and ever-present option in discourse. The development of multicompetence in a classroom setting is just a potential and not a necessity. It depends on several variables such as, for example, the intensiveness of studies, availability of and exposure to target-language cultural material, and student motivation.

### Preconditions for conceptual fluency

Conceptual fluency is an essential condition of native-like language production and comprehension. Metaphorical competence is an important constituent of conceptual fluency, but not its only constituent. Our study demonstrated that the average metaphorical density (AMD) index is low even in the language production of immersion and specialised classes. This confirms the hypothesis of Pavlenko (1996), who claimed that immediate contact with the target-language culture and speakers is an inescapable condition for the development of conceptual fluency.

### Gender differences

The experiment highlighted some interesting differences between the learning strategies of the two genders. Boys tended to use more metaphors in their writings than girls, but girls produced better results in structural well-formedness. This claim, however, needs to be confirmed by further research.

### The position of English in Hungary

English language education in Hungarian schools and colleges has always been at a high level in Hungary, especially prior to 1990 when only a relatively small number of people were involved in it. This is demonstrated in our study too, in the way the English specialised class were able to compete with the French immersion class. After 1990, however, the situation changed: there was an enormous and ever-increasing demand for English teaching and the country did not have the necessary number of well-prepared teachers to meet it. But the necessary measures were taken by the educational authorities and the quality of English education has improved considerably as a result.

### Notes

1. Take, for instance, the difference between Russian aspect and English aspect.

2. Until 1989 Russian was a compulsory language from Grade 4 to Grade 12 inclusive in Hungarian elementary and high schools. With some exceptions, schools usually had a system of three Russian classes a week. For political and cultural reasons Russian was not popular in Hungarian schools. As a result, average Hungarian students usually had a very weak command of Russian. Several elementary schools had the facilities to teach languages other than Russian. They usually offered English and German. High schools required the study of two languages: one of these had to be Russian and the other (English, German, French, Italian, Spanish, etc.) could be chosen by the student. From 1989, with Russian having ceased to be a compulsory language, this system started to dissolve.
3. This does not mean of course that high-quality Russian language education did not exist in Hungary before 1990. There were excellent Russian teachers whose methodology was as good as that of the Western language teachers, and sometimes even better. What we are talking about here is mass education. A huge number of people were involved in Russian language teaching and a considerable number of teachers, for several reasons, were not well prepared for the task.
4. On the common underlying conceptual base (CUCB) see Kecskés & Papp, 2000.
5. In the examples no corrections were made. Student productions are quoted as they appeared in the original texts.

### References

Bouton, L. (1994) Can NNS skill in interpreting implicatures in American English be improved through explicit instruction? A pilot study. In L. Bouton and J. Kachru (eds) *Pragmatics and Language Learning* 5, 88–110.

Cook, V. (1991) The poverty-of-the-stimulus argument and multicompetence. *Second Language Research* 7, 103–17.

Cook, V. (1992) Evidence for Multicompetence. *Language Learning* 42, 557–91.

Danesi, M. (1992) Metaphorical competence in second language acquisition and second language teaching: The neglected dimension. In J.E. Alatis (ed.) *Georgetown University Round Table on Languages and Linguistics* (pp. 489–500). Washington, DC: Georgetown University Press.

De Bot, K. (1992) A bilingual production model: Levelt's 'speaking' model adapted. *Applied Linguistics* 13, 1–24.

Gentner, D. and Gentner, D.R. (1982) Flowing waters or teeming crowds: Mental models of electricity. Report No. 4981, prepared for the Office of Naval Research Personnel and Training Research Programmes. Boston: Bolt Beranek and Newman Inc.

Humboldt, W. von (1903/1936) *Wilhelm von Humboldts Werke* (Vol. 4). A. Leitzmann (ed.). Berlin: B. Behr.

Hunt, E. and Agnoli, F. (1991) The Whorfian hypothesis: A cognitive psychology perspective. *Psychological Review* 98, 377–89.

Irujo, S. (1993) Steering clear: Avoidance in the production of idioms. *IRAL* 21, 205–19.

Jacobson, R. (1953) Results of the conference of anthropologists and linguists. *IJAL Supplement* 8, 19–22.

Johnson, M. (1987) *The Body in the Mind*. Chicago: University of Chicago Press.
Kecskés, I. (1995) Concept formation of Japanese EFL/ESL students. In M. Ahmed, T. Fujimura, Y. Kato and M. Leong (eds) *Second Language Research in Japan* (pp. 130–49). Yamato-matchi: IUJ.
Kecskés, I. (1998) The state of L1 knowledge in foreign language learners. *WORD*, 49(3), 321–41
Kecskés, I. and Papp, T. (1991) *Elméleti nyelvészet, alkalmazott nyelvészet, nyelvoktatás* [*Theoretical Linguistics, Applied Linguistics, Language Teaching*]. Budapest: Ts-Programmeiroda.
Kecskés, I. and Papp, T. (1995) The linguistic effect of foreign language learning on the development of mother-tongue skills. In M. Haggstrom, L. Morgan, L. and J. Wieczorek (eds) *The Foreign Language Classroom: Bridging Theory and Practice* (pp. 163–81). New York/London: Garland.
Kecskés, I. and Papp, T. (2000) *Foreign Language and Mother Tongue*. Hillsdale, NJ: Lawrence Erlbaum.
Kövecses, Z. and Szabó, P. (1996) Idioms: A view from cognitive semantics. *Applied Linguistics* 17, 326–55.
Lakoff, G. (1987) *Women, Fire and Dangerous Things*. Chicago: University of Chicago Press.
Lakoff, G. and Johnson, M. (1980) *Metaphors We Live By*. Chicago: University of Chicago Press.
Lenneberg, E. (1953) Cognition in ethnolinguistics. *Language* 29, 463–71.
Loban, W. (1963) The language of elementary school children. NCTE Research Report No.1. Champaign, IL.
Locke, J. (1690/1959) *An Essay Concerning Human Understanding*. (Edited by A.C. Fraser). New York: Dover Publications.
Osgood, C., May, W. and Miron, M. (1975) *Cross-cultural Universals of Affective Meaning*. Urbana, IL: University of Illinois Press.
Papp, T. (1991) Az anyanyelvi tudás és az eredményes idegennyelv tanulás összefüggései egy többszintü longitudinális vizsgálat alapján [The study of the interrelation of mother-tongue development and foreign language learning in a multi-level longitudinal experiment]. Unpublished dissertation for candidate degree of the Hungarian Academy of Sciences, Budapest.
Paradis, M. (ed.) (1995) *Aspects of Bilingual Aphasia*. Pergamon: Elsevier Science.
Pavlenko, A. (1996) Bilingualism and cognition: Concepts in the mental lexicon. In A. Pavlenko and R. Salaberry (eds) *Cornell Working Papers in Linguistics: Papers in Second Language Acquisition and Bilingualism* (pp. 49–85). Ithaca: Cornell University Press.
Pavlenko, A. and Salaberry, R. (eds) (1996) *Cornell Working Papers in Linguistics. Papers in Second Language Acquisition and Bilingualism*. Ithaca: Cornell University Press.
Sapir, E. (1921) *Language*. New York: Harcourt, Brace and World.
Searle, J. (1969) *Speech Acts: An Essay in the Philosophy of Language*. Cambridge: Cambridge University Press.
Sweetser, E. (1990) *From Etymology to Pragmatics*. Cambridge: Cambridge University Press.
Taylor, J.R. (1993) Some pedagogical implications of cognitive linguistics. In R.A. Geiger and B. Rudzka-Ostyn (eds) *Conceptualizations and Mental Processing in Language* (pp. 200–23). Berlin/New York: Mouton de Gruyter.

Valeva, G. (1996) On the notion of conceptual fluency in a second language. In A. Pavlenko and R. Salaberry (eds) *Cornell Working Papers in Linguistics* (Vol. 14, pp. 22–38). Ithaca: Cornell University Press.

Vygotsky, L.S. (1962) *Thought and Language*. Boston: MIT Press.

Vygotsky, L.S. (1978) *Mind in Society: The Development of Higher Psychological Processes*. Cambridge, MA: Harvard University Press.

Wierzbicka, A. (1993) A conceptual basis for cultural psychology. *Ethos* 21, 205–31.

Whorf, Benjamin L. (1956a) Science and linguistics. In J.B. Caroll (ed.) *Language, Thought and Reality* (pp. 207–19). Cambridge, MA: MIT Press.

Whorf, Benjamin L. (1956b) The relation of habitual thought and behavior to language. In J.B. Caroll (ed.) *Language, Thought and Reality* (pp. 134–59). Cambridge, MA: MIT Press.

Winner, E. (1982) *Invented Worlds: The Psychology of the Arts*. Cambridge, MA: Harvard University Press.

## Chapter 7
# Word-fragment Completions in the Second and Third Language
## A Contribution to the Organisation of the Trilingual Speaker's Lexicon

UTE SCHÖNPFLUG

The structure of a trilingual lexicon and its underlying representational system is usually considered to be an extended bilingual structure governed by one organisational principle: either interdependence, or independence, of the language systems involved. The triad of languages may, however, not be organised homogeneously. The three dyads of languages, first and second, second and third, and first and third, respectively, may differ in their organisation. Indeed, the results of Abunuwara (1992), Clyne (1997) and Voorwinde (1981) suggest that the three dyads of languages may not be ruled by the same principles. The results of Abunuwara's Stroop Colour Test indicate that when neither of the two languages is very dominant a trilingual's first and second and second and third languages seem to be independently organised. However, the relationship of the first language to the third seems to be one of interdependence characterised by great interference. Thus the pattern of relationships between the three dyads does not confirm everyday experiences of interference, suggesting a greater contamination between second and third languages. When the experimental paradigm was changed, similar results were obtained (e.g. Clyne, 1997; Voorwinde, 1981). Abunuwara interprets the differential relationship between first and second and second and third languages on the one hand and first and third on the other as the result of developmental processes: the distinctly weaker last language learned still seems to be processed via the first (see Dufour & Kroll, 1995).

One further question remains, however: whether, as novices, trilinguals process their third language via their first language, or through their strong second language, when these are both functionally active. With proficient trilingual speakers Dufour and Kroll would claim a direct access to a common conceptual store from all three languages. This leaves open the problem of whether the second and even more so the third language will ever reach this expert stage, or whether in most cases the second and the first only might have this kind of common conceptual storage, the third language remaining, in relation to the first and second, in the novice interdependent stage. Kroll's revised hierarchical model of the lexicon–concept relationship (Kroll & Michael, 1997; Kroll & Stewart, 1994) questions whether the second language may develop an equally strong access to the corresponding conceptual units as the first language. There would be no question of this with the third language.

More specifically, Abunuwara (1992) tested trilingual subjects in Israel with Arabic as their first language (L1), Hebrew as their second (L2) and English as their third (L3). The tests were guided by the developmental interdependence–independence distinction. In a first experiment Abunawara looked at the Stroop interference effects between the three verbal systems of trilingual subjects. The Stroop Colour Test measures the interference in naming the colour in which a colour word is written when discrepant from the semantics of the word (e.g. the word 'green' written in red colour) or reading the colour word 'green' written in red colour. Stroop interference is accepted as an indicator of the way different languages are connected in the underlying representational (conceptual) system. Within the Stroop paradigm used here the independent hypothesis was supported for L2 and L3, Hebrew and English, respectively. In addition, the developmental hypothesis, predicting a transition from L1-mediated conceptual access from L2 to a direct, though weaker access to the conceptual representations from L2, was also supported by showing different patterns of interference effects among these two languages, L2 and L3, respectively and Arabic, the subjects' first language.

In the second experiment, latencies for translations between the subjects' three languages were compared to their picture-naming latencies. The rationale was that if any of the three languages were to be translated into any of the others and revealed the same latencies for these translations as for picture-naming of the respective languages, direct access to the conceptual representations might be assumed. The results obtained provided additional support for the developmental hypothesis by comparing Hebrew (L2) and English (L3) latencies with those of Arabic (L1). Hebrew seemed to act like another L1. On the other hand, English picture-naming was slower than translating L1 words. The fact that the mean reaction times for translations between Hebrew and English were the longest supports the idea that an independent relationship exists between these two languages. The two experiments were concerned with understanding the relationships among different language systems which are on different levels of proficiency. They provide evidence for independence and interdependence of the trilingual speaker's language systems; and also for a developmental hypothesis stating that independence may be expected for the relationship between two proficiently known languages, whereas interdependence is more likely between a proficient and a non-proficiently known language.

Mägiste (1986) reported studies with Finnish students living in Sweden and learning English as a third language. Various assessments of performance in the third language showed a decrement when trilinguals used their first language, Finnish, actively, but not when they did not use their L1 actively. Bilingual subjects were faster in their L1 and L2 performance than trilinguals in the same languages when in the L2 and L3 position. With increasing number of languages, reaction times increased; in the case of active L1 use more than in the case of passive L1 knowledge.

The lack of other studies testing relations between different verbal systems using trilingual subjects restricts the scope of interpretation of the data from these two studies (e.g. Clyne, 1997; Voorwinde, 1981). Voorwinde studied the speech in three languages of young Dutch–English bilinguals acquiring German as their third language in Australia. He found a substantial influence from English on the other two languages, with German affecting Dutch least. The extent of Dutch influence on German depended on the level of their proficiency in the former. Voorwinde concluded that trilingualism was more complex than bilingualism but not essentially different from it. Clyne reports on 'some of the things trilinguals do', looking at the Australian situation. Intensity and extent of language use, language dominance hierarchy, language similarity will all affect the relative influence of each language on the others. What language production strategies trilinguals employ generally follow the 'principle of least effort'.

This chapter is concerned with understanding of what happens when trilingual subjects have to perform in either their second or their third language. The participants in the study we shall discuss were Polish-speakers with German as their second and English as their third language. They were asked to reconstruct words from word-beginnings which were part of either their second or their third language's lexical repertoire. In terms of language similarity we have a clear dissimilarity between the first language, Polish, on the one hand, and German and English on the other, and a similarity between the second and third languages, German and English, respectively. In addition, German was the language of the social environment; the participants had to use it daily for pursuing their studies at the German-speaking Europe-University Viadrina.

According to the transfer-appropriate processing approach (TAP) suggested by Roedinger (1990), priming is most efficient when priming stimuli and test stimuli are very similar. Word-fragment completion is primarily determined by data-driven processing, i.e. the word form dominates in processing. Conceptual processing, however, may also influence the performance, since in Roedinger's study, priming occurred even when surface forms were quite different in the study and in the test. But in the study, words primed word-fragment completion more than did pictures, although pictures did produce slight but significant priming as well. Weldon and Roedinger (1987) interpreted the latter result as evidence for a weaker conceptually driven component in word-fragment completion. Similar results were reported by Challis and Brodbeck (1992). They demonstrated that semantic processing of target words yielded greater priming than did physical processing of targets in word-fragment completion. Thus, in addition to physical resemblance of prime and target, although the effects are typically small, conceptual processing may contribute to priming in word-fragment completion. After summarising various results Weldon (1991) proposed that word-fragment completion may be mediated by a combination of data-driven and conceptually-driven processing components.

Weldon recently revised the TAP framework to include lexical access in addition to conceptual processing and perceptual overlap as processing components. The lexical access hypothesis suggests that priming depends on prior activation of or access to the representation of the lexical (word) unit of the test item. With his first experiment Weldon was able to find evidence for all three component processes: conceptual processing, lexical access and perceptual overlap, by introducing four study conditions. In the first, participants simply read Spanish target items and later completed the corresponding word-fragments in English. Reading was assumed to involve a combination of conceptual processes, lexical access and perceptual overlap of study and test items. In the second study condition Spanish targets were presented auditorily; and in the third, Spanish targets were generated from associative cues. Both the second and the third study conditions were assumed to involve only conceptual processing and lexical access. In the fourth study condition, subjects studied pictures; this task was assumed to involve only conceptual processing. Consistent with Weldon's predictions, priming was greatest in the read condition, next in the auditory presentation and with the generation of associations, and least in the picture condition.

Basden et al. (1994) added two other priming conditions: mental translation of the Spanish target items to English, and writing Spanish translations of English words to be completed from word-fragments under test conditions. Their experiments also yielded support for a revised TAP framework involving the three processes of conceptual processing, lexical access and perceptual overlap. Hence word-fragment completion seems to be a task tapping important processing components of lexical organisation in multilingual persons. Brasden et al.'s findings are in opposition to those of Smith (1991), who found no evidence for conceptual processing in word-fragment completion tasks involving cross-linguistic priming.

The study described in this chapter uses the performance of word-fragment completion to analyse just two of the processing components involved: conceptual processing and lexical access. As an alternative to a priming paradigm it was hypothesised that conceptual processing is indicated by the effects of the concreteness or abstractness of the lexical items involved. This hypothesis is based on experiments reported by Paivio et al. (1988), who found that with bilingual 'semantic' repetition via translation equivalents from a list used for free recall, concrete words profited more from bilingual repetition than did abstract words. Schönpflug's (forthcoming) partial repetition and extension of their experiment found evidence that refuted the concreteness effect and redefined the number of translation equivalents that concrete and abstract words have. Concrete words have, in general, fewer translation equivalents than do abstract words. In semantic priming tasks this effect, when controlled for, seems to override the concreteness effect. This implies that the number of cross-linguistic associations plays a decisive role in the priming of words by means of translations.

The study aims to find additional support for the hypothesis that the number of translation equivalents overrules the concreteness effect in word-fragment completion. It is assumed that in word-fragment completion, concreteness impacts on the conceptual component and the number of translations on the lexical access component.

The following three hypotheses were derived from the research reported:

H1 The concreteness of words to be completed from word-fragments will influence performance in this test, as word-fragment completion is known to be – in part – concept-driven. Concrete words should be less efficiently completed than abstract words, as abstract words are assumed to be predominantly verbally coded in long-term memory.

Abstract words may thus profit more than concrete words from a data-driven processing in addition to conceptual processing.

H2 German words will be completed from smaller word-fragments than will English words, as lexical access is easier for the second than for the third language.

H3 The number of translations of words to be completed impacts on word-fragment completion in a multiple language context: the more translations are possible for a lexical item the greater the fragment has to be in order to result in a correct completion.

## Method

## Material and procedure

*Questionnaire*

An English translation of the questionnaire used is included at the end of this chapter. Originally it was given in German, the language spoken by the students in their current studies at Europe-University Viadrina (see description of sample below). The questions covered sociodemographic information, the history of language learning, current language use, self-ratings of language competence and language use preferences.

**Table 7.1** Word list for word-fragment completion test

| | Word Category | | | |
|---|---|---|---|---|
| | German | | English | |
| | Short | Long | Short | Long |
| Concrete/ 1 Translation | Harfe Buch | Bleistift Kartoffel | Harp Book | Potato Bottle |
| Concrete >1 Translation | Vieh Puppe | Fahrkarte Schlinge | Bowl Flag | Steamer Ticket |
| Abstract/ 1 Translation | Stolz Tod | Wahrheit Notwendigkeit | Thought Truth | Advantage Freedom |
| Abstract/ >1 Translation | Tugend Anschein | Ehrfurcht Vertrauen | Awe Anger | Confidence Virtue |

## Word-fragment completion test

The word-fragment completion test comprised 32 words (see Table 7.1) which had been used in other experiments and possessed known translation reaction times, numbers of translations given by a sizeable sample of students (n = 403), word frequency and concreteness ratings. They were all high-frequency words, occurring – in English – 100 and more times per million words (Thorndike & Lorge, 1957 for English words; Baschek *et al.*, 1977 for German words). Concreteness ratings were taken from the Paivio *et al.* (1968) norms for English words and the Baschek *et al.* norms for German words. Concrete words had ratings of 6 or higher, abstract words of 3 or lower (full range from 1 to 7). Long and short words were distinguished by number of syllables and number of letters: short words had one to two syllables and two to six distinguishable sound units (e.g. 'sch' in German); long words had two to four syllables and four to 13 distinguishable sound units. There were 16 English and 16 German words, 16 abstract and 16 concrete, 16 long and 16 short; 16 had only one translation and 16 had more than one translation in the experiments preceding this study. Each combination of word categories had two exemplars.

The participants first went through the same list of 254 English and German concrete and abstract words as those who took part in the previous experiments, trying to find as many translations or translation equivalents as they could think of for each word. (The 32 words of the word-fragment completion test were spread around among the 254.) After this procedure had been completed they were given the word-fragment completion test.

The word-fragments, presented in a random order, were given with their initial letter and a blank marked for each of the rest ( e.g. P _ _ _ _ for Puppe). The participants were asked to fill in the remainder of the letters of the word they had in mind. They were told that it could be either a German or an English word. If when they had filled in the letters the word was not correct, they were given the second letter as well (e.g. PU _ _ _ ) and were again asked to complete the word. The correct letters were provided one by one until the last. Each line with its word-fragment at the beginning and the blanks marking missing letters was presented on its own, with neither previous nor subsequent lines visible. The presentation of each line was self-timed, but must not exceed one minute. If completion was not achieved during this period the participants were advised to start straightaway on the next line. At the end of each word test, marked blanks equivalent to the word length were provided to give some idea of what alternative words the students might have in mind (e.g. anger/angel).

The factors measured were *uniqueness*, i.e. the number of given letters necessary to complete the word correctly divided by the total number of letters in the word, and *errors*, i.e. the number of incorrectly completed words divided by 32, the total number of words including the amount not completed.

## Sample

Thirty students from Europe-University Viadrina in Frankfurt/Oder, Germany, near the Polish border, volunteered to participate in this study. One student's language competence in English was not good enough, so his data were excluded. Half the participants belonged to the School of Cultural Sciences, the rest were studying economics or law. Their average age was 21.

Of those students included in the analyses, 21 were born in Poland, two in Russia, one in Germany, one in Italy, one in Costa Rica, one in the Ukraine and one in France. They had spent most of their lifetime, an average of 20 years, in their home country. Their nationality was mostly Polish (23 students); only six had other nationalities: Russian, Ukrainian, Serbian, Swedish, Italian and French. Their average number of visits to a German-speaking country lasting several weeks was 8.66: 50% had spent up to 8 years; the maximum was 20 years. The average number of visits to an English-speaking country was 7.93: 50% had spent up to 6 years and the maximum here was also 20 years.

For 21 of the students German was the first and English the second foreign language they had learnt at school. Four students gave the reverse sequence, but in terms of length of stay and self-rated competence in the two languages they still revealed the required sequence of German as first and English as second foreign language. The last three gave no language learning sequence or deviations from the required one.

Self-rated language competence in terms of the four criteria of comprehension, speaking, reading and writing was on average rated as 'good' (59%), 'very good' (28%) and 'like a native speaker' (13%) for German, whereas 52% assessed their competence in English as 'little', 31% as 'good', 14% as 'very good' and only 3% as 'like a native speaker'. When their mother tongue was excluded from the spectrum of choices, they chose to spell and count in German rather than in English.

## Results

All analyses to be published were carried out twice before the full data were presented. In a first series of analyses only the 21 'pure' cases were used, those of Polish nationality with Polish as their first language, German as their second and English as third foreign language. In a second series of analyses all 29 participants were included. The results were strikingly similar, so the full data set is given.

## Self-rated language competence

Self-ratings of language competence showed without exception that German was perceived as dominant over English. Table 7.2 gives the means, standard deviations and results of the tests for significance of mean differences for the various measures assessed.

**Table 7.2** Mean self-ratings ($M$) and standard deviations ($SD$) of trilingual students' self-ratings of language competence

|  | Language | |
| --- | --- | --- |
| Competence domain | German (L2) $M$ ($SD$) | English (L3) $M$ ($SD$) |
| Comprehension | 2.83 (0.71) | 2.22 (0.73)** |
| Speaking | 2.39 (0.70) | 1.61 (0.70)*** |
| Reading | 2.72 (0.67) | 2.06 (0.73)*** |
| Writing | 2.44 (0.62) | 1.50 (0.51)*** |
| Active[1] | 2.42 (0.60) | 1.56 (0.48)*** |
| Passive[2] | 2.78 (0.60) | 2.14 (0.70)*** |

** Significant mean difference at p<0.01   *** Significant mean difference at p<0.00
1 Average of speaking and writing means   2 Average of comprehension and reading means

Significant differences between the two languages were observed in the self-ratings in all domains of competence, confirming other indicators of second and third language dominance in the participants of this study. Self-ratings of passive competence (comprehension and reading) were higher than active competence (speaking and writing). The active competencies showed greater discrepancies between the two languages than the passive competencies.

## Uniqueness point and word categories

In a comprehensive univariate analysis of variance including the integral factors of concreteness (concrete, abstract), number of translation equivalents (one and more than one), language (German, English), and length of words (short, long) and with uniqueness point as dependent variable all factors yielded significant main effects. Figure 7.1 depicts the mean values corresponding to the four main effects. Abstract words had an earlier uniqueness point than concrete words ($F(1.28) = 18.39$, $p<0.00$; $Eta^2 = 0.40$); words with one translation equivalent had a later uniqueness point than words with more than one ($F(1.28) = 48.53$, $p<0.00$; $Eta^2 = 0.63$); German words had a later uniqueness point than English words ($F(1.28) = 21.41$, $p<0.00$; $Eta^2 = 0.43$); and short words were recognised earlier than long words ($F(1.28) = 168.28$, $p<0.00$; $Eta^2 = 0.86$).

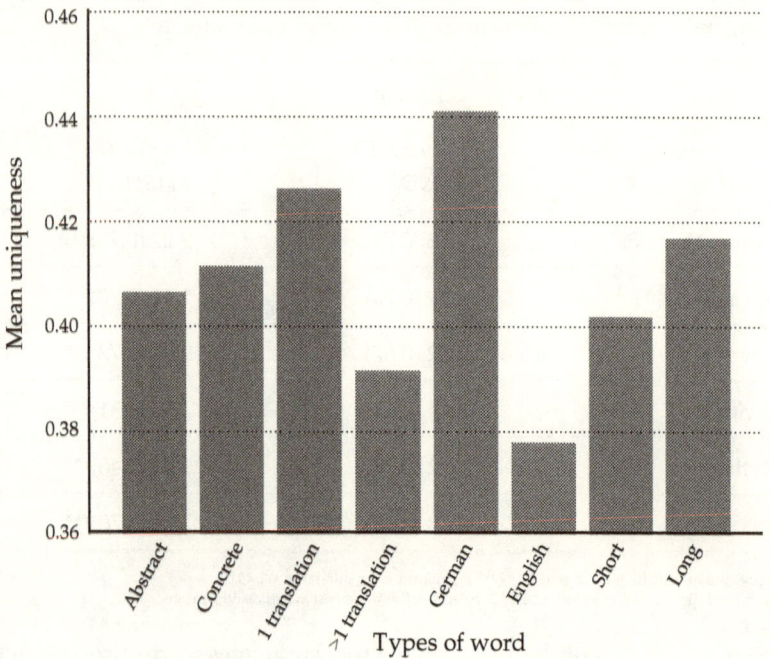

**Figure 7.1** Mean uniqueness point of the word categories concreteness, number of translations, language and word length (significant main effects of each factor)

All significant higher order interactions included the term of the length of words factor indicating that word length moderated the theoretically relevant other factors. Therefore two separate analyses of variance were carried out, one for short words and one for long words. The results of the separate analyses of variances are reported in Tables 7.3 and 7.4. The results give a more differentiated picture of the effects of the word categories in word-fragment completion tasks.

**Table 7.3** Results of univariate analysis of variance of uniqueness point in word-fragment completion of short words

| Factor | F-value (df = 1.28) | Size of effect |
|---|---|---|
| Concreteness (C) | 18.33*** | 0.40 |
| Number of translation equivalents (N) | 1.84 | 0.06 |
| Language (L) | 0.96 | 0.03 |
| C × N | 3.49 | 0.11 |
| C × L | 3.15 | 0.10 |
| N × L | 21.05*** | 0.43 |
| C × N × L | 22.91*** | 0.45 |

\*\*\* p<0.00

**Table 7.4** Results of univariate analysis of variance of uniqueness point in word-fragment completion of long words

| Factor | F-value (df = 1.28) | Size of effect |
|---|---|---|
| Concreteness (C) | 5.88* | 0.17 |
| Number of translation equivalents (N) | 94.82*** | 0.77 |
| Language (L) | 25.54*** | 0.48 |
| C × N | 8.57** | 0.23 |
| C × L | 0.10 | 0.00 |
| N × L | 34.49*** | 0.55 |
| C × N × L | 5.27* | 0.16 |

\*\*\* p<0.00  \*\* p<0.01  \* p<0.05

The two separate analyses revealed an important difference between long and short words. While concreteness had a significant effect on their uniqueness point regardless of the length of the words, the number of translations only had a significant effect when long words were completed. But the main effects should not be evaluated when higher-order interactions involve the term of the given main effect. In this study, for both the long and the short words the interaction concreteness × number of translations × language is significant. Figures 7.2 and 7.3 depict the mean differences for short and long words separately.

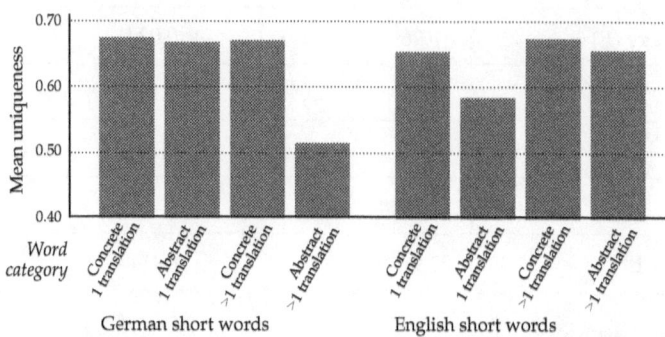

**Figure 7.2** Mean uniqueness point (number of letters necessary to complete word-fragment correctly/total number of letters in word) for German and English correctly completed short words, respectively (interaction of concreteness, number of translations and language)

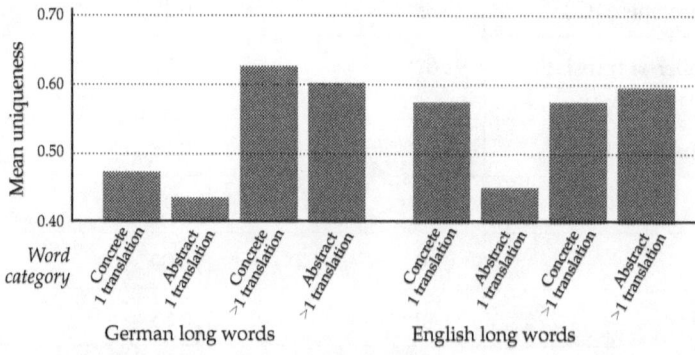

**Figure 7.3** Mean uniqueness point (number of letters necessary to complete word-fragment correctly/total number of letters in word) for German and English correctly completed long words, respectively (interaction of concreteness, number of translations and language).

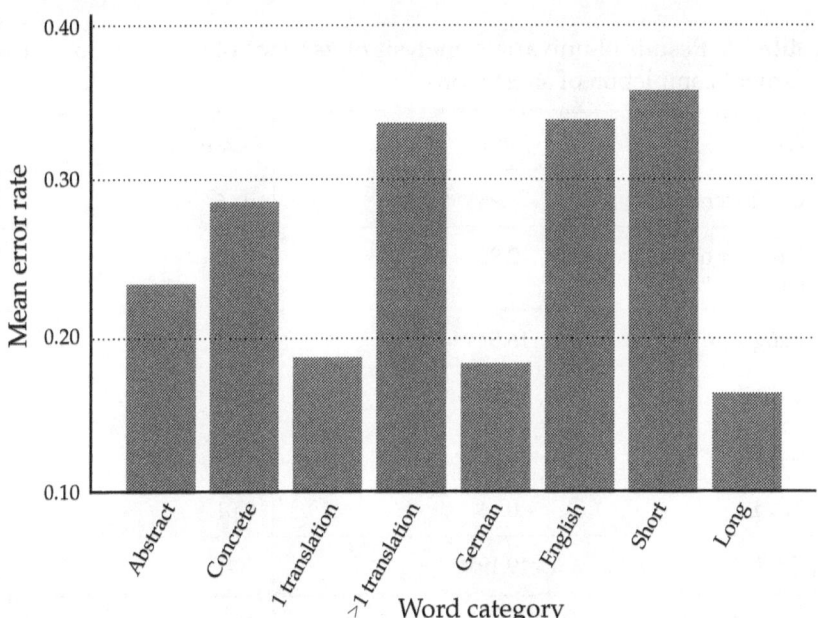

**Figure 7.4** Mean error rate of word categories, concreteness, number of translations, language and word length (significant main effects)

The results for short and long words correspond when they are recognised to be English: abstract words with one translation need fewer letters to be correctly completed than all other word categories. The effect is particularly distinct among long words. For short German words we find a different result: Abstract words with more than one translation reveal distinctly shorter uniqueness points than the other word categories.

*Error rate of word categories*

The strategy for analyses was the same as that in the section on correctly completed words. First all data were included in a univariate analysis of variance with error rate as dependent variable and the four integral subject factors of concreteness, number of translations, language and word length, with two levels for each factor as described above. Figure 7.4 depicts the main effects. Participants made significantly more errors when they completed concrete words as compared to abstract ones, when completing words with more than one translation as compared to just one, when solving English as compared to German words and when tackling short as compared to long words.

**Table 7.5** Results of univariate analysis of variance of error rate in word-fragment completion of short words

| Factor | F-value (df = 1,28) | Size of effect |
|---|---|---|
| Concreteness (C) | 23.95*** | 0.46 |
| Number of translation equivalents (N) | 2.96 | 0.10 |
| Language (L) | 16.51*** | 0.37 |
| C × N | 1.84 | 0.06 |
| C × L | 12.66** | 0.31 |
| N × L | 0.16 | 0.01 |
| C × N × L | 19.19*** | 0.41 |

\*\*\* p<0.00  \*\* p<0.01

**Table 7.6** Results of univariate analysis of variance of mean error rate in word-fragment completion of long words

| Factor | F-value (df = 1,28) | Size of effect |
|---|---|---|
| Concreteness (C) | 3.32 | 0.11 |
| Number of translation equivalents (N) | 71.56*** | 0.72 |
| Language (L) | 13.10** | 0.32 |
| C × N | 2.43 | 0.08 |
| C × L | 0.02 | 0.00 |
| N × L | 10.50** | 0.27 |
| C × N × L | 0.03 | 0.00 |

\*\*\* p<0.00  \*\* p<0.01

Again word length was involved in all significant interactions. Thus again, two separate analyses for short and long words were carried out. The results are given in Tables 7.5 and 7.6. In the case of short words concreteness has a powerful effect on error rate while the number of translations has none, whether on its own or in interaction with either concreteness or language. Only the triple interaction of concreteness, number of translations and language was significant. Figure 7.5 depicts the means involved in this interaction.

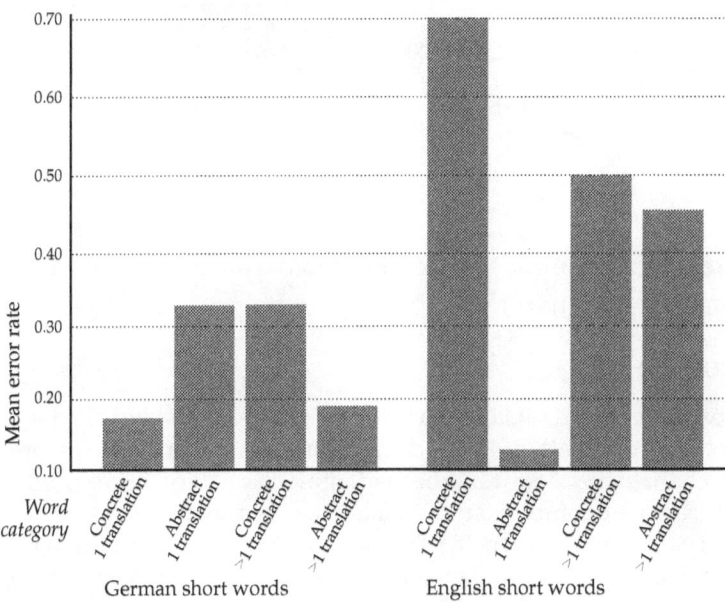

**Figure 7.5** Error rate of word categories of short words (interaction concreteness × number of translations × language)

There seems to be no clearly interpretable pattern. The corresponding analysis for long words, however, yielded more consistent results. Table 7.6 shows no concreteness effect, but the number of translations is a powerful factor. Language and number of translations x language are the only significant other effects. Figure 7.6 depicts the means involved in this simple interaction effect. For German words with one and more than one translation the mean difference was much less than for the corresponding English word categories. The greater number of possible translations raised the error rate.

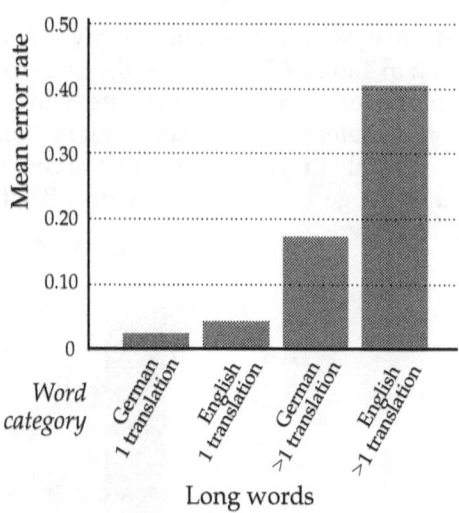

**Figure 7.6** Mean error rate of long words (interaction of number of translations × language)

## Discussion

Our study aimed to clarify some of the processes involved in the performance of trilinguals in a word-fragment completion task. In previous research three processes have been identified as having priming effects on word-fragment completion: (a) conceptual processing, (b) lexical access and (c) perceptual overlap. In this study a different approach from priming was introduced. The influence of conceptual processing was tested by examining the effect of word concreteness (e.g. Paivio, 1986) on word-fragment completion. The concreteness of words is clearly represented at the conceptual level; both the uniqueness point of correctly completed words, i.e. the number of letters necessary for a correct completion of the words (divided by word length), and the error rate are affected by concreteness. Concrete words had in general a later uniqueness point than abstract words. This result was modified when interactions with word length, language and number of translations were considered. Except for German short words the impact of abstractness was most clear among words with just one translation equivalent: abstract words with one translation equivalent were recognised earliest. But as already evident from previous research the effect of conceptual processing alone, in our case represented by the influence of the concreteness factor, was relatively small as compared to the other factors examined. The conceptual processing hypothesis

(H1) in word-fragment completion gets further support from the dual-coding approach taken in this study.

We also get evidence of the effects of differential lexical access on word-fragment completion from our study. Words from two languages, English and German, belong to two different lexical pools. Fragment completion of words from the lexicon of both languages show differential uniqueness points and error rates. German words had a late uniqueness point but a low error rate while English words had an early uniqueness point and a high error rate. This might be a finding peculiar to the lexical access of trilinguals in their second and third languages. Lexical access in their second language is slower because of the larger lexicon they have in that language as compared to their third language. The lexicon of the third language is smaller, as the high error and missing rates demonstrate, and thus the correct words – if known – are probably more easily accessible in the third language. They should be of the highest frequencies and availability.

The number of translations of words to be completed from word fragments also indicates lexical access processes. The task context provided for the participants was bilingual in that they could expect either a German or an English word. This enforced the use of interlanguage as well as intralanguage lexical search. Both lexicons were seemingly activated and a choice had to be made among items from both. The number of possible translations may play a crucial role in the activation of possible target items. They may be among the first to be accessed for a match with the word fragment. If there are many translations the matching takes longer; if there is just one the matching is more quickly achieved. The results confirm the earlier uniqueness point of words with one translation over those with more postulated by these considerations. Abstract words with one translation have the shortest uniqueness point, except for German short words. Easy lexical access for words with one translation and an increased data-driven processing for abstract words postulated by the dual-coding approach combine to achieve the most efficient word-fragment completion of abstract words with one translation, but not necessarily the lowest error rates.

The differential results for long and short words are dominant. Completing a three letter word like *Tod* (death) leaves the participant with very few alternatives for completion when the first letter is presented: e.g. *Ton*. It is the last letter that decides the uniqueness point for these short words. We may thus – when considering the research questions tackled in this study – put more emphasis on inspecting the results from the long words. These do indeed provide a clearer picture of the effects of the factors tested in this experiment.

A last thought has to reflect what Mägiste (1986) considers important in the use of the first of a trilingual speaker's languages. Her findings suggest that passive competence in a trilingual's first language enhances the use of the second and third language, reducing the probability of their interdependence. The participants in our study had active and intensive use of their first and second language, which made conditions less favourable for the third language. It may be suspected that the early uniqueness point and the number of errors obtained were due more to a data-driven and lexical processing and less to conceptual processing. Furthermore, less proficiency in the third language provides few intra- and interlanguage connections, thus restricting lexical access to very few matching alternatives in the lexical repertoire of the third language. The abstract English words with one translation support this argument; they are responsible for the generally shorter completion performance of the trilinguals.

Further research is needed to clarify the questions raised in this discussion. A most valuable complementary study with German–English bilinguals would be able to focus on findings typical for trilinguals, as opposed to bilinguals. If more were known about possible similarities and differences, then more of the results already obtained for bilinguals could be used for evaluating the performance of trilinguals.

## References

Abunuwara, E. (1992) The structure of the trilingual lexicon. *European Journal of Cognitive Psychology* 4, 311–22.

Baschek, I.L., Bredenkamp, J., Oehrle, B. and Wippich, W. (1977) Bestimmung der Bildhaftigkeit (I), Konkretheit (C) und der Bedeutungshaltigkeit (m) von 800 Substantiven. *Zeitschrift für experimentelle und angewandte Psychologie* 24, 353–96.

Basden, B.H., Bonilla-Meeks, J.L. and Basden, D.E. (1994) Cross-language priming in word-fragment completion. *Journal of Memory and Language* 33, 69-82.

Challis, B.H. and Brodbeck, D.R. (1992) Level of processing affects priming in word-fragment completion. *Journal of Experimental Psychology: Learning, Memory, and Cognition* 18, 595–607.

Clyne, M. (1997) Some of the things trilinguals do. *International Journal of Bilingualism* 1, 95–116.

Dufour, R. and Kroll, J.F. (1995) Matching words to concepts in two languages: A test of the concept mediation model of bilingual representation. *Memory and Cognition* 23, 166–80.

Kroll, J.F. and Michael, E. (1997) A model of bilingual representation and its implications for second language acquisition. Unpublished manuscript.

Kroll, J.F. and Stewart, E. (1994) Category interference in translation and picture naming: Evidence for asymmetric connections between bilingual memory representations. *Journal of Memory and Language* 33, 149–74.

Mägiste, E. (1986) Selected issues in second and third language learning. In J. Vaid (ed.) *Language Processing in Bilinguals* (pp. 97–122). Hillsdale, NJ: Lawrence

Erlbaum.
Paivio, A. (1986) *Mental Representations: A Dual-coding Approach*. New York: Oxford University Press.
Paivio, A., Clark, J.M. and Lambert, W.E. (1988) Dual-coding theory and semantic repetition effects on recall. *Journal of Experimental Psychology: Learning, Memory and Cognition* 14, 163–72.
Paivio, A., Yuille, J.C., and Madigan, S. (1968) Concreteness, imagery and meaningfulness values for 925 nouns. *Journal of Experimental Psychology Monograph Supplement* 76.
Roedinger, H.L. (1990) Implicit memory: Retention without remembering. *American Psychologist* 45, 1043–56.
Schönpflug, U. (forthcoming) Bilingual organisation of the lexicon: Concreteness and number of translation equivalents.
Smith, M.C. (1991) On the recruitment of semantic information for word-fragment completion: Evidence from bilingual priming. *Journal of Experimental Psychology: Learning, Memory and Cognition* 17, 234–44.
Thorndike, E.L. and Lorge, I. (1957) *The Teacher's Wordbook of 30,000 Words*. New York: Columbia University Teachers' College.
Voorwinde, S. (1981) A lexical and grammatical study in Dutch–English–German trilingualism. *International Review of Applied Linguistics* 52, 3–30.
Weldon, M.S. (1991) Mechanisms underlying priming on perceptual tests. *Journal of Experimental Psychology: Learning, Memory and Cognition* 17, 526–41.
Weldon, M.S. and Roedinger, H.L. (1987) Altering retrieval demands reverses the picture superiority effect. *Memory and Cognition* 15, 269–80.

# Appendix

## QUESTIONNAIRE

**I. Personal information**

1. *Age*: _____

2. *Gender*:         male         female

3. a) *Nationality*:_____

   b) *Country and town of birth*: _____

**For students**

4. a) *School background*: _____

   b) *Sequence of languages learned*: 1._____
   2._____
   3._____
   4._____

**For university students**

5. *major subject*:_____

**For working people**

6. *employment*: _____

**II. Current language use**

| 7. With whom do you speak German? | How intensively? | Dominant language of partner German? |
|---|---|---|
| Close partner you live with | 0--------0--------0--------0<br>hardly  sometimes  often  very often | yes   no |
| Own children | 0--------0--------0--------0<br>hardly  sometimes  often  very often | yes   no |
| Persons you live with | 0--------0--------0--------0<br>hardly  sometimes  often  very often | yes   no |
| Best friend | 0--------0--------0--------0<br>hardly  sometimes  often  very often | yes   no |
| A friend | 0--------0--------0--------0<br>hardly  sometimes  often  very often | yes   no |
| On certain occasions | 0--------0--------0--------0<br>hardly  sometimes  often  very often | yes   no |

## III. Language Learning History

*German*

1-2-3-4-5-6-7-8-9-10-11-12-13-14-15-16-17-18-19-20-21-22-23-24-25-26-27-28-29-30 years of age

Mark those years with a cross in which you actively learned German (include German lessons in your country or lessons and time spent in a German speaking country)

*English*

1-2-3-4-5-6-7-8-9-10-11-12-13-14-15-16-17-18-19-20-21-22-23-24-25-26-27-28-29-30 years of age

Mark those years with a cross in which you learned English (include English lessons in your country or lessons and time spent in an English speaking country)

*First language*

1-2-3-4-5-6-7-8-9-10-11-12-13-14-15-16-17-18-19-20-21-22-23-24-25-26-27-28-29-30 years of age

Mark those years of age with a cross in which you actively learned and used your first language

## IV. Language preferences

For each of the functions below indicate the order of preference with 1, 2, and 3.

| | |
|---|---|
| *Which language do you most prefer to <u>speak</u>?* | First language<br>German<br>English |
| *Which language do you most prefer to <u>write</u>?* | First language<br>German<br>English |
| *In which language do you most prefer to <u>read</u>?* | First language<br>German<br>English |
| *In which language do you most prefer to <u>listen</u> to?* | First language<br>German<br>English |

## V. Language competence (self ratings)

**GERMAN**

*How well do you speak German?*   O---------O---------O---------O
                                   not very well   well   very well   like my first language

*How well do you write German?*     O---------O---------O---------O
                                                                   not very well    well    very well   like my first language

*How well do you read German?*      O---------O---------O---------O
                                                                   not very well    well    very well   like my first language

*How well do you understand*       O---------O---------O---------O
*German?*
                                                                   not very well    well    very well   like my first language

**ENGLISH**

*How well do you speak English?*      O---------O---------O---------O
                                                                   not very well    well    very well   like my first language

*How well do you write English?*       O---------O---------O---------O
                                                                   not very well    well    very well   like my first language

*How well do you read English?*        O---------O---------O---------O
                                                                   not very well    well    very well   like my first language

*How well do you understand*        O---------O---------O---------O
*English?*
                                                                   not very well    well    very well   like my first language

**VI. <u>Automatisation in language use</u>**

(Mark the appropriate language with a cross)

*In which language do you spell out most easily?*      German
                                                                                                 English

*In which language do you count most easily?*        German
                                                                                                 English

## Chapter 8
# Towards the Construction of a Theory of Cross-linguistic Transfer

CHRISTINE BOUVY

For some 40 years, research into second language acquisition has focused on mother-tongue influence. It seems obvious, however, that when learners try to compensate for lack of knowledge, other foreign languages may also be sources of borrowing. The positive or negative impact the (relative) knowledge of a third language (L3) may have on the acquisition of a second one (L2) or vice versa has seldom been studied systematically to date.

This chapter examines the impact of knowledge of a second Germanic language (Dutch or German) on the acquisition of English in a formal setting. We shall demonstrate that though apparently very similar to mother-tongue transfer in motivation and output, cross-linguistic transfer is more a compensatory performance phenomenon than a phenomenon of intellectual compensation, comparable to mother-tongue transfer. In other words, L2/L3 transfer is a feature of language *use* and not of language *structure*. Hence, presumably, the relatively low frequency (under 5% of the total errors in this study) and relative non-persistence of L2/L3 transfer phenomena. Cross-linguistic transfer does, however, reflect learners' metalinguistic awareness, i.e. not just their typological knowledge but also their psychotypology, their perception of the linguistic similarities and differences between their L2 and their L3, and therefore only involves those elements that are transferable or that learners themselves regard as such. The transferability constraint prevents pure randomness, even though cross-linguistic transfer nevertheless remains a largely unconscious interaction phenomenon between evolving sets of imperfectly acquired structures.

## Sample Structure and Data Collection

The subjects in our study were students aged 18 to 22 studying business administration at the University of Liège in Wallonia (the French-speaking part of Belgium). At this university, students in business administration have to study two foreign languages, namely English plus either Dutch,

German or Spanish.[1] Most of them choose the two languages they have been studying in secondary school, i.e. English and either Dutch (for over two-thirds of them) or German. Indeed, French-speaking Belgian pupils study two foreign languages at secondary school, choosing from English, Dutch, German and, in rare cases, Spanish. They pick Dutch, English or German at age 12, and opt for a second foreign language (English, Dutch, German or exceptionally Spanish) two years later.

In business administration, languages are an integral part of the students' university curriculum, together with mathematics, statistics, corporate law, sociology, economics, management and so on. The students are taught English and Dutch or German for about 60 classroom hours a year, which represents two hours a week of each language. During these two-hour classes they discuss articles on economics taken from current magazines and do various types of linguistic exercise based on the texts. They are also encouraged to watch TV and listen to radio programmes in the target language and to do additional exercises in the language laboratory. At the end of the academic year there are written and oral exams in both languages. The oral exams consist in presenting newspaper articles, essays or papers the students have prepared; the written ones – which are held on two successive days, which certainly favours L2/L3 interference – consist of short essays, answers to open questions, lexical and grammatical exercises and translations.

As L2/L3 interference often surfaced in examination papers, we decided to study its occurrence systematically. All instances of cross-linguistic interference found in end-of-year written exams were noted and classified in order to determine the relative impact of L2/L3 interference. Using these data, we hoped to analyse the mechanisms and evolution of such interference as a function of learners' linguistic proficiency, examine whether it is in any way comparable to mother-tongue influence, and ultimately understand how to remedy it. Clearly L2/L3 interference requires an explanation on the basis of transfer. We suggest, however, that, unlike mother-tongue transfer, which has been shown to affect learners' grammar (Corder, 1992), L2/L3 transfer is simply a performance-induced phenomenon, brought about by virtue of learners' use of the semantic–syntactic access file to the 'mental lexicon' in the production task. Indeed, as we shall see, L2/L3 transfer is limited to specific parts of speech or linguistic phenomena and consists almost exclusively of a process of relexification, that is, the replacement of lexical items in L3 by those in L2, leaving the syntactic structure unaffected (Zobl, 1980a, 1980b). But the fact that there were many (over 20) occurrences of 70% of L2/L3 errors in the corpus suggests that these are not just individual performance data attributable to utterly arbitrary behaviour.

The error corpus is composed of 1683 errors found in the exam papers of business administration students and in two translation exercises subsequently given to business administration and economics students. The students are divided into four categories or levels: A, B, C and D. Level A students (310), i.e. first-year university students, can be considered representative of the foreign language standard achieved by French-speaking secondary school graduates in Belgium. Students in Levels B (250), C (192) and D (184) are respectively in their second, third and fourth years and have had complementary university training, or else first-year students who have been living or studying abroad and have therefore been directly streamed into upper levels.

The error corpus was compiled in three stages:
(1) All errors due to cross-linguistic influence in the examination papers were noted and classified according to type, frequency and context. This first error corpus, comprising 874 entirely unsolicited errors that highlight L2/L3 interference at Levels A, B, C and D, enabled us to make preliminary observations.
(2) These observations were verified through a short translation exercise given to all incoming Level A students the following year. Note that these were new students, whose errors had never been considered. This second corpus consisted of 394 errors.
(3) These observations were further verified through an exercise given to all business administration and economics students; the latter were to be used as a control group as English is the only foreign language they study at university. This third corpus comprised 415 errors. The purpose of this exercise was to see how L2/L3 errors evolved with linguistic competence and to what extent they were due to the activation of the L2.

**Table 8.1** Error total and distribution

| Errors  | Written exams | Translation 1 | Translation 2 |
|---------|---------------|---------------|---------------|
| Total   | 874           | 394           | 415           |
| Level A | 453           | 394           | 206           |
| Level B | 284           |               | 131           |
| Level C | 91            |               | 56            |
| Level D | 46            |               | 22            |

## Types of Error

There were three main types of error: a very small number of syntactic interference errors such as inversion; a small percentage (8%) of morphological errors; and an overwhelming number of lexical errors.

### Morphological errors

These are of two main types:

*Morpho-syntactic code-mixing*

Examples (1%, almost exclusively in Level A) included applying L2 syntactic rules to English phrasal verbs or word clusters, such as the replacement of the passive voice or 'you' by *men* (Dutch) or *man* (German), or converting 'take over' to *overtake*, 'set off' to *offset*:

*They will the firm overtake.*
*They fear that it will a conflict offset.*
*If men asks you ..* (<Dutch) = If they ask you ...
*Man doesn't know.* (<German) = You never know.
*If man the head attacks ..* (<German) = If you attack the head ...

*Morpho-semantic code-mixing*

These (7%) fell into four categories:

(1) An English lexeme and an L2 rule and suffix: *help-t* for 'helped', using the Dutch suffix *-t* ; *agenda's, quota's, product-en* and *good-eren* for 'goods', using Dutch plural formation rules and suffixes;
(2) A Dutch root and an English suffix: *wacht-ed* for 'waited'; *goed-s* for 'goods';
(3) An English lexeme and an English prefix used according to an L2 rule: *singer-ess* corresponding to 'zanger-in' (female singer) in Dutch; *Canadese* for 'Canadian' corresponding to 'Canadees' in Dutch with the English suffix *-ese* as in 'Chinese'; and
(4) Half-Dutch half-English compounds and word clusters: *avondlunch* for 'dinner', corresponding to Dutch 'avondeten'; *Great Britannië* for 'Great Britain'; *Zuid Europeans* for 'South Europeans'; *achteen* for 'eighteen', from Dutch 'achtien'; *begin of the year* for 'beginning of the year'; *minder strong* and *less sterk* for 'less strong', corresponding to Dutch 'minder sterk'.

### Lexical errors

As previously stated, L2/L3 transfer appears to be almost exclusively a process of relexification. Errors attributable to relexification represent 92%

of the error corpus. They are classified into five categories on the basis of both form and relevance.

*Direct borrowing (gap-filler)*

Direct borrowing accounts for 22% of the errors, almost exclusively in Levels A and B. It consists of substituting a Dutch/German lexeme having the same meaning but a completely different form, often incompatible with English spelling and phonetics. Some examples are given in Table 8.2.

**Table 8.2** Direct borrowing

| Dutch | German |
|---|---|
| aantal (number) | bei (at) |
| bouw (build) | genug (enough) |
| inwoner (inhabitant) | kein (no) |
| eeuw (century) | Leute (people) |
| Engels (English) | mehr (more) |
| ongeveer (about) | nicht (not) |
| s'avonds (in the evening) | oder (or) |
| tijdens (during) | Reiziger (traveller) |
| zelfs (even) | Stunde (hours) |

The assumption here is that while encoding an L3 utterance learners not only realise they have no matchable lexeme in their lexicon, but can find no phonetically plausible target-like lexeme in their L2 store either. What is less clear, however, is whether they are aware of merely filling a gap – which is certainly the case when they fall back on the mother-tongue lexeme they intended to translate, or simply retrieve one word for the other accidentally (Bouvy, 1989).

*Spelling Interference*

Spelling interference, which involves the use of a Dutch/German lexeme having the same meaning and a form close to that in English, accounts for 28% of the errors in the corpus. It typically involves L2/L3 doublets, for example the Dutch words 'nieuw, vieuw, tekst, produkt, balans, Sovjet, miljonair, januari, probleem' and the English 'new, view, text, product, balance, Soviet, millionaire, January, problem'. Such errors could be accounted for as 'slips of the pen' if they were not so commonplace in the lower proficiency levels of study (Levels A and B). Other examples are shown in Table 8.3.

**Table 8.3** Spelling interference

| Dutch | German |
|---|---|
| beter (better) | hundert (hundred) |
| Japanees (Japanese) | komm (come) |
| miljoen (million) | prozent (percent) |
| salaris (salary) | tausend (thousand) |
| sinds (since) | |
| tien (ten) | |

*Lexeme Copying*

This consists in using a Dutch/German lexeme, often anglicised, which has the same meaning as in English yet quite a different form, although one that is consistent with English spelling and phonetics rules: *minder* (less), *grens* (border), *streek* (area), *want* (for).

Here the learner cannot retrieve the English word he or she is looking for and thus retrieves its Dutch/German equivalent, which is modified according to spelling and phonetics rules. Being limited by the possibility of using a Dutch/German lexeme according to English phonetic rules, lexeme copying only accounts for 13% of errors, all the more so as the strategy is very close to lexeme matching, which is reinforced by the existence of the English lexeme used erroneously.

*Lexeme matching*

Lexeme matching involves 18% of the corpus errors. It consists in using an L2 word form which exists in English (often after minor anglicisation) with its Dutch or German meaning (see Table 8.4).

**Table 8.4** Lexeme matching

| Dutch | German |
|---|---|
| arm (for poor, <arm) | also (for thus, <also) |
| breed (for broad, <breed) | become (for obtain, <bekommen) |
| deal (for distribute, <delen) | fast (for almost, <fast) |
| handle (for trade, <handel) | kind (for child, <kind) |
| loan (for wages, <loon) | spare (for save, <sparen) |
| mate (for size, <maat) | |
| middle (for means, <middel) | |
| tell (for count, <tellen) | |
| wet (for law, <wet) | |

The assumption here is that at a given stage in the encoding process the learner matches an English sememe with an L2 one, so that the associated lexeme can be accessed, retrieved and copied into the part of the semantico-syntactic structure being processed. Schematically, this gives us, for example:

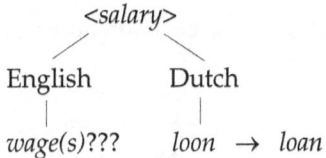

In this example the learner is trying to remember the English word 'wage(s)' and instead retrieves its Dutch equivalent 'loon', which is then anglicised and used under its English form *loan*. Hence:

*They want their loans (= wages) to be over £140 a week.*

### Generalisation

Being limited to few words, generalisation represents only 7% of errors. It consists in using an English word of specialised, restricted use, on the basis of its more common Dutch/German equivalent: *great* (big), *land* (country), *wares* (goods).

Here the erroneous use of *great*, *land* and *wares* for 'groot', 'land' and 'waren' in Dutch is encouraged by the existence of the English words 'great', 'land' and 'wares', which have a similar meaning but a more restricted use. Schematically, we have one L2 word (groot) semantically related to three or more L3 words (big, great, large), one of which is also related phonetically; hence it is likely that the learner will retrieve 'great' on the basis of 'groot' (e.g. *a great company, great problems, great difficulties, great profits* ..).

## Horizontal and vertical comparative studies

Though L2/L3 interference errors proved to be mainly relexification phenomena falling into the five different categories listed above, it was also noteworthy that an impressive number of errors involved particular categories of word: numbers, nouns and adjectives of nationality, names of months and countries, short linking words and prepositions. The question that then arises is, why were these words more likely candidates for L2/L3 interference than others? Why should learners transfer nationality words and numbers more often than other categories? Our hypothesis is that they do so because such words are often related both phonetically and semantically, which makes them twice as likely to be transferred as phonetic doublets like 'become' (<German *bekommen* used with the meaning of 'get')

and semantic ones like 'streek' (<Dutch *streek* used to mean 'area') that can be transferred on a phonetic or semantic basis only. Given the model we have outlined above, where L2/L3 transfer is seen as a performance process due to interference between imperfectly acquired languages, it seems logical that closely related words should be retrieved more easily for one another than those with no obvious connection.

In order to verify this observation, made on the basis of unsolicited errors found in answers to open questions and in translation exercises in the examination papers of students from all levels, A–D, we asked Level A students (298 in all) the following year to translate this passage, which contains many words we suspected would create L2/L3 interference:

> Des millions d'<u>Allemands</u> <u>économisent</u> de l'argent en achetant leurs marchandises en <u>Pologne</u>. Depuis <u>août</u> de l'année passée, des <u>milliers</u> de voitures passent la <u>frontière</u> entre les deux <u>pays</u> chaque jour. Hier <u>soir</u>, par exemple, on a compté pas moins de <u>2000</u> voitures à la douane <u>polonaise</u> entre <u>18</u> et <u>24</u> heures.[2]

Of the words underlined (the most likely candidates for interference, as they all belong to one of the categories mentioned, namely nationality words, numbers etc.), those which gave rise to the most numerous and varied errors were: *Allemand* (German: 38 interference errors, 13%); *Polonaise* (Polish: 69 errors, 23%); *Pologne* (Poland: 68 errors, 22%); *pays* (country: 47 errors, 16%); *août* (August: 60 errors, 20%); and *économiser* (save: 34 errors, 11%). Other interference errors were made for 'goods' (*produkten, producten, gooderen, goeds, wares*); 'border' (*grens, Grenze, greans*); 'no less than' (*not minder that, no minder than*); 'and' (*en*); 'for example' (*bij/bei exemple/example*); 'since' (*sinds*); 'thousands' (*duizends* and *tausend*, but also hybrid word forms like *thausands, thousand, tausent, thousent, thausend, thuisends*); 'eighteen' (*eightien, achtien*); and 'twelve' (*twelf, twaalf*). This confirmed our hypothesis that such words are indeed very likely candidates for L2/L3 interference.

Subsequently all A, B, C and D Level business administration and economics students were asked to translate the following passage:

> A l'avenir, des milliers d'Allemands économiseront de l'argent en achetant leurs marchandises en Pologne. En effet, on sait que tous les nouveaux produits sont plus chers en Allemagne depuis août 1990.[3]

There were 493 students in all (136 in economics and 357 in business administration), distributed as follows: 148 in Level A (101 in business administration and 47 in economics), 157 in Level B (110 in business administration and 47 in economics), 106 in Level C (83 in business administration and 23 in economics), 82 in Level D (63 in business administration and 19 in economics). Their errors were classified according to section, year of study, L2 and language proficiency (weak/fair/good). The words which provoked the greatest interference phenomena were, in decreasing order of occurrence: *août* (August: 27%); *économiser* (save: 23%); *Pologne* (Poland: 17%); *Allemands* (Germans: 9%) and *Allemagne* (Germany: 7%). The number of different versions dropped from level to level, and idiosyncratic word forms at Levels A and B had disappeared in favour of L3 correct forms by Level D (see Table 8.5).

**Table 8.5** Comparative table of interference error frequency for the word *Poland*

| Level | Business Administration | Economics |
|-------|------------------------|-----------|
| A     | 39%                    | 26%       |
| B     | 23%                    | 14%       |
| C     | 12%                    | 9%        |
| D     | 9%                     | 6%        |

Note here that in order to assess the possible influence of English on either Dutch or German interlanguage, the students were asked to translate the sentences into the two languages studied (English and either Dutch or German). This visual element undoubtedly had a correcting function; many students did indeed correct interference errors they had made in English after seeing the Dutch or German forms.

## Conclusion

The process of language acquisition is now generally described as cognitive, one of creating a body of implicit knowledge upon which L2 or L3 utterances are based. Acquiring a language is a creative process in which learners interact with their environment to produce an internalised representation of the regularities they discover in the linguistic data to which they are exposed (Corder, 1981). This internal representation is their interlanguage competence, which keeps changing and developing so long as learners continue to learn. Second language acquisition research has shown that the developmental sequence of acquisition is largely independent of external processes such as teaching or variation in the data or internal ones such as affective factors. The mother tongue does not appear to affect the order of development either, but it does play a heuristic and facilitative role in the process of learning (Corder, 1992). The very nub of the classical position (Lado, 1964) was that the relative ease or difficulty of acquiring some feature of a target language heavily depended on the similarity or difference it bore to the mother tongue. Similarity implied ease of learning, difference implied difficulty. This being so, if transfer occurs, it is from the mental structure which is the implicit knowledge of the mother tongue, to the separate and independently developing knowledge of the target language. But the mother tongue also plays a role in the use of a target language in communication. Both structural and communicative in nature, mother-tongue transfer naturally gives rise to structural and communicative transfer errors, i.e. phenomena of language structure and use that are difficult to distinguish (Kellerman, 1977; Tarone, 1977). The only difference between the two is presumably the more persistent occurrence of incorrect mother-tongue-like features due to structural transfer, what Schachter (1978) has called 'resident errors'.

Taking this into account, it appears clearly from the data compiled in our study that, though very similar to mother-tongue transfer in motivation and output, L3/L2 transfer cannot be a by-product of learning but must be a performance process, attributable to the discrepancy between learners' linguistic competence and their communicative needs. Like mother-tongue transfer, it is motivated by the learners' need to fall back on previous knowledge when 'new' L3 knowledge is lacking, that is, when they have to express themselves beyond their linguistic competence. Its mechanism is one of linguistic – essentially lexical – interference (unconscious) or borrowing (conscious). It seems conceivable that learners may have access – consciously or not – to an L2 word stored in their mental lexicon instead of the corresponding L3 one. One can equally argue that the closer phonetically and semantically two L2/L3 words are to one another, the more easily they can be substituted for one another in production. As L2/L3 transfer also reflects learners' relative knowledge of similarity between L2 and L3, it will only involve elements that are transferable or regarded as such by learners as a function of their metalinguistic awareness. This transferability constraint prevents pure randomness and individual variation and accounts for the gradual disappearance of the grossest errors. Thus, L2/L3 transfer can be described as *elaborative, evolutive, selective* and *mixed*.

## Types of L2/L3 transfer

### Elaborative

As suggested by Kellerman (1978, 1983), elaborative transfer consists in using L2/L3 elements to fill interlanguage gaps. It allows learners to resort to L2/L3 surface structures when they fail to remember or simply do not know the L2/L3 equivalents. Being a compensatory phenomenon, it is temporary and evolving by nature, as it depends on learners' individual levels of knowledge and communicative needs.

*Evolutive*

Our comparative study of L2/L3 errors in Levels A, B, C and D shows that, fortunately, not all kinds of transfer errors persist throughout the four years. Direct borrowing and spelling interference, which are rough-and-ready compensatory phenomena, are numerous at Level A and have virtually disappeared by Level D. Other errors, however, such as lexeme matching and generalisation, only appear regularly in the upper levels (C and D). This is not surprising, since such errors require a better knowledge of both languages (L2/L3) and thus a more elaborate perception – or implicit knowledge – of the linguistic distance between the two languages.

*Selective*

The fact that all the words transferred – except gap-fillers and spelling doublets – are perfectly compatible with English phonetic spelling structure is a first indication of the type of word likely to be transferred. In the absence of specific knowledge, learners will seek to maximise the systematic, the explicit and the logical in their productions. This attitude determines the selection of those elements that can be transferred. Since learners' selection processes are directly dependent on their individual notion of linguistic distance, interference phenomena are bound to evolve in parallel with the 'regular' system, because learners are substituting a system based on rules for one based on memory.

Accordingly, it is apparent in the error corpus that the only elements that will ever be transferred are those perceived as transferable, i.e those whose word forms are seen as resembling English. By the next level only those that do not correspond to generalisable rules will remain candidates for longer-term transfer, while errors based on L2 spelling and morphology rules will disappear. Of these, the only potential candidates responsible for recurring, persistent errors in Levels C and D are categories of word that appear to be more easily confused because they are formally and semantically very close in L2 and L3. Such L2/L3 doublets are clearly words too close to one another formally not to be associated in learners' memories, whether they mean the same or not (e.g *Dutch/Deutsch* – similar form with a different meaning, or *August/Augustus* – very similar form and same meaning). This remains typically the case for, first, specialised vocabulary that is not activated enough or has only been activated for a short while (*handle, wages, quotas, agendas, goods*), and second, semantically neutral or too obvious words whose forms presumably do not catch learners' attention, namely linking words (*the/de/der, or/of/oder, thus/dus, what/wat*), numbers (*ten/tien, three/drie, eleven/elf; hundred/honderd, million/miljoen, percent/prozent*), nationality words and names of countries (*Belgium/ België, Europe/Europa, the Netherlands/Nederland*).

*Mixed*

Spelling, morphemic–semantic, morphemic–syntactic and lexical–semantic mixing show that the different levels of the two systems can interact closely and that the learner can graft or transplant L2 rules to L3 words and vice versa.

Mixing is interesting for two reasons. First, it shows there are no barriers between the different codes because of learners' imperfect knowledge of L2, which may be seen as a better source of borrowing than the mother tongue (enjoying a unique status), and because of their incomplete knowledge of English. As mentioned earlier, transferred words are possible in English. It seems clear that L2 influence is filtered and thus reinforced by ill-known English elements. Does the English verb *overtake*, for instance, reinforce the learner's temptation to change 'take over' into 'overtake' in subordinate clauses? Does the plural form *families* encourage the use of the Dutch form 'familie' in the singular? Second, it seems to prove that the ultimate purpose of learners is not so much to incorporate particular L2 elements, but rather to establish bonds between rules which are too similar not to be associated in their memories for economy's sake.

Finally, it follows from what precedes that L2/L3 transfer will be reinforced by the following factors : the activation level of the L2, the relative (lack of) knowledge of both L2 and L3, the linguistic despecification of the candidates for transfer, the degree of linguistic constraint implicit in the context of production and the communicative pressure.

### Reinforcing factors

*Activation of the L2*

There can only be an interaction between two systems in memory if the two are equally easily accessible, and the ease of access to a memorised word depends on its frequency of use. As soon as one of the two systems is no longer used it falls into the background, and transfer phenomena become rarer. The smaller percentage of L2/L3 interference errors made by economics students, whose only foreign language at university is English, shows that cross-linguistic interference only takes place in a conspicuous way when L2 is activated. Clearly, there is an activation threshold under which an element is no longer disruptive.

### Knowledge of L2/L3

Cross-linguistic transfer requires some knowledge of the elements transferred; one cannot transfer what one does not know. Similarly, erroneous transfer diminishes as learners improve their (implicit) knowledge of two systems and develop more realistic perceptions of the linguistic distance between the two languages. This confirms the assertion that L2/L3 transfer is not a phenomenon of intellectual compensation comparable to mother-tongue transfer, which necessarily goes from the better known to the less well known, but rather an interaction phenomenon between imperfectly acquired elements associated in learners' individual memories.

### Despecification of the candidates for transfer

As transferability is a feature of the perception of the relationship between second and third languages, it seems obvious that the frequency of L2/L3 associations will depend on how imperfectly learners perceive L2/L3 differences. As Kellerman (1983) showed for L1 transfer, the transferability of a term is indirectly proportional to its degree of markedness. Psycholinguistically marked terms will seldom be transferred. As we saw, the only real candidates for cross-linguistic transfer are words that are sufficiently despecified not to be considered strictly L2. Those which are not will not be transferred unless they undergo a morphological–phonological transformation in order to become transferable. The students, for example, will use *sparen* (save) to mean 'save', but not *bezuinigen* (save). If *bekommen* (obtain) is a likely candidate for interference, it is so under the form and with the meaning of 'become'.

### Communicative needs and context

Wherever we find communicative pressure exceeding knowledge we get the strongest L2/L3 transfer. Systematic analysis of the data suggests that transfer errors are more numerous in guided exercises such as translation or rephrasing, and in semantically complex ones like short essays, than in less constraining tasks such as answers to questions or summaries. This indicates that interference errors are heavily dependent on, first, the degree of linguistic constraint implicit in the context of linguistic production due to the neccessity to use a given word or structure imposed by the exercise, and second, the level of difficulty (linguistic or semantic). As compensatory phenomena, errors will naturally appear more often when learners have to express themselves beyond their L3 competence.

To conclude – quite positively – we reiterate that the proportion of cross-linguistic transfer errors remains low (under 5% of the total errors in the data) and that it spontaneously diminishes in the course of learning. Therefore cross-linguistic transfer errors do not have important teaching implications and can in fact be seen as a necessary by-product of multilingual education.

Further research might address the possibility of a reverse effect of English vs. Dutch/German linguistic transfer. Systematic analysis of English as a source of interference errors in both learner Dutch and learner German would enable us to disprove or, hopefully, to confirm the present conclusions.

## Notes

1. The students who studied Spanish and English were not included in the study.
2. Millions of Germans are saving money by buying goods in Poland. Since August 1998, thousands of cars have crossed the border every day. Yesterday evening, for instance, at least two thousand cars went through Polish customs between 6 p.m. and midnight.
3. In the future, thousands of Germans are expected to save money by buying goods in Poland. Indeed, new products have been more expensive in Germany than in Poland ever since August 1990.

## References

Bouvy, C. (1989) Exploration of early second language acquisition in a formal setting. PhD thesis, University of Liège.

Corder, S.P. (1981) *Error Analysis and Interlanguage*. London: Oxford University Press.

Corder, S.P. (1992) A role for the mother tongue. In S. Gass and L. Selinker (eds) *Language Transfer in Language Learning* (pp. 18–31). Amsterdam/Philadelphia: John Benjamins.

Kellerman, E. (1977) Towards a characterisation of the strategy of transfer in second language learning. *Interlanguage Studies Bulletin* 2, 58–146.

Kellerman, E. (1978) Giving learners a break: Native language intuitions as a source of predictions about transferability. *Working Papers on Bilingualism* 15, 59–92.

Kellerman, E. (1983) Now you see it, now you don't. In S. Gass and L. Selinker (eds) *Language Transfer in Language Learning* (pp. 112–34). Rowley: Newbury House.

Lado, R. (1964) *Language Teaching*. New York: McGraw-Hill.

Schachter, J. (1978) Interrelationships between total production and error production in the syntax of adult learners. *Papers in ESL*. NAFSA.

Tarone, E. (1977) Conscious communication strategies in interlanguage. In *TESOL 77: Teaching and Learning English as a Second Language: Trends in Research and Practice* (pp. 194–203) Washington: TESOL.

Zobl, H. (1980a) The formal and developmental selectivity of L1 influence on L2 acquisition. *Language Learning* 30, 43–57.

Zobl, H. (1980b) Developmental and transfer errors: Their common bases and (possibly) differential effects on learning. *TESOL Quarterly* 14, 469–83.

## Chapter 9
# Bilingualism and Trilingualism in School Students in Catalonia

CARMEN MUÑOZ

Catalan is spoken by more than six million people, four million of whom live in Catalonia. The remaining Catalan-speakers are found in Valencia, the Balearic Islands, Andorra, the 'Franja' in Aragon, the French Roussillon, and l'Alguer in Sardinia. Catalonia itself dates its birth back to the ninth century. Since then its language has been in close contact, when not in conflict, with other more largely extended languages, mainly Latin, French and Spanish Castilian.[1] The standardisation of Catalan took place at the beginning of the present century and sprang from the strong nationalist movement of the nineteenth century. There followed two brief periods of autonomous government when Catalan was used as the medium of instruction at schools, during which the language underwent a process of revitalisation that was brought to an abrupt end by the Civil War. Defeat in the War – since the Catalans had largely supported the legitimate Republican government – led to a period of political and linguistic repression in which words such as 'freedom' or 'democracy' were banned from public speech, doubly so if uttered in Catalan.

Spanish-speaking immigrants from other parts of Spain flooded in during the 1950s, 1960s and early 1970s. They concentrated in new neighbourhoods on the urban periphery of big towns, particularly around Barcelona, and usually maintained minimal interaction with the autochthonous population. The effect of the Spanish mass media (in particular, since 1958, of television) was also a determinant factor in the domination of Castilian over Catalan. However, in 1975 the death of General Franco marked the beginning of a new period of revitalisation for Catalan. An indication of how low its status was at that time is that only a little over 10% of the population were then literate in the language (compare with Table 9.2 below). But the Spanish democratic constitution of 1978 permitted the introduction of Catalan in schools, and this began just two years later: first as a language subject for three hours a week, then for four hours, and soon as the language of instruction for a number of other subjects. The subsequent statutes of autonomous government were followed by laws of 'linguistic normalisation' in those 'autonomies' which had their own autochthonous languages (Galician in Galicia, Basque in the Basque Country, and Catalan in Catalonia, Valencia and the Balearic Islands). The *Llei de normalització lingüística* in Catalonia (1983) dictated language policies in the education domain and marked the official beginning of the Catalan immersion programme for children of Spanish-speaking families (although earlier experiences date back to 1978–9), and the progressive generalisation of Catalan to higher levels of education.

The introduction of Catalan in schools was expected to have linguistic, educational and social benefits for the children involved. Several studies conducted in the 1980s soon showed that immersion in Catalan had generally beneficial effects for the pupils, specially as far as reading comprehension was concerned (Bel, 1990; Serra, 1989), or at worst no negative effects (Arenas, 1986). On the other hand, the very strong social presence of Castilian guaranteed a very high command of Spanish, as found by studies conducted in recent years. For example, it was shown that pupils at the end of obligatory education in 1990 (then at age 14) still had a better command of Spanish than of Catalan (Arnau *et al.*, 1994; Serra & Vila,

**Table 9.1** Recent changes in distribution of primary schools and students in Catalonia

|  | 1986–7 | 1995–6 |
|---|---|---|
| *Distribution of schools* | | |
| Catalan | 24% | 68% |
| Bilingual (Evolutionary)* | 39% | 27% |
| Bilingual | 35% | 5% |
| Spanish | 2% | 0% |
| *Distribution of students* | | |
| Catalan | 42% | 81% |
| Bilingual | 33% | 18% |
| Spanish | 25% | 0.5% |

*Source*: Sedec (Servei d'Ensenyament del Català)

* 'Evolutionary' bilingual schools are in the process of becoming monolingual Catalan

1991). At the same time, the level of written Catalan was shown to be dependent on the degree of use of Catalan at the different types of school (see Table 9.1), while oral abilities in Catalan seemed affected only by the family language (Bel *et al.*, 1991), although differences were seen to be disappearing (Vila, 1993).

In 1992 an act passed by the Catalan Parliament decreed that Catalan was to be the language of instruction and use in educational institutions at all levels, which gave a new impulse to the generalisation of the minority language. The evolution of the process outlined in the preceeding passage can be seen in Table 9.1, where primary schools are classified in terms of their use of Catalan and Spanish and the corresponding proportion of pupils who are instructed in these languages. Figure 9.1 shows the differences in the proportion of use of the two languages in primary and secondary education. And in Table 9.2 we can observe the effects of the school system and other wider changes on Catalonians' command of Catalan in recent years.

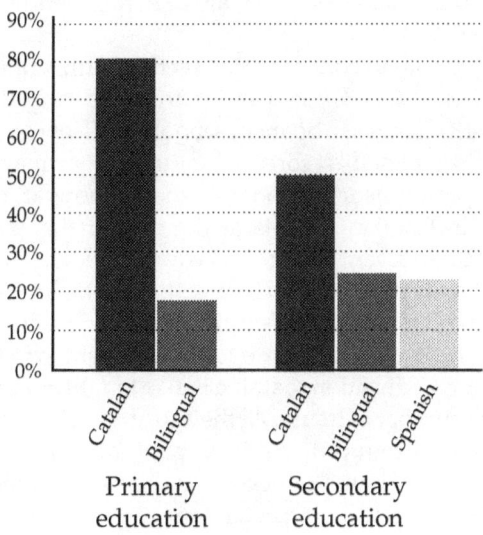

**Figure 9.1** Distribution of students per language of instruction, 1995–6

Source: Sedec (Servei d'Ensenyament del Català)

**Table 9.2** Percentage of population competent in Catalan for each skill

| Skills | 1986 | 1991 |
|---|---|---|
| Listening | 90.3% | 94% |
| Speaking | 64.0% | 68% |
| Reading | 60.5% | 68% |
| Writing | 31.5% | 40% |

Source: Reixach (1997)

While the figures that refer to the population's proficiency in Catalan are positive, and in particular with reference to young people (Boix, 1997), social use of the minority language lags behind, especially in those zones, mostly around Barcelona, where there are high numbers of Spanish-speaking immigrants (Vila, 1996).

It seems appropriate to conclude this section with a brief report on the new Education Law (LOGSE), also dating from the early 1990s, which has brought important changes to Spanish schools at all levels, among them an earlier introduction of the first foreign language in primary schools and a longer period of compulsory schooling, ending now at age 16. The language situation in Catalan schools at the end of the 1990s reflects the incorporation of these recent changes, as we will see. The pre-school period (from age 3 to 6) still consists of an immersion period in Catalan for those children from Castilian-speaking families. Castilian is introduced as a language subject at the age of 6 in Grade 1, and is taught for a total number of 768 hours in primary education. Catalan is also taught as a language subject for an equivalent number of hours. At the age of 8 the first foreign language (usually English) is introduced, and is taught for two and a half hours per week until the end of primary education at the age of 12, and for a total of 350 hours. Optionally, a second foreign language (usually French) may be introduced at the age of 10, although this is not common.

In secondary education, Catalan and Castilian are each taught for three hours a week (a total number of 432 hours). The foreign language is taught for two or three hours a week, for a total of 316 hours; a second foreign language may also be taken as an optional subject, for the same number of hours. Students can choose whether to take some credit courses in the first foreign language and/or in a second foreign language. In the following section we will present an analysis of the position of English in the school system and of its status in Catalonia.

### English in Catalonia

English in Catalonia is a foreign language. That is, following Stern (1983) we consider English to be a foreign language because it is learned with reference to a speech community outside (rather than inside) the national or territorial boundaries in which such learning takes place. We agree with Berns (1990), however, that the 'foreign–second' dichotomy deserves some reconsideration and refinement, and that the different situations can be better accounted for by means of a 'cline of language status', with 'foreign' on one pole and 'second' on the other. Some situations will not be at either pole, and their distance from one or the other may be more finely defined by means of instruments such as sociolinguistic profiles, which typically include information about the users of a language and their attitude toward it, the functions of this language and learners' various motives for learning it (Berns, 1990: 4).

In Catalonia today, English is the most widely used foreign language, but until some 15 years ago French was still the first foreign language in schools, which explains the generally low levels of English ability among adults.[2] Furthermore, following the long years of General Franco's dictatorship, the replacement of French by English has coincided with the opening up of the Catalonian community to the international arena, which has made achieving a communicative competence in English seem much more urgent. A case in point is tourism, of crucial interest to the economic development of both Spain and Catalonia during the past decades. Another consideration is Spain's integration into the European Community, which is of great political and economic importance and has awakened the hope of a European political organisation in which all nations, big and small, may find their own place, over and above political state borders.

English language instruction in Catalan (and Spanish in general) state schools now begins at age 8 in the third grade, following the recent change outlined above. The change in the starting age of foreign language instruction, from age 11 to age 8, was one of the modifications concerning foreign languages brought in by the new Education Law (LOGSE). Among other important innovations we also find official support for a communicatively oriented approach to the teaching of foreign languages, an appreciation of the use of the language as medium of instruction for other subjects, and an acknowledgement of the importance of promoting communication strategies and metalinguistic awareness (see Muñoz & Nussbaum, 1997). Should these changes be fully implemented, coming generations will develop a higher level of proficiency in English and one that is better suited to present-day needs, particularly in terms of communicative ability.

The amount of teaching has not been increased, however, and remains low, particularly in bilingual communities like Catalonia, where the foreign language has to share curriculum time with the two official languages; as a result, foreign language instruction does not usually receive more than two and a half hours per week.[3]

As in other countries, learning English is a popular free-time activity, one in which many children and adults engage after school or work. In the case of children, pressure usually is put on them by their parents, who were generally taught French at school, and who only learnt English – the few who did – as their second foreign language, in adulthood. Their own lack of competence in English is one of the factors that seems to explain the eagerness of parents for the early introduction (that is, before the age of 8) of English in schools. In a recent study of parents' views on the early introduction to English of their pre-school children, their own personal experience is reflected in comments such as those of a mother who said at the interview: 'It's so that they don't do like us, who came late [to learn English]', and their frustration with trying to achieve some competence in English in adulthood: 'After 20 it's too late' (Torras *et al*. 1997: 146).[4]

Schoolchildren's own motivation towards English, as a recent study (Tragant, 1998)[5] shows, is predominantly instrumental, and no doubt influenced by their parents' belief in the importance of English for their future careers. Young people are also attracted to English because of its value as a *lingua franca* for use in travelling abroad and communicating with foreign people. Third comes the metalinguistic factor, that is the value of the English language *per se*, which is also a driving force for many students.

Many adults also join English classes, either at work or at language schools. The youngest among them usually begin at intermediate levels, having already studied English at school and setting out now to improve their communicative skills and their general knowledge. Those who did French at school are fewer these days and therefore the best-attended levels are no longer those for beginners. In-house training is often oriented toward the specific needs of employees. For example, among the services required from the Language School at the University of Barcelona in the past few years we find the training of administrative staff to answer international telephone calls in English and of groups of researchers interested in attending and participating in international conferences to be conducted in English.

Opportunities for using English outside the classroom are not as frequent in Catalonia, or in Spain, as in other European communities, such as the Scandinavian countries or the Netherlands. English is not used in the media, and yet the borrowing of English words is very frequent in the written press; in fact more frequent than borrowings from Spanish (Freixa *et al.*, in press). A strong tradition of dubbing foreign films into Spanish, and these days a few also into Catalan, has resulted in less exposure to spoken English than is the case in other European countries, where movies and television programmes in their original versions are a permanent source of English input.[6] However, a combination of school exchanges via European programmes and families' arrangements for children's summer courses in Ireland, Britain, Canada or the United States is already having an impact on the communicative skills in English of both Spanish and Catalonian adolescents in the late 1990s.

At the workplace, contacts in English are more frequent today as a result of increasing dependence on trade relations with other European countries. Job opportunities, in a community with a high percentage of unemployment, may much depend on a knowledge of English, which results in a strong motivation for adults to learn the language.

To sum up, on the 'cline of language status', English in Catalonia is somewhere near the foreign language end, and clearly nearer to that pole than it is in some other European countries such as Germany (Berns, 1990), or in Scandinavia (Phillipson, 1991).

## The Research Study

In our study we have set out to explore two main issues. The first relates to trilingual acquisition. We are interested in examining the linguistic competence in Catalan, Spanish, and English, from the results obtained in a series of tests, of three groups of students, aged 10, 12 and 17. The tests were administered to the older group in 1997 and to the two younger groups in 1996, that is, 14 and 13 years respectively after the Law of Linguistic Normalisation and the beginning of the Catalan Immersion Programme in schools; and five and four years respectively after the Catalan Parliament's own Act (March 1992) by which Catalan became the language of instruction and use in all educational institutions at all levels (see above). Our subjects have, therefore, learnt two languages, Catalan and Spanish or Spanish and Catalan, at different points in childhood, and English later on (see Cenoz, Chapter 3, for a revision of research on trilingual acquisition).

The second issue in our study relates to the influence of age on foreign language acquisition. As we saw above, the new curriculum for compulsory education has brought in an earlier introduction of the foreign language, from the age of 11 (Grade 6 of EGB or basic general education) to the age of 8 (Grade 3 of EP or primary education).[7] The 12-year-old subjects in our study started English at the age of 11, while the 10-year-old group began, under the new curriculum, at 10. The number of teaching hours when the tests were administered was the same for the two groups, which permits inter-group comparison. In the next section we will briefly review previous research on the age factor and implications of this for the acquisition of English in the Catalan school context.

### Age and second language acquisition

Ever since Penfield (1953) placed an optimum age for language learning within the first decade of life, the idea that children have an advantage over adults in second language acquisition has not remained undisputed. Lenneberg (1967) applied the 'critical period' concept – widely used in relation to various aspects of behavioural development in animals and humans – to human language development. His critical period hypothesis came to reinforce, and was in turn reinforced by, the innatist proposals made by Chomsky at around the same time, and also initiated a so far unfinished debate on the possible neurological basis for the decline in language capacity, which he situated at puberty (see, for example, the paper by Eubank & Gregg, 1995).

In the field of second language acquisition, the existence of a critical period, or rather of more gradual and flexible, multiple *sensitive* periods, which would allow for the differences observed between the different language components (Scovel, 1988; Patkowski, 1994), has also found ample support among researchers (Long, 1990).

This 'consensus' view (Singleton, 1995) includes the generalisations, first stated by Krashen *et al.* in 1979, according to which, adults and older children proceed through early stages of syntactic and morphological development faster than young children, while acquirers who are naturally exposed to a second language during childhood generally achieve higher second language proficiency than those beginning as adults (Krashen *et al.*, 1982, reprint: 161). These generalisations show the relationship that pertains between age, rate, and eventual attainment in second language acquisition. Of particular interest is the distinction between *rate* on the one hand, that is, the speed at which learning takes place, and eventual or ultimate *attainment* on the other; that is, the highest level of proficiency that learners achieve.

This question of rate appears to be a crucial one in age studies in foreign language situations, much more so than the question of ultimate attainment. In fact, in a context with very little exposure, regardless of age, ultimate attainment cannot be very high. As Lightbown and Spada state, one or two hours a week –even over seven or eight years – 'will not produce very advanced second language speakers' (1993: 113). Moreover, although the younger children, given enough time and exposure, are better candidates for attaining a native-like proficiency in a second language, existing evidence also shows that they need a certain period of time before they can catch up with the quicker older children and adults, that is, before their advantage will show. The study carried out by Snow and Hoefnagel-Höhle (1978), for example, demonstrated that after 12 months in a situation of naturalistic acquisition the young children in their study were overtaking the adults in several of the areas measured, but that it was still the adolescents who had the highest global scores.

The question remains, therefore, as to how long the period of instruction must be in order for young children to overtake older learners; that is, how long before they will have received enough exposure for long-term advantages to show. In this respect, Singleton has estimated that 'more than 18 years would need to be spent in a formal instructional setting in order to obtain the same amount of second language input as seems to be required for older learners' initial advantage to begin to disappear' (1995: 3), having taken as the basis for his estimate the 12-month period used in the study conducted by Snow and Hoefnagel-Höhle and referred to above. Although one can not equate a given quantity of input received over 12 months with the same amount of exposure spread over 18 years, as the author admits, the estimate is illuminating, and the span of time involved is clearly beyond the school education period.

Furthermore, long-term studies on taught foreign language acquisition are scarce and, unfortunately, not without problems. The study carried out by the British National Foundation for Educational Research (NFER) is a case in point (Burstall, 1977). One of the criticisms has been that pupils who had started learning a foreign language at an earlier age were at some point integrated into classes with pupils who had begun later. In these circumstances, the early starters did not seem to be able to maintain their initial advantage for more than a relatively short period of time, and by the age of 16 they were significantly better only in listening comprehension. In addition, before mixing the various levels, these early starters only rated higher on a speaking test than an older group who had begun at age 11, while the latter were ahead on all three of the other skills tested: reading, writing and listening.

It is therefore essential that our research into the acquisition of English by schoolchildren in Catalonia should take into account differences in the degree of exposure between second language acquisition in a situation of immersion in the community of the second language (e.g. Catalan for Spanish-speaking children), and foreign language acquisition (English for these same children). Likewise, in this type of study it is important to distinguish between different language skills, since these may be differently affected, as previous studies have shown, by both the starting age and the length of instruction.

### Subjects

There are three groups of subjects in our study. The first group is composed of 284 schoolchildren aged 10, and in Grade 5 of EP (the new curriculum), that is those who began English classes in the third grade with two and a half hours per week and had had some 200 hours of instruction in the foreign language by the time they were given the tests. The second group is composed of 286 schoolchildren aged 12, and in Grade 7 of EGB (the former curriculum), that is those who began English classes in the sixth grade with three hours per week and who had also had 200 hours of instruction in the foreign language by the time they were given the tests. The third group is composed of 296 secondary education students aged 17, enrolled in COU, the pre-university course; these had had approximately 725 hours of instruction in English by the time they took the tests, and represent the highest level of proficiency in English that can be attained via the former official school curriculum. That is, these subjects represent, in cross-section, the last measurement possible of the second group mentioned above, those starting English at 11 years old.

In our study, analysis of competence in Catalan and Spanish is carried out on data from these three subject groups, while analysis of proficiency in English is performed only on data from the subgroup of subjects, in each age level, who had not had any additional or previous instruction in English, nor any additional exposure to the language. Subjects valid for the age study (VA) in each group were 170, 129, and 95, respectively (see Table 9.3, where the proportion of VA subjects with respect to the total number in each group is also shown).

Since Catalan instruction was progressively implemented throughout the 1980s, all the students in our sample, including the oldest ones who were born around 1980, should have a good level of Catalan, but differences in language command do exist; these may be related to the language spoken in the family, Catalan, Spanish or both. Hence a three-way classification has been established on the basis of the speaker's answers to specific questions about the language normally spoken – with the mother, with the father, with brothers and sisters, and with other persons living in the

**Table 9.3** Subjects in the study

| Age | Number | VA* | % |
|---|---|---|---|
| 10 | 284 | 170 | 59.86 |
| 12 | 286 | 129 | 45.10 |
| 17 | 296 | 95 | 32.09 |
| Total | 866 | 394 | 45.49 |

*VA: valid for the age study

household. The three categories were: Catalan (C) with all family members (mother, father, brothers and/or sisters, others); Spanish (S) with all family members; and both Catalan and Spanish (B), in a variety of dominance vs. balance situations. It must be made clear, though, that the two first groups are not monolingual speakers: due to the status of Spanish as a majority language in the community, there cannot be any Catalan monolingual speakers. Similarly, because Catalan has been the school language for the majority of these children for as long as they have been attending school, and because of the extensive use of Catalan in the media and for social interaction in the neighbourhood, there cannot be any Spanish monolingual speakers either (with the exception of a few students who have only recently come to Catalonia). Therefore, although among the S group there may be subjects with no more than passive competence in Catalan, all the subjects are to be considered bilingual, at different points in the continuum towards balanced bilingualism.

Figure 9.2 shows the distribution of our subjects in the three major descriptive categories, while Table 9.4 shows the absolute frequencies of these categories per age.

As we can see, the largest group is that of students who use both languages at home, while in C and in S the numbers are almost identical. There are 53 further subjects who either do not fall into any of these categories (those who speak Galician, Basque, or another foreign language at home, either exclusively or in combination with Catalan or Spanish), or else did not provide this information.

We cannot, however, generalise from our sample to the whole population, since not all the age groups were equally distributed in the different schools, and the schools themselves differed in terms of the proportion of speakers in the three categories. A comparison of our data, including the subset from the subjects in primary education, with those from a survey of 681,811 primary school subjects carried out in Catalonia in the same year (1996) is shown in Table 9.5.

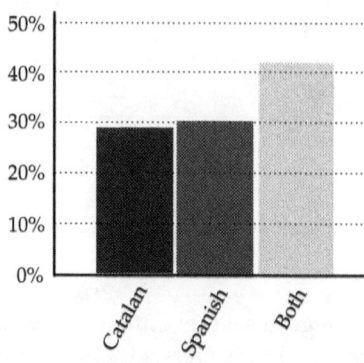

**Figure 9.2** Global distribution of language categories: percentages

**Table 9.4** Distribution of language categories in our sample by age

| Age | Catalan | Spanish | Both | Total |
|---|---|---|---|---|
| 10 | 88 | 86 | 85 | 259 |
| 12 | 75 | 89 | 92 | 256 |
| 17 | 75 | 64 | 148 | 287 |
| Total | 238 | 239 | 325 | 802 |

**Table 9.5** The home language of primary school children

| Language | Our total sample | Our primary sample | Catalonia primary sample* |
|---|---|---|---|
| Catalan | 29.6% | 34.0% | 36% |
| Spanish | 29.8% | 33.2% | 47% |
| Both | 40.5% | 32.8% | 15% |
| Number | 802 | 259 | 681,811 |

*Source: Sedec

As we can see in this table, the proportion of subjects in our study who declare themselves to come from a bilingual household is twice that of the larger sample; this may be due to the character of Barcelona, which has a very mixed population, and/or to that of our own sample.

All the students come from a total of 11 state schools located in the central area of Barcelona. The families of the children in these schools provide a good mixture of social classes and cultural backgrounds: a few from working-class families, both unskilled (12.3%) and skilled workers (13.6%); most from middle-class families, with a medium sociocultural background (27.7%) or else a university education (30.2%). It is interesting to note that for some of these parents, taking their children to a Catalan state school may symbolise democratic and nationalistic rights, those important emblems of a not so distant past, as well as following in a tradition of sound pedagogic principles that dates back to an earlier period of political autonomy under the Spanish Second Republic, before the Civil War.

## Procedures

A series of tests were administered to the subjects in intact groups, and in a randomised order to control for order effects. In this chapter we will analyse a subset composed of two Catalan tests, two Spanish tests and four English tests.

Prior to the tests the subjects were asked to fill in a questionnaire which asked for biographical information, information about their parents' jobs and the language/s spoken in the family (as we saw above), and information about English: type and intensity of exposure (oral and written); motivation; language attitude; and learning and communication strategies.

## Materials

The two types of test in which the subjects were examined in the three languages were dictation and cloze test. These two types were chosen for two important reasons. First of all, they are both considered to meet the 'naturalness' requirements for pragmatic or integrative language tests, understood by Oller (1979: 38) as:

> any procedure or task that causes the learner to process sequences of elements in a language that conform to the natural contextual constraints of that language, and which requires the learner to relate sequences of linguistic elements via pragmatic mappings to extralinguistic context.

Secondly, both the dictation and the cloze test are said 'to offer economical ways to measure overall ability in a language' (Hughes, 1989: 62), which made their use very convenient in a large-scale study such as the one described here.

The cloze tests in our study had 30 blanks, one every tenth word, and there were two forms of each. Both the Catalan and the Spanish texts were adaptations of journal articles written by the same bilingual writer, so as to minimise differences in style and the degree of difficulty of the language. The two English forms were adaptations of popular children's tales, well known to our subjects. The cloze tests were scored for correct words (that is, following the 'exact word' scoring procedure), except for a few items in which more than one alternative was allowed, based on the answers given by a control native-speaker group, and the contextually appropriate scoring method was then followed.

The dictations consisted of 50 words, and examinees were given a mark for each correct word (and in the Catalan and Spanish dictations, for each correct punctuation mark). All of the texts were adaptations of literary texts for use with school students. For convenience of administration all the subjects took the same form of dictation in each measured period.

The other two English tests were a multiple choice grammar test and a listening comprehension test. For the two younger groups there were two alternative forms with 25 items each; the two forms for the oldest group contained 50 (more difficult) items. The listening comprehension test consisted of 30 items in increasing order of difficulty; for each item, subjects were asked to recognise (out of three possibilities represented by drawings) the stimulus they heard from a tape.

### Research questions and hypotheses

Our first hypothesis was that high levels of competence in L1 and L2 would correlate positively with a high level of competence in L3, which could be explained from a cognitive point of view (Cummins, 1976, 1981), and would confirm the results of previous studies (Cenoz, 1992; Lasagabaster, 1997). Furthermore, we set out to explore which, if any, of the three home language situations described above (C, S, B) has a more positive influence on the acquisition of the third language.

With regard to the question of age, there seems to be enough evidence from previous research that older children will have a faster pace in the early stages of second (third, etc.) language acquisition. Therefore we hypothesised that, after only 200 hours of instruction, the 12-year-olds would have higher results than the 10-year-olds in all these tests, particularly in those in which the morphosyntactic aspects of the language are more important.

## Results

We will first look at the results obtained in the Catalan and Spanish tests, to compare the command these students have of their first two languages, and gain a more accurate profile of our bilingual foreign language learners. The mean scores obtained in the Catalan and Spanish tests by the three age groups are shown in Table 9.6. In the last three columns the results correspond to the total sample.

**Table 9.6** Results of the Catalan and Spanish tests

| Test | 10-year-olds | | | 12-year-olds | | | 17-year-olds | | | Total | | |
|---|---|---|---|---|---|---|---|---|---|---|---|---|
| | Mean | SD | N | Mean | SD | N | Mean | SD | N | Mean | SD | N |
| C.cl. | 16.2 | 12.1 | 265 | 27.4 | 14.4 | 275 | 54.7 | 12.8 | 289 | 33.3 | 20.9 | 829 |
| C.d. | 79.6 | 12.8 | 264 | 87.1 | 9.1 | 272 | 97.2 | 3.2 | 284 | 88.2 | 11.6 | 820 |
| S.cl. | 19.0 | 12.1 | 240 | 31.6 | 15.7 | 193 | 59.9 | 12.3 | 289 | 38.7 | 22.3 | 722 |
| S.d. | 77.0 | 13.2 | 239 | 85.9 | 11.2 | 196 | 95.7 | 3.0 | 284 | 86.8 | 12.6 | 719 |

Analysis of the scores in both the dictations and the cloze tests shows a high direct correlation between results in the two languages. The Spanish cloze test and the Catalan cloze test obtain a correlation coefficient of 0.8491, which is highly significant ($p = 0.000$). The Spanish dictation and the Catalan dictation obtain a correlation coefficient of 0.7754, which is again highly significant ($p = 0.000$).

In order to examine the possible effect of the home language on the scores in these tests, we performed a one-way analysis of variance (ANOVA) for each age group, preceded by a test of homogeneity of variances. The only significant difference was obtained from the Catalan dictation done by the 17-year-olds, where Group C obtained significantly higher results than Group S ($p = 0.0094$ in a Kruskal-Wallis test[8]). A comparison of the averages from the remaining eleven statistical tests shows that the highest score is not always obtained by the group whose home language is the language of the test. On the whole, then, the home language of our subjects does not seem to have a significant influence on their command of Catalan and Spanish, as measured by our two tests.[9]

As mentioned above, analysis of the English test results was carried out for a subset of the subjects, those who were not taking any extra English

**Table 9.7** English test results for subset in all three age groups

| Test | 10-year-olds | | | 12-year-olds | | | 17-year-olds | | |
| --- | --- | --- | --- | --- | --- | --- | --- | --- | --- |
| | Mean | SD | N | Mean | SD | N | Mean | SD | N |
| Cloze | 6.52 | 6.80 | 164 | 11.73 | 11.68 | 125 | 79.86 | 14.79 | 94 |
| Dict. | 14.10 | 12.72 | 167 | 22.45 | 13.86 | 124 | 81.66 | 10.72 | 95 |

classes. Table 9.7 shows the scores obtained by these subjects in the English cloze test and the English dictation.

Correlations were computed for the three sets of scores in each of the tests, that is for the scores on the cloze test and the dictation in the three languages (this time with just the VA subjects). The correlation coefficients found on the cloze tests in the three languages are all direct and highly significant, and so are those between the English, Catalan and Spanish dictations (p = 0.000). The coefficients obtained between Spanish and English (0.8410 and 0.6908 in the cloze and dictation tests respectively) are slightly higher than those between Catalan and English (0.8005 and 0.6538), while those between Catalan and Spanish are the highest (0.8704 and 0.7534).

A one-way analysis of variance (ANOVA) was performed with both the English cloze test and the English dictation as dependent variables, and the linguistic categories (Catalan only, Spanish only, and both) as independent variables. No significant differences were found between the results obtained for each age group between those students who spoke Catalan at home, Spanish, or both languages.

In order to examine our hypothesis about the influence of age on foreign language acquisition, we focused on the two groups with the same number of hours of instruction. The means and standard deviations in the four tests of the two age groups, 10-year-olds and 12-year-olds, appear in Table 9.8.

T-tests for independent samples were performed for each test. In the cloze test, the dictation and the grammar test, the differences between the means of the two groups were found to be highly significant (t-value = 4.44; 5.33 and 4.49 with p = 0.000 in all cases). However, in the listening comprehension test the difference was not significant (t-value = 0.50; 2-tail significance = 0.62). We can conclude, therefore, that the 12-year-olds did significantly better on the first three tests than the 10-year-olds, in spite of having had the same number of hours of instruction, while there is no

Table 9.8 English test results for the two younger age groups

| Test | 10-year-olds | | | 12-year-olds | | |
|---|---|---|---|---|---|---|
| | Mean | SD | N | Mean | SD | N |
| Cloze | 6.52 | 6.80 | 164 | 11.73 | 11.68 | 125 |
| Dictation | 14.10 | 12.72 | 167 | 22.45 | 13.86 | 124 |
| Grammar | 28.62 | 12.61 | 168 | 35.57 | 13.45 | 121 |
| List./comp. | 36.55 | 13.32 | 168 | 37.32 | 12.81 | 124 |

reason not to ascribe the small difference observed in the listening test to a chance factor.

## Discussion and Conclusions

First, we have found significant correlations between the scores on the tests in Catalan and Spanish (both in the cloze tests and in the dictations). Those subjects with a high score on a Catalan test also have a high score on the corresponding Spanish test, and vice versa. The fact that the scores for the tests in the two languages are similar, as are the dispersion measures, seems to confirm the hypothesis of the interdependence between languages (Cummins, 1981) from a theoretical point of view, while from a sociolinguistic point of view it confirms the trend towards a better command of Catalan among school students in Catalonia (Arnau et al., 1994; Vila, 1993).

Likewise, the patterns of language use at home do not seem to produce any differences in the type of bilingualism present in our subjects that are strong enough to influence their results in the third language. Instruction in the minority language seems to be successfully achieving balanced bilingualism in our subjects. Different situations, with, for example, higher concentration of Spanish-speaking families, or very different socioeconomic backgrounds, may very well produce different results. On the other hand, though our tests seem to measure overall competence in the languages, no implications can be drawn as to their social use, in which area differences may still be strong (Vila, 1996).

Second, we have seen that the correlation coefficients between the tests in the three languages are also high, so that our first hypothesis, that those students with high levels of competence in L1 and L2 would have a high level of competence in L3, is confirmed. This result is in line with that obtained by other researchers (Lasagabaster, 1997; Möhle, 1989), although in our case neither of the two languages seems to have a higher influence on the third, and neither of the two is formally closer to English.

Our second hypothesis, that the age of the children will have an influence on the scores obtained in the English tests, was also confirmed. According to our results, the 12-year-old subjects attained a significantly better command of English, as measured by three out of the four tests analysed. This would confirm our hypothesis, according to which the older subjects advance at a higher rate (that is, are more efficient than the younger learners) in the first stages of language acquisition. Differences were very high on the grammar test, as predicted, but slightly higher still on the dictation, which may be due to the youngest subjects' lack of experience of this type of task. The 12-year-olds did not do better than the 10-year-olds in the listening comprehension test, however. This seems to confirm that an early start particularly favours listening comprehension, as was found in the NFER study in which this was the only skill at which the early starters did consistently better over all the different measurement times (Burstall, 1977). It remains to be seen whether our younger subjects overtake the older ones, and if so, when, in this and the remaining skills – a question that can only be answered when results from the long-term longitudinal study are available.

The poorer results from the younger subjects in the first three tests may be due to several factors: first of all, cognitive factors, such as the more demanding effort involved in reading the text of the cloze test, in segmenting sequences of speech and writing them down in the dictation test, or in processing the grammatical constraints of the grammar test. All of these tasks are certainly of a context-reduced academic type, those in which previous studies have also found that more mature children do better than the less mature younger ones (Cummins, 1979), although superior test-taking skills cannot fully explain the older learners' rate advantage in all situations (for a discussion, see Harley, 1986).

Second, methodological and instruction factors may also be influential on the results. In fact, under the current school curriculum (LOGSE) more attention is paid to oral and communicative skills in the previous two years (the third and fourth grades of primary education), and therefore the Grade 5 children, the 10-year-olds, have probably had more training in listening comprehension than in the other skills such as reading and writing in the foreign language, or in learning grammar rules. In this sense it is possible that the test of listening comprehension is the only one that, for the youngest school children, realistically measures achievement, that is, how well subjects do with respect to material or skills for which they have been trained. A further influence on the results may be the amount of teaching, which is less intensive in the new curriculum now followed by the younger children, so that the same number of hours was distributed over three academic years for the younger subjects, and only two for the older ones.

Finally two issues mentioned above should be kept in mind for the continuation of a rate study, such as this one. First, the study should be followed up over the longest possible stretch of time, in order to see how the two groups have progressed, both at mid-term and in the long term. The outstanding question is whether the end of secondary education will come too soon for the advantage expected in the young children to become apparent.

The second consideration has to do with the importance of separating the different aspects of L2 competence (listening comprehension, reading comprehension, pronunciation, discourse-building abilities, etc.) at each measurement time, in order to examine in which ones young school-age children can be expected to be as competent, or more so, than older children. If these conditions are met we believe the results of our study will significantly contribute to the issue of age wherever foreign languages are taught.

## Notes

1. In this paper Spanish Castilian is referred to variously as Spanish or Castilian.
2. As an illustration, in the academic year 1996–7 the proportion of compulsory secondary education schools (for pupils aged 12 to 14) having French as their first, compulsory, foreign language was 0.1%, while those which had French as an optional subject represented 1.2% of all the schools. (My thanks to the Centre de Recursos de la Generalitat de Catalunya for this information.)
3. Furthermore, experience of content-based teaching, which could be a way of increasing exposure to the foreign language in such circumstances (Muñoz, 1997), is less common than in other European countries.
4. This study forms part of a larger research project on the age factor in foreign language acquisition which is being conducted in schools in Barcelona.
5. Idem.
6. The tradition owes much to Franco's 1941 prohibition of films in any language other than Castilian.
7. EGB and EP are Spanish acronyms for Basic General Education (the former curriculum), and Primary Education (the new curriculum), respectively.
8. Variances were not homogeneous, and a non-parametric test had to be used. Both a Scheffée and a Tukey-B test were also significant.
9. On the other hand, the family language and the socio-cultural class are not independent, as shown by a chi-square test of association ($p = 0.0001$), which shows that the Catalan-speaking families tend to be found in the two groups with

higher instructional levels, while the Spanish-speaking families are more frequently found among the lower instructional levels, and the bilingual families show more variability. That knowledge of Catalan increases with the level of instruction has been shown in previous studies, which have also shown that the association is stronger for reading and writing than for speaking and listening comprehension (Torres, 1997).

## References

Arenas, J. (1986) *La immersió lingüística. Escrits de divulgació.* Barcelona: La Llar del Llibre.
Arnau, J., Bel, A., Serra, J.M. and Vila, I. (1994) A comparative study of the knowledge of Catalan and Spanish among 8th-grade schoolchildren in Catalonia. In C. Laurén (ed.) *Vaasan Yliopiston Julkaisuja [Evaluating European Immersion Programmes. From Catalonia to Finland]* (pp. 107–28). Vaasa: Vaasa University.
Bel, A. (1990) El programa d'immersió: Alguns resultats. *Escola Catalana* 274, 26–7.
Bel, A., Serra, J.M. and Vila, I. (1991) Estudi comparatiu del coneixement del català i castellà al final del Cicle Superior. Paper given at the XVI Seminari Llengües i Educació. Sitges, 28–30 November.
Berns, M. (1990) 'Second' and 'foreign' in second language acquisition/foreign language learning: A sociolinguistic perspective. In B. Van Patten and J.F. Lee (eds) *Second Language Acquisition – Foreign Language Learning* (pp. 3–11). Clevedon: Multilingual Matters.
Boix, E. (1997) Llengua i edat. In M.Reixach (ed.) *El coneixement del català. Anàlisi de les dades del cens lingüístic de 1991 de Catalunya, les Illes Balears i el País Valencià* (pp. 141–60). Barcelona: Generalitat de Catalunya.
Burstall, C. (1977) Primary French in the balance. *Foreign Language Annals* 10, 245–52.
Cenoz, J. (1992) *Enseñanza–aprendizaje del inglés como L2 o L3.* Leioa (Spain): University of the Basque Country.
Cummins, J. (1976) The influence of bilingualism on cognitive growth: A synthesis of research findings and explanatory hypotheses. *Working Papers on Bilingualism* 9, 1–43.
Cummins, J. (1979) Cognitive/academic language proficiency, linguistic interdependence, the optimum age question and some other matters. *Working Papers on Bilingualism* 19, 198–205.
Cummins, J. (1981) *Bilingualism and Minority Language Children.* Ontario: Ontario Institute for Studies in Education.
Eubank, L. and Gregg, K.R. (1995) Et in amygdala ego? UG, (S)LA and Neurobiology. *Studies in Second Language Acquisition* 17, 35–57.
Freixa, J., Solé, E. and Cabré, M.T. (in press) Observació de la variació i el contacte de llengües en els neologismes. In *Actes del CLUB-4: Col.loqui de Lingüística de la Universitat de Barcelona.* Barcelona: Universitat de Barcelona.
Harley, B. (1986) *Age in Second Language Acquisition.* Clevedon: Multilingual Matters.
Hughes, A. (1989) *Testing for Language Teachers.* Cambridge: Cambridge University Press.
Krashen, S.D., Long, M.H. and Scarcella, R. (1979) Age, rate and eventual attainment in second language acquisition. *TESOL Quarterly* 9, 573–82. Reprinted in

S.D. Krashen, R. Scarcella and M.H. Long (eds) (1982) *Child-adult Differences in Second Language Acquisition* (pp. 202–26) Rowley, MA: Newbury House.

Lasagabaster, D. (1997) *Creatividad y conciencia metalingüística: Incidencia en el aprendizaje del inglés como L3*. Leioa: University of the Basque Country.

Lenneberg, E. (1967) *Biological Foundations of Language*. New York: Wiley.

Leprêtre, M. (1992) *La llengua catalana en l'actualitat*. Barcelona: Generalitat de Catalunya, Departament de Cultura.

Lightbown, P. and Spada, N. (1993) *How Languages are Learned*. Oxford: Oxford University Press.

Long, M.H. (1990) Maturational constraints on language development. *Studies in Second Language Acquisition* 12, 251–85.

Möhle, D. (1989) Multilingual interaction in foreign language production. In H.W. Dechert and M. Raupach (eds) *Interlingual Processes* (pp. 179–94). Tübingen: Gunter Narr.

Muñoz, C. (1997) Age, exposure and foreign language acquisition. In *Second Language Acquisition: Early Childhood Perspectives*. APAC Monographs 2, 16–24.

Muñoz, C. and Nussbaum, L. (1997) Les enjeux linguistiques dans l'éducation en Espagne. In C. Muñoz, L. Nussbaum and M. Pujol (eds) *Appropriation des langues en situation de contact. AILE* 10, 3–20.

Oller, J. (1979) *Language Tests at Schools*. London: Longman.

Patkowski, M. (1994) The critical age hypothesis and interlanguage phonology. In M. Yavas (ed.) *First and Second Language Phonology* (pp. 209–21). San Diego: Singular Publishing Group.

Penfield, W. (1953) A consideration of the neurophysiological mechanisms of speech and some educational consequences. *Proceedings of the American Academy of Arts and Sciences* 82, 201–14.

Phillipson, R. (1991) Some items on the hidden agenda of second/foreign language acquisition. In R. Phillipson, E. Kellerman, L. Selinker, M. Sharwood-Smith and M. Swain (eds) *Foreign/Second Language Pedagogy Research* (pp. 38–51). Clevedon: Multilingual Matters.

Reixach, M. (1997) El coneixement del català a Catalunya, Illes Balears i País Valencià. In M. Reixach (ed.) *El coneixement del català. Anàlisi de les dades del cens lingüístic de 1991 de Catalunya, les Illes Balears i el País Valencià* (pp. 13–79). Barcelona. Generalitat de Catalunya.

Scovel, T. (1988) *A Time to Speak: A Psycholinguistic Inquiry into the Critical Period for Human Speech*. Cambridge, MA: Newbury House.

Serra, J.M. (1989) Resultados académicos y desarrollo cognitivo en un programa de inmersión dirigido a escolares de nivel socio-cultural bajo. *Infancia y Aprendizaje* 47, 55–65.

Serra, J.M. and Vila, I. (1991) Estudio comparativo del conocimiento del catalán y el castellano en Octavo de EGB. Paper given at I Seminario Internacional de Planificación Lingüística. Santiago de Compostela, 25–8 September.

Singleton, D. (1995) A critical look at the critical period hypothesis in second language acquisition research. In D. Singleton and Z. Lengyel (eds) *The Age Factor in Second Language Acquisition* (pp. 1–29). Clevedon: Multilingual Matters.

Snow, C. and Hoefnagel-Höhle, M. (1978) The critical period for language acquisition: Evidence from second language learning. *Child Development* 49, 1114–28.

Stern, H.H. (1983) *Fundamental Concepts of Language Teaching*. Oxford: Oxford University Press.

Torras, M.R., Tragant, E. and García, M.P. (1997) Croyances populaires sur l'apprentissage précoce d'une langue étrangère. In C. Muñoz, L. Nussbaum and M. Pujol (eds) *Appropriation des langues en situation de contact*. *AILE* 10, 127–58.

Torres, J. (1997) Llengua i estructura social. In M.Reixach (ed.) *El coneixement del català. Anàlisi de les dades del cens lingüístic de 1991 de Catalunya, les Illes Balears i el País Valencià* (pp. 177–91). Barcelona. Generalitat de Catalunya.

Tragant, E. (1998) Individual differences, age and language learning. Report for Euroconference on The Teaching of Foreign Languages in European Primary Schools. Saint-Cloud, September.

Vila, I. (1993) *La normalització lingüística*. Barcelona: Generalitat de Catalunya.

Vila, X. (1996) When classes are over. Language choice and language contact in bilingual education in Catalonia. Unpublished doctoral dissertation. Université Libre de Bruxelles.

Chapter 10
# Three Languages and Three Linguistic Models in the Basque Educational System

DAVID LASAGABASTER

The Basque Country covers an area bordering the Pyrenees and the Bay of Biscay, that in the north of the Pyrenees being part of France and that in the south belonging to Spain. The Spanish Basque Country is made up of two political entities, the Basque Autonomous Community (BAC) and Navarre. This chapter will deal with the former. Under the 1979 statute of autonomy it was established that the BAC would consist of three provinces: Araba, Bizkaia and Gipuzkoa. Since 1982, and as a result of the Basic Law on the Standardisation of Basque, this has become a bilingual community where both Basque (the minority language) and Spanish (the majority language) are official languages.

During the dictatorship (1939–1975), use of the Basque language was forbidden by law. This had an obvious and damaging impact on the number of Basque speakers and numbers fell dramatically, although during the final decade (1965–1975) this linguistic repression lessened somewhat, as the regime was breaking down and was not as harsh as it had been. Since Basque acquired co-official status with Spanish, however, positive efforts to revive the language have been made on the part of both public and private institutions (Cenoz & Perales, 1997).

The Basque Statistical Institute (Eustat) divides the different groups of speakers present in the Basque Country into three categories:

(1) **Basque speakers:** those who can speak and understand Basque without problems;
(2) **Quasi-Basque speakers:** those who can speak Basque with difficulty but who can understand it well or with only slight trouble; and
(3) **Spanish speakers:** those who can neither speak nor understand Basque.

Between 1981 and 1991 the number of speakers in each of these groups evolved as follows:

**Table 10.1** Basque and Spanish speakers in the Basque Autonomous Community

|  | 1981 | | 1991 | |
| --- | --- | --- | --- | --- |
| **BAC** | N | % | N | % |
| Basque speakers | 447,776 | 21.56 | 542,387 | 26.22 |
| Quasi-Basque speakers | 300,394 | 14.47 | 350,454 | 16.94 |
| Spanish speakers | 1,328,278 | 63.97 | 1,176,086 | 56.84 |
| Population older than 2 | 2,076,448 | | 2,068,927 | |

Source: Eustat, Isasi (1994)

It can be observed that the number of Spanish speakers has decreased by more than 7% between 1981 and 1991, which matches the percentage increase in Basque and quasi-Basque speakers. Nevertheless, it is the use of a language in society that really demonstrates its vitality. A study (Iñigo, 1994) completed in the BAC in 1993 in which more than 275,000 people's language use was examined by means of direct observation showed that the use of the Basque language in each of the three provinces was as follows: Araba (2.56%), Bizkaia (6.21%) and Gipuzkoa (19.66%). Yet a comparison of these results with those of a similar study carried out four years previously in 1989 proves that in just this short period of time the overall use of Basque had increased by 18.74%. It can be therefore stated that there is a steady, albeit small increase in the number of people who both can and do speak Basque in their everyday life, especially children and youngsters, although despite this, Basque clearly remains a minority language.

There is no doubt that school is one of the main contributing factors to the increase in the use of Basque. In the Basque educational system, and due to the existence of different social sensibilities towards bilingualism, there are currently three linguistic models through which children can complete their studies (see also Cenoz, 1998):

- Model A: this is a regular programme in which Spanish is the vehicle language and Basque is taught only as a subject (for four to five hours per week). The L1 of the students is Spanish. Research studies have shown that these students' competence in Basque is extremely poor (Gabiña et al., 1986; Lasagabaster & Cenoz, 1998; Sierra & Olaziregi, 1989).

- Model B: this is an early partial immersion programme in which both Basque and Spanish are used as means of instruction. These students' L1 is usually Spanish, although there may be some rare exceptions with Basque as their L1. These subjects attain a higher level of competence in Basque than Model A students, but lower than that of Model D students (Gabiña et al., 1986; Sierra & Olaziregi, 1991a).

- Model D: this is a total immersion programme for those students whose L1 is Spanish, and a maintenance programme for those whose L1 is Basque. These students are the ones who achieve the highest scores in Basque and hence the ones who are closer to balanced bilingualism, that is to say, bilinguals with a high level of competence in both languages. As regards Spanish, research studies have not found any significant difference between the three models. These results could be due to the social importance of Spanish in society as a majority language (Lasagabaster & Cenoz, 1998; Sierra & Olaziregi, 1990; Sierra & Olaziregi, 1991a).

As far as the English language is concerned, due to the considerable amount of support and confirmation that the European Union has been receiving over the past decade (monetary union being a very good case in point), also to the role of English as a *lingua franca* (see James, Chapter 2) and to ever-increasing migratory movements, this is now without any doubt the most widespread foreign language in our community. Furthermore, in 1995 the European Union proposed the introduction to secondary education of a second foreign language, which has led to a four-languages-in-contact curriculum in those areas of Europe which are bilingual. It seems obvious that everybody (society at large, but politicians and parents above all) agrees to the need for a multilingual Europe, which is why there are ever more educational systems wherein three languages are taught. In this sense it is worth remembering that 35 languages coexist just within the European Union, and about 75 on the European continent as a whole.

## English in the Basque Educational System

Until the 1970s French was the most widespread foreign language in the Basque educational system, but as we have already seen, this leading position is today occupied by English; in fact some 97% of pre-university students learn English as their first foreign language at school. In the three models described above English is taught only as a subject (for three to four hours per week) and the variety taught, due to historical links, geographical proximity and the important presence of British publishing houses, is usually British English. Before the school year 1993–4 the teaching of English did not start until Grade 6 (11- to 12-year-olds), but since then, due to social concern about the need to learn foreign languages on the grounds that this would make it easier for our students to tackle a new Europe without borders, English has been taught as a subject from Grade 3 onwards (8- to 9-year-olds). Cenoz and Lindsay (1994: 203) draw attention to the fact that some parents and even teachers thought that the learning of a third language would confuse students, since they are also being introduced to reading and writing in their second language (Spanish or Basque) at this age. Nevertheless, parents who were interested in the early introduction of English clearly outnumbered those who were more reluctant and the Department of Education of the Basque Government therefore set up compulsory teaching of English from the earlier age.

Teachers of English are required to have completed a degree in English studies. Those who aim to teach in primary education need a degree from a teacher training college; aspiring secondary school teachers need a degree from a university. It must be noted that the degree of command of English exhibited by teachers depends very much on their interests. The administration offers several courses throughout the school year on English language and methodology, as well as offering grants for those wishing to go on summer courses in English-speaking countries. This means that teachers willing to improve or maintain their English proficiency have several possibilities available.

There is a sharp contrast between the methodology on which teachers fall back in primary education and that of secondary education. The basic curricular design (DCB) established by the Ministry of Education for primary education does not mention in its main objectives any ideas on forms of language, which means that in the first few years special attention is paid to speaking and listening abilities, while reading and writing activities are put off till Grades 5 and 6. On the other hand, one of the main objectives in the foreign languages area in secondary education is 'to reflect on the functioning of the linguistic system in communication as a facilitative element in the learning of the foreign language and as an instrument to improve students' own output' (DCB, 1992: 101). This means that from Grade 7 onwards teachers concentrate harder on linguistic issues and set aside the predominantly communicative method of previous grades, although keeping it in mind. Several other reasons could account for this change, the following ones being most probable: the number of students per class is higher in secondary education; adolescents are not so willing to speak in the foreign language as younger children are; and above all, the pre-university exam or *Selectividad*, the results of which will decide whether or not students can take the degree of their choice. This is a written exam in which oral skills are not evaluated.

These methodological differences also have a considerable impact on the materials used for teaching English. In primary education teachers have recourse to more active activities like those focused on the TPR (Total Physical Response) approach, games or performances. There is usually a basic textbook, but many other activities are carried out. In secondary education, on the contrary, teachers tend to centre their lessons on the textbook, although there are exceptions, and the learning of grammar plays a much more important role than in previous grades. It is nowadays very fashionable to resort to videos and cassettes, and even multimedia when available, in both primary and secondary education.

The number of evaluations of language teaching in the BAC is small and all of them have been carried out during the past decade. The first of these studies that is relevant here is that of Cenoz (1991), which examined the English proficiency of 321 students from the pre-university grade or *Curso de Orientación Universitaria* enrolled in Models A and D. Bilingual students (Model D) outperformed monolingual students (Model A). After analysing their results in the various tests, Cenoz concluded that the level of foreign language competence these students attained at school was insufficient, an opinion shared by the subjects themselves and by their parents. In fact many of the students were also having private English lessons outside school. Performance was significantly poor in the oral test, some of the subjects never having done this sort of test prior to the research study. These data confirm the neglect of the speaking and listening activities in secondary education to which I have already referred.

The second study was that carried out by Cenoz *et al.* (1994) on the Federation of Ikastolas (Basque medium schools), the main aim of which was to observe the influence of very early teaching of English, at the age of 4, on the L1 and L2 of the students. There were no differences between the control and the experimental groups in Spanish and Basque. The authors accordingly concluded that the early teaching of English did not hold back the learning of Basque and Spanish at all.

Thus despite the limited number of studies completed in our community, it can be affirmed that the results obtained in the BAC coincide with those of research studies from many other different contexts (Bild & Swain, 1989; Lewis & Massad, 1975; Orpwood, 1980), since the Spanish–Basque bilingual students perform significantly better than their monolingual peers when it comes to learning an additional language.

## The Research Study

The study presented here was aimed at evaluating the levels of competence in Basque, Spanish and English attained by students from six different schools who were enrolled in the three linguistic models currently available in the Basque educational system, half of them in Grade 5 and the other half in Grade 8. It analysed the interrelation of the scores obtained in the three languages and was carried out in Vitoria-Gasteiz (Araba), capital of the BAC and one of the areas of the community where Basque is less widely used (Iñigo, 1994), certainly much less than in Gipuzkoa where Cenoz's study was done. In theory, the absence of Basque as a means of everyday communication may have different implications for bilingual education by comparison with areas where the language is more widely spoken.

According to Cummins' 'threshold' hypothesis, 'the level of competence attained by a bilingual child may mediate the effects of his bilingual learning experiences on cognitive growth' (1976: 36). For the purposes of our study, this suggests that those students who have attained high levels of competence in both languages (most Model D students and some Model B students) will take advantage of some positive cognitive effects. Model A students, however, who cannot be considered to be bilingual since their command of the Basque language is extremely poor, will become highly proficient just in their L1; if Cummins is correct, the cognitive effects will be neither positive nor negative. The threshold hypothesis has been borne out by many studies: Barik and Swain (1976), Duncan and De Avila (1979), Kessler and Quinn (1982), Goncz and Kodzopeljic (1991), to name but a few.

There are thus many studies which show that bilingual students outperform monolinguals in the learning of an additional language: Bild and Swain (1989), Cenoz (1991), Eisenstein (1980), Enomoto (1994), Klein (1995), Lewis and Massad (1975), Orpwood (1980), Cenoz and Genesee (1998a). There are also studies (Lasagabaster, 1998a; Thomas, 1988) which show balanced bilinguals performing significantly better than the non-balanced.

A second noteworthy issue has to do with the closeness of the relationship between learning the three languages. This relationship could be explained in terms of the 'developmental interdependence' hypothesis (Cummins, 1979), which states that the learning of the L2 will be closely related to the proficiency of the learner in his or her L1: if L1 proficiency is high it will facilitate L2 learning; if low it may impede it. This hypothesis could be applied by extension to L3 learning: those who have a high level of competence in the two local languages, Basque and Spanish, will succeed when it comes to learning the L3 because of their highly developed common underlying proficiency, which will facilitate the transfer of cognitive/academic abilities from one language into the other. On the other hand, those with a low competence in Basque and Spanish will have many problems in achieving a high command of the L3 because their common underlying proficiency is less developed. Since the context of this research study is an additive one, where the learning of both the L2 and the L3 does not mean any risk to the L1, interdependence between the three languages seems plausible.

In the sociolinguistic context of this research those students who become highly proficient in Basque will be the ones who are closer to balanced bilingualism. It is therefore presumed that this will lead to a closer relationship between English and Basque, despite the fact that these two languages are not as closely related typologically as Spanish and English are (unlike the latter, Basque is one of the few European languages which does not stem from the Indo-European).

This theoretical context led us to put forward the following two hypotheses:
(1) The degree of bilingualism will have a significant effect on the English scores. It is expected that Model D students will score significantly higher in Basque and English than Model A and B students. Similarly, it is hypothesised that Model B students will score significantly higher in Basque and English than Model A students, but that no difference whatsoever will be observed concerning competence in Spanish.
(2) The scores obtained in the three languages, Basque, Spanish and English, will be interrelated. However, the relationship between English and Basque is expected to be more significant than that between English and Spanish.

## Research Methodology

Our study followed a cross-sectional approach: there was controlled measurement, and it was outcome-oriented and generalisable in that a large group of subjects took part (Larsen-Freeman & Long, 1991: 12).

### The sample

The participants were 252 students from Grade 5 (10–11 years old) and

Grade 8 (13–14 years old), 42 of them from each of the three linguistic models in each grade. The mean age of the Grade 5 subjects was 10.22 and of those in Grade 8, 13.27. In terms of gender distribution, 50.4% were males and 49.6% females. All were studying in Vitoria-Gasteiz, where 80% of the students of the province are gathered. The students from each of the three linguistic models were matched on age, gender, IQ (except for Model B in Grade 5, whose results were significantly lower than those of Models A and D), socioeconomic status, English classes outside school and motivation (Lasagabaster, 1997).

As we saw earlier, it is only since the 1993–4 academic year that the teaching of English has been compulsory from Grade 3 (8–9 years old) onwards. This means that our Grade 5 sample started learning English in Grade 4 (9–10 years old), but that our Grade 8 students did not start until they were in Grade 6, at 11–12 years old, as was then customary. Grade 5 students were chosen for the study because they were in their second year of learning English at school. Although they were still at an early stage in their learning, the differences between them would be easier to distinguish than had they been tested in Grade 4. Grade 8 was chosen because it represented the final year of compulsory education and would allow us to compare the beginning of English teaching with its end.

### Controlled variables and instruments

*Dependent variables*

**Competence in English:** this dependent variable was measured via a vocabulary and a grammar test and by tests corresponding to the four language skills, except that Grade 5 did not do a writing test; this was thought to be too difficult for children who were unaccustomed to writing in English.

The reading comprehension test for Grade 5 consisted of two activities. In the first of these, students had to answer five multiple-choice questions about an alien. In the second one they had to match six sentences dealing with weather conditions with their corresponding pictures. The minimum score was 0 and the maximum 11. Grade 8 had to read a text about some famous places in London and answer ten questions, formulated to evaluate their ability to understand general as well as specific information. Five of these were multiple-choice questions, and the other five invited students to help a couple of tourists who had several limitations on their visiting scope. The minimum score here was 0 and the maximum 10.

In the listening comprehension test, Grade 5 students listened to a short text where a character called John talked about himself and then had to answer five multiple-choice questions. The minimum score was 0 and the maximum 5. For Grade 8 the text was about an interview between a teacher and the mother of one of his students, who were discussing the student's schoolwork. Students had to answer nine multiple-choice questions, some of them focused on general information and the rest being more specific, the minimum score being 0 and the maximum 9.

Grade 5, as already stated, did no written test. Grade 8 students had to write a letter to a pen-friend in England after having seen her advertisement in a newspaper. They had to write at least eight lines and were rated on five aspects, following Jacobs et al.'s (1981) model: content, organisation, vocabulary, language use and mechanics. The minimum score was 34 and the maximum 100.

The oral test was the same for both grades and its maximum score was 50. Students had to talk about a six-picture story they were shown. It was the story of a cat and a dog who, taking advantage of the fact that they were alone at home, had a fight over an apple. Oral tests were marked on the basis of pronunciation, vocabulary, grammar, fluency and content. Both written and oral tests were marked by two assessors, who carefully studied the evaluation criteria before going twice through each one.

The vocabulary and grammar tests were aimed at assessing the students' command of the vocabulary and grammar normally taught in each grade. The activities were set out in ascending order of difficulty. The maximum scores were 38 for Grade 5 and 40 for Grade 8.

The overall English score was the sum of the results from the five tests. Since the range of marks varied we resorted to Z-scores, which allowed us to compare variables measured in different scales. Once we had obtained the Z-scores the mean for the new distribution became zero, those above the mean having a positive score and those below it a negative score.

**Competence in Basque:** this variable was measured via standardised tests, the Galbahe tests created by the Department of Education of the Basque Government (Olaziregi & Sierra, 1988; Sierra & Olaziregi, 1991b). For the Grade 8 sample these tests consisted of two activities, reading comprehension and writing; Grade 5 also had a listening comprehension activity. In the Grade 5 listening and reading tests the minimum score was 0 and the maximum 10; in the writing test, 0 and 60. In the Grade 8 reading test the minimum score was 0 and the maximum 15; in the writing test 0 and 60. Here again we resorted to Z-scores in order to obtain overall figures for Basque.

**Competence in Spanish:** to assess Spanish proficiency we again used Galbahe tests (Sierra & Olaziregi, 1986; Olaziregi & Sierra, 1992), which were made up of the same kinds of activity as the Basque ones. The range of marks for each grade was the same as for the Basque tests; as with the other two languages, we then used Z-scores so that we could compare the results.

*Independent variables*

**Intelligence:** non-verbal intellectual capacity was controlled by means of Raven's progressive matrices test.

**Background information:** students completed a questionnaire which asked for personal details such as gender, age, socioeconomic status, English classes outside school, and motivation.

*Data collection procedure*

Before the final sample of students did the tests we carried out some English pre-tests with two groups of 20 (one group enrolled in Grade 5 and the other in Grade 8) so that we could iron out as many deficiencies and problems as possible in advance before settling on a definitive format for each test. All the tests were completed in groups except for the English oral, which was done individually and tape-recorded so that it could be marked by the two assessors. Three sessions of about an hour were needed for the completion of all the tests, always with an interval of two or three days between. Once the students' answers had been marked and codified, these results were treated by means of the SPSS (statistical package for social sciences).

## Results

### Competence in the three languages

In order to test our first hypothesis, concerning the levels of competence attained by students from each of the three linguistic models in each of the three languages present in the curriculum, we performed ANOVA analyses. The results for Basque (Grade 5) are shown in Table 10.2.

**Table 10.2** Competence in Basque, Grade 5.

|  | Model A | Model B | Model D | F |
|---|---|---|---|---|
| Listening | 2.50 | 7.61 | 9.33 | 289.257** |
| Reading | 2.33 | 7.57 | 9.28 | 380.329** |
| Writing | 4.52 | 41.90 | 50.00 | 516.321** |
| Overall | −1.27 | 0.39 | 0.87 | 750.640** |

** $p < 0.001$  *p $< 0.05$  # $p < 0.9$

In every case Model D students achieved the highest scores, Model B students came second and Model A scores were lowest. T-test analyses revealed that Model D students outperformed Model A students in all the tests: listening (t = 25.69, p <0.001), reading (t = 32.17, p <0.001), writing (t = 30.77, p <0.001) and overall Basque score (t = 46.23, p <0.001). They also outperformed the Model B students: listening (t = 6.26, p <0.001), reading (t = 5.04, p <0.001), writing (t = 6.42, p <0.001) and overall Basque score (t = 7.95, p <0.001).

Model B students did however significantly outperform Model A students in all the Basque tests; listening (t = 15.01, p <0.001), reading (t = 24.88, p <0.001), writing (t = 18.01, p <0.001) and overall Basque score (t = 25.40, p <0.001). In Grade 8 these were the results:

**Table 10.3** Competence in Basque, Grade 8

|  | Model A | Model B | Model D | F |
|---|---|---|---|---|
| Reading | 3.23 | 8.52 | 10.59 | 79.419** |
| Writing | 13.80 | 39.76 | 48.80 | 278.223** |
| Overall | −2.25 | 0.60 | 1.65 | 203.019** |

** $p < 0.001$   * $p < 0.05$   # $p < 0.9$

In Grade 8 Model D students also obtained the highest scores and Model A the lowest. T-test analyses showed significant differences in favour of Model D over Model A: reading (t = 24.80, p <0.001), writing (t = 14.27, p <0.001) and overall Basque score (t = 23.62, p <0.001), as well as over Model B: reading (t = 5.57, p <0.001), writing (t = 3.06, p <0.05) and overall Basque score (t = 4.60, p <0.001).

Similarly, and as with Grade 5, Model B students also performed significantly better than Model A students in all the Basque tests: (t = 8.77, p <0.001), writing (t = 16.45, p <0.001) and overall Basque score (t = 14.08, p <0.001). As far as proficiency in Spanish was concerned, the results for the Grade 5 sample were as shown in Table 10.4.

**Table 10.4** Competence in Spanish, Grade 5

|  | Model A | Model B | Model D | F |
|---|---|---|---|---|
| Listening | 7.90 | 7.85 | 7.97 | 0.059 |
| Reading | 7.50 | 7.80 | 7.69 | 0.538 |
| Writing | 45.95 | 48.33 | 47.14 | 1.251 |

| Overall | −0.09 | 0.08 | 0.01 | 0.671 |

** p <0.001    * p <0.05    # p <0.9

Although both Model B and Model D students had had less teaching time in Spanish, they achieved higher scores than Model A students. However in no case were the differences significant. T-test analyses bore out these results. For Grade 8 the following results were obtained:

**Table 10.5** Competence in Spanish, Grade 8

|  | Model A | Model B | Model D | F |
|---|---|---|---|---|
| Reading | 9.02 | 9.11 | 9.71 | 0.814 |
| Writing | 45.00 | 46.07 | 45.23 | 0.178 |
| Overall | −0.14 | 0.01 | 0.13 | 0.336 |

** p <0.001    * p <0.05    # p <0.9

Once again bilingual students scored higher than the Model A students, but these differences were not significant either. Lastly, ANOVA analyses gave the following results for the Grade 5 sample in English:

**Table 10.6** Competence in English, Grade 5

|  | Model A | Model B | Model D | F |
|---|---|---|---|---|
| Listening | 2.28 | 2.38 | 2.64 | 0.939 |
| Reading | 6.97 | 8.52 | 8.59 | 6.595** |
| Speaking | 24.57 | 26.19 | 28.80 | 3.569* |
| Grammar | 28.00 | 28.09 | 30.92 | 2.461# |
| Overall | −0.29 | −0.04 | 0.21 | 4.156* |

** p <0.001    * p <0.05    # p <0.9

Model D also performed significantly better than the rest in the English tests, Model B students obtained the next best scores, and Model A students the lowest. T-test analyses showed us the tests in which Model D outperformed both Model A: reading ($t = 3.25$, $p < 0.001$), speaking ($t = 2.65$, $p < 0.05$), grammar ($t = 2.15$, $p < 0.05$), overall English score ($t = 3.08$, $p < 0.05$) – and Model B: speaking ($t = 1.90$, $p < 0.05$) and grammar ($t = 2.03$, $p < 0.05$). Yet there were no significant differences between Model D and Model B as to their overall English scores.

On the other hand, Model B outperformed Model A in only one of the tests, reading (t = 2.91, p < 0.05), although no difference was observed in the overall English score between these two linguistic models. The results for the Grade 8 sample are shown in Table 10.7.

**Table 10.7** Competence in English, Grade 8

|  | Model A | Model B | Model D | F |
|---|---|---|---|---|
| Listening | 4.95 | 4.59 | 5.88 | 4.716* |
| Reading | 4.42 | 5.52 | 6.30 | 6.149** |
| Speaking | 27.21 | 28.40 | 29.90 | 3.219* |
| Grammar | 25.80 | 23.73 | 25.30 | 0.733 |
| Writing | 72.11 | 70.77 | 76.59 | 5.314* |
| Overall | –0.10 | –0.10 | 0.30 | 4.201* |

** $p < 0.001$   * $p < 0.05$   # $p < 0.9$

In Grade 8 Model D also got the highest scores, whereas Models B and A achieved very similar results, even to the extent of sharing the same overall English score (-0.10). The differences in favour of Model D with respect to Model A were observable in all the tests but grammar: listening (t = 2.16, p <0.05), reading (t = 3.65, p <0.001), speaking (t = 3.01, p <0.05), writing (t = 2.72, p <0.05) and overall English score (t = 2.98, p <0.05); and with respect to Model B in the listening test (t = 2.95, p <0.05), the writing test (t = 3.00, p <0.05) and the overall English score (t = 2.28, p <0.05). Model B performed better than Model A only in the reading test (t = 2.12, p <0.05).

### Relationship between the three languages

According to our second hypothesis there will be a significant relationship between all three languages in both grades. The results of the correlational analyses in Grade 5 were these:

**Table 10.8** Correlations: Basque, Spanish and English in Grade 5

|  | Spanish | English |
|---|---|---|
| Basque | 0.1936<br>(p = 0.030) | 0.3628<br>(p = 0.000) |

| | |
|---|---|
| Spanish | 0.4989 (p = 0.000) |

Since these results showed that the scores in the three languages were interrelated, multiple regression analyses were performed, with the aim of assessing which of the two community languages, Basque or Spanish, had a greater effect on the English scores:

**Table 10.9** Multiple regression (method = stepwise); dependent variable = English, Grade 5

| | $R^2$ | T | P |
|---|---|---|---|
| Spanish | 0.24 | 6.41 | 0.000 |
| Spanish and Basque | 0.32 | 3.65 | 0.000 |

Despite the fact that both Spanish (T = 6.41; Sig T = 0.000) and Basque (T = 3.65; Sig T = 0.000) had a significant effect on English, the Spanish influence appears more significant than the Basque. The same statistical analyses were carried out as respects Grade 8:

**Table 10.10** Correlations: Basque, Spanish and English in Grade 8

| | Spanish | English |
|---|---|---|
| Basque | 0.3076 (p = 0.000) | 0.3791 (p = 0.000) |
| Spanish | | 0.4925 (p = 0.000) |

As with Grade 5 the results of the three languages turned out to be significantly interrelated, which led us to perform multiple regression analysis, the outcome being as shown in Table 10.11.

**Table 10 11** Multiple regression (method = stepwise); dependent variable = English, Grade 8

| | $R^2$ | T | P |
|---|---|---|---|

| | | | |
|---|---|---|---|
| Spanish | 0.24 | 6.30 | 0.000 |
| Spanish and Basque | 0.29 | 3.17 | 0.001 |

Once again Spanish (T = 6.30; Sig T = 0.000) emerged as more influential on English than was Basque (T = 3.17; Sig T = 0.001). Therefore our hypothesis was not confirmed, since we had thought that Basque would show a greater effect on English than would Spanish.

## Discussion

As far as levels of proficiency in the three languages were concerned, our results showed that learning an L2 or an L3 did not imply any negative effect on the normal development of the L1, whether this was a majority language (Spanish) or a minority one (Basque). These results coincide with those from many different contexts (Byram & Leman, 1990; Cenoz et al., 1994; Genesee, 1998; Genesee & Lambert, 1983). In fact Model B and D students whose L1 was Spanish attained the same level of competence in Spanish as their colleagues in Model A, although the number of hours devoted to teaching in Spanish was less. And the same holds good for those Model D students whose L1 was Basque, since in no instance were differences observed in their competence in Spanish, although they were the most proficient in Basque.

Models B and D attained a higher command of Basque than the regular programme (Model A), whereas Model D achieved higher scores than Model B. It should be remembered that for those students who are native speakers of Basque, Model D is not an immersion programme but rather a maintenance programme. This leads us to the conclusion that when teaching takes place in a minority language, the development of the majority one (in our context, Spanish) is not retarded, since its social presence is sufficient to guarantee the attainment of as good a level of competence in it as that of those who are taught in it. On the other hand, use of the minority language as a teaching medium *does* have an important effect on student levels of competence in that language – in our case, Basque – since this has little presence in society and learning it at school turns out to be a key factor in the level of proficiency achieved.

As regards the foreign language, the results showed that Model D students were the ones who obtained the best scores in both grades, outperforming Model A in Grade 5 and both Models A and B in Grade 8, whereas no significant difference whatsoever was observed between Model A and Model B. In conclusion it could be stated that only those students who achieved a high level of competence in both languages, that is to say balanced bilinguals (Cummins, 1976), were able to take advantage of their bilingualism in connection with the learning of English as an L3. In such a Spanish-speaking context as Vitoria-Gasteiz, it seems clear that only those students enrolled in the total immersion or maintenance programme (Model D) can reach this high competence in both languages, one which then goes on to benefit their learning of English. These results support the idea that the special attention given to the L1 where this is a minority language (as in the case of Basque) does not impede in any way the normal acquisition of an L2 and an L3, an assertion which agrees with those of Appel and Muysken (1987), Thomas (1988), Byram and Leman (1990) and Swain et al. (1990).

The presence of three languages in the curriculum is therefore not as problematic as some parents, politicians and even teachers think it may be. It has been suggested (Lasagabaster, 1998a) that the presence of three languages, instead of being a stumbling-block for students, should rather be seen as fostering a highly developed level of metalinguistic awareness which will result in greater competence, not just in the L3 but in all the languages in the curriculum.

Nevertheless one should bear in mind the huge range of bilingual situations, which means that results obtained in one place cannot be directly applied in another. The ideal situation would be one of additive bilingualism, where it is clearly understood that achieving the objective of balanced bilingualism is more feasible, since in the majority of the research studies it is balanced bilingual subjects who reveal the positive effects of bilingualism. In the Basque context the number of balanced bilingual subjects is increasing, with the number of students who achieve a high degree of competence in the L1 and the L2 increasing all the time. This is due to the evident improvement which has been effected in immersion programmes, not only from a methodological point of view but also in the training and quality of the teaching staff.

It is also worth remembering that if the learning of a second language in a school context is already an extremely complicated task, one which depends on a multitude of variables, then the learning of a third language is even more so. In spite of our trying to control those variables we considered most relevant, there were others in our study which could not be controlled, among them class methodology, the teachers' proficiency in English and how much support the English language received in each school. Our study is thus limited in all these respects.

The study clearly shows, however, that if a high degree of competence is achieved in L1 and L2, then the L3 can be seen as having a beneficial effect in that it may promote and assist the development of greater metalinguistic awareness. This may result in greater competence not just in the L3, but in all the languages in the curriculum, a supposition confirmed by the important relationship produced here between the scores obtained in the three languages and which could be taken as corroboration of the threshold hypothesis (Cummins, 1976) in a situation of three languages in contact. Since balanced bilinguals are primarily those who achieve a high proficiency in Basque (a high proficiency in Spanish being easier to achieve due to its social role), a closer relationship between Basque and English than between Spanish and English was assumed. However, and contrary to what was expected, it is the score for Spanish which has had the greatest effect on the English score. This could be due to the fact that Spanish and English are much closer to each other from a typological point of view than are Basque and English, which means students can use the similarities between these first two languages to their advantage.

Finally, it could be pointed out that the number of European contexts in which at least three languages are taught at school is ever-increasing. Although during the past few decades researchers' interests have been mainly focused on bilingualism, it is the study of the coexistence of three or more languages that will definitely grasp their attention in the years to come. This will result from increasing worldwide interest in the learning of international and minority languages alike (Lasagabaster, 1998b, Cenoz & Genesee, 1998b; see also Björklund & Suni, Chapter 11, Muñoz, Chapter 9, and Ytsma, Chapter 12). Although for those interested in this all too real issue there is already a good deal of information available, there is no doubt that the number of research studies on trilingualism (or even more languages in contact) will greatly increase in the future.

### References

Appel, R. and Muysken, P. (1987) *Language Contact and Bilingualism*. London: Edward Arnold.
Barik, H. and Swain, M. (1976) A longitudinal study of bilingual and cognitive development. *International Journal of Psychology* 11, 251–63.
Bild, E.R. and Swain, M. (1989) Minority language students in a French immersion programme: Their French proficiency. *Journal of Multilingual and Multicultural Development* 10, 255–74.
Byram, M. and Leman, J. (1990) *Bicultural and Trilingual Education: The Foyer Model in Brussels*. Clevedon: Multilingual Matters.
Cenoz, J. (1991) *Enseñanza–aprendizaje del inglés como L2 o L3*. Leioa: University of the Basque Country.
Cenoz, J. (1998) Multilingual education in the Basque Country. In J. Cenoz and F. Genesee (1998a) *Beyond Bilingualism: Multilingualism and Multilingual Education* (pp. 175–91). Clevedon: Multilingual Matters.

Cenoz, J. and Lindsay, D. (1994) Teaching English in primary school: A project to introduce a third language to eight-year-olds. *Language and Education* 8, 201–10.
Cenoz, J., Lindsay, D. and Espi, M.J. (1994) Plurilingüismo desde edades tempranas. Evaluación 1993–4. Unpublished manuscript. Donostia: Federación de Ikastolas.
Cenoz, J. and Perales, J. (1997) Minority language learning in the administration: Data from the Basque Country. *Journal of Multilingual and Multicultural Development* 18, 261–70.
Cenoz, J. and Genesee, F. (1998a) *Beyond Bilingualism: Multilingualism and Multilingual Education*. Clevedon: Multilingual Matters.
Cenoz, J. and Genesee, F. (1998b) Psycholinguistic perspectives on multilingualism and multilingual education. In J. Cenoz and F. Genesee (1998a) *Beyond Bilingualism: Multilingualism and Multilingual Education* (pp. 16–32). Clevedon: Multilingual Matters.
Cummins, J. (1976) The influence of bilingualism on cognitive growth: A synthesis of research findings and explanatory hypotheses. *Working Papers on Bilingualism* 9, 1–43.
Cummins, J. (1979) Linguistic interdependence and the educational development of bilingual children. *Review of Educational Research* 49, 222–51.
DCB (Basic Curricular Design), Departamento de Educación, Universidades e Investigación del Gobierno Vasco (1992) *Diseño curricular base de la Comunidad Autónoma Vasca. Lenguas Extranjeras*. Vitoria-Gasteiz: Servicio Central de Publicaciones del Gobierno Vasco.
Duncan, S.E. and De Avila, E.A. (1979) Bilingualism and cognition: Some recent findings. *Journal of the National Association for Bilingual Education* 4, 15–50.
Eisenstein, M. (1980) Childhood bilingualism and adult language learning aptitude. *International Review of Applied Psychology* 29, 159–72.
Enomoto, K. (1994) L2 perceptual acquisition: The effect of multilingual linguistic experience on the perception of a 'less novel' contrast. *Edinburgh Working Paper on Bilingualism* 5, 15–27.
Gabiña, J.J., Gorostidi, R., Iruretagoiena, R., Olaziregi, I. and Sierra, J.(1986) *EIFE-1 Euskararen irakaskuntza: Faktoreen eragina*. Vitoria-Gasteiz: Central Publications of the Basque Government.
Genesee, F. (1998) Immersion and multilingualism. In J. Arnau and J.M. Artigal (eds) *Els programes d'immersió: Una perspectiva europea* (pp. 151–61). Barcelona: Universitat de Barcelona.
Genesee, F. and Lambert, W.E. (1983) Trilingual education for majority-language children. *Child Development* 54, 105–14.
Goncz, L. and Kodzopeljic, J. (1991) Exposure to two languages in the preschool period: Metalinguistic development and the acquisition of reading. *Journal of Multilingual and Multicultural Development* 12, 137–63.
Iñigo, J.J. (1994) Euskararen kale erabilpena Euskal Herrian: EKBren neurketaren emaitzak. *BAT-Soziolinguistika Aldizkaria* 13/14, 51–76.
Isasi, X. (1994) Hiztun erroldak, labelak eta euskaldunak. *BAT-Soziolinguistika Aldizkaria* 13/14, 27–50.
Jacobs, H.L., Zinkgraf, S.A., Wormuth, D.R., Hartfiel, V.F. and Hughey, J.B. (1981) *Testing ESL Composition*. Newbury: Rowley.
Kessler, C. and Quinn, M.E. (1982) Cognitive development in bilingual environments. In B. Hartford, A. Valdman and R. Foster (eds) *Issues in International*

Bilingual Education: The Role of the Vernacular (pp. 53–79). New York: Plenum Press.
Klein, E.C. (1995) Second versus third language acquisition: Is there a difference? Language Learning 45, 419–65.
Larsen-Freeman, D. and Long, M.H. (1991) An Introduction to Second Language Acquisition Research. New York: Longman.
Lasagabaster, D. (1997) La motivación hacia el aprendizaje del inglés dependiendo del modelo lingüístico. Paper presented at the XXI Seminar on Languages and Education. Sitges, Catalunya.
Lasagabaster, D. (1998a) Creatividad y conciencia metalingüística: Incidencia en el aprendizaje del inglés como L3. Leioa: University of the Basque Country.
Lasagabaster, D. (1998b) The threshold hypothesis applied to three languages in contact at school. International Journal of Bilingual Education and Bilingualism 1 (2), 119–33.
Lasagabaster, D. and Cenoz, J. (1998) Language learning in the Basque Country: Immersion versus non-immersion programmes. In J. Arnau and J.M. Artigal (eds) Immersion Programmes: A European Perspective (pp. 494–500). Barcelona: European Institute of Immersion Programmes.
Lewis, E.G. and Massad, C.E. (1975) The Teaching of English as a Foreign Language in Ten Countries. Stockholm: Almquist and Wiksell.
Olaziregi, I. and Sierra, J. (1988) Galbahe-E2 hizkuntza testa. Gida liburua. Vitoria-Gasteiz: Central Publications of the Basque Government.
Olaziregi, I. and Sierra, J. (1992) Pruebas de lengua. Vitoria-Gasteiz: Central Publications of the Basque Government.
Orpwood, S. (1980) Trilingual children in a French immersion programme. Unpublished manuscript. Toronto: Ontario Institute for Studies in Education.
Sierra, J. and Olaziregi, I. (1986) Galbahe-C1 y C2. Tests de lengua. Vitoria-Gasteiz: Central Publications of the Basque Government.
Sierra, J. and Olaziregi, I. (1989) EIFE-2 Euskararen irakaskuntza: Faktoreen eragina. Vitoria-Gasteiz: Central Publications of the Basque Government.
Sierra, J. and Olaziregi, I. (1990) EIFE-3 Euskararen irakaskuntza: Faktoreen eragina. Vitoria-Gasteiz: Central Publications of the Basque Government.
Sierra, J. and Olaziregi, I. (1991a) Hine. Hizkuntza idatziaren neurketa eskolan. Vitoria-Gasteiz: Central Publications of the Basque Government.
Sierra, J. and Olaziregi, I. (1991b) Euskara probak. Vitoria-Gasteiz: Central Publications of the Basque Government.
Swain, M., Lapkin, S., Rowen, N. and Hart, D. (1990) The role of mother-tongue literacy in third language learning. Language, Culture and Curriculum 3, 65–81.
Thomas, J. (1988) The role played by metalinguistic awareness in second and third language learning. Journal of Multilingual and Multicultural Development 9, 235–46.

## Chapter 11
# The Role of English as L3 in a Swedish Immersion Programme in Finland
## Impacts on Language Teaching and Language Relations

SIV BJÖRKLUND AND IRMELI SUNI

In many ways, Finland is linguistically a very homogeneous nation. Even though it is officially bilingual, with Finnish and Swedish as its national languages, and though there is a third language (the Sàmi language) represented by indigenous people in the north of the country, the people who speak these three languages vary both in total numbers and geographically. The great majority belong to the Finnish-speaking population, which in 1993 was estimated to include more than 4,710,000 speakers.[1] The next biggest group, the Swedish-speaking population, consisted at that date of a little over 290,000 speakers (which is about 6% of the total population) and this language group is mainly situated on the west and south coasts of Finland. The Sàmi-speaking population were not ranked among the ten biggest language groups in Finland and numbered fewer than 2000 speakers.

The same statistics reveal that there is no large-scale language diversity in Finnish society. Apart from Finnish and Swedish, the biggest language populations in Finland were those of two neighbouring nations (Russian-speakers about 9330, Estonian-speakers about 5900), sign language (about 5000) and English (about 4500) (Latomaa, 1993).

The populations representing foreign languages in Finland are thus modest in size. The same picture also clearly emerges in the Finnish school system, where at the beginning of the 1990s there were approximately 4700 migrant children/students in comprehensive or secondary schools (Martin, 1992). The lack of native speakers of different foreign languages in many Finnish schools has not, however, hindered a language programme which has developed out of both historical and geographical reasons. Since Finland is an officially bilingual nation, both Finnish-speaking and Swedish-speaking children there have to study the other official national language during their compulsory period of education. Both language groups have to learn the same curriculum content, but students attend separate schools according to the language of instruction. Their motivation for studying the other official national language, and the length of time they study it for, vary greatly in different parts of the country. The unofficial status of Finland's third language, Sàmi, has led to a situation where the provision of teaching both of and in Sàmi still has significant gaps, even though it has been permissible for comprehensive and secondary schools to use it as their language of instruction since 1985 (see e.g. Aikio, 1991).

The study of either Finnish or Swedish as part of the language programme is not considered sufficient for Finnish students, who also need knowledge of languages that are more widely used internationally. It is therefore common for students to learn three or four different languages during their compulsory education. Normally the first foreign language, which in this case may also be Swedish for Finnish-speakers and Finnish for Swedish-speakers, is introduced at the age of 9 in Grade 3, though many schools nowadays choose to introduce the first foreign language in lower grades (1–2).[2] In addition, students can opt for a second foreign language as early as in Grades 4–6 (usually in Grade 5, at the age of 11). For students who have not done this, the study of a second foreign language becomes compulsory in the upper grades (Grades 7–9). On the other hand, language-oriented students, who have already been taking two foreign languages in the lower grades, can choose to study a third foreign language (usually in Grade 8, at the age of 14) during Grades 7–9. Hence, by the time students leave compulsory education, which covers Grades 1–9, they will all have studied their first language plus at least two foreign languages, possibly three.[3] Language lessons are usually held for 45 minutes once or twice a week; language teachers concentrate on teaching the language, rather than focusing on teaching content.

## Trends within Language Programmes in Finland and in Europe

Over the past decade there has been a lot of vivid discussion in Finland about the effectiveness of the traditional language teaching programmes. In many cases these programmes have not achieved their goals: students leaving them have good theoretical knowledge of the languages learnt but do not seem willing to use these languages in practice.

The trend towards implementing more intensive and effective language programmes so as to enhance students' communicative competence in foreign languages is by no means an isolated Finnish phenomenon. All over

Europe there is a growing interest in developing efficient language programmes, as the supranational character of politics and economics increases and communication barriers based on language differences have to be overcome. The European Community has been, and remains, one of the most significant driving forces behind the building of this 'global village'. Such a concept, however, necessitates communication skills in many languages.

Fortunately there are a lot of sources available to turn for inspiration and guidance in establishing new kinds of language programme. According to Wode *et al.* (1994), a valuable source for Europeans is the development in North America, especially in Canada, of immersion teaching. These programmes have initiated an enormous amount of research; it has been estimated that there have been almost a thousand studies on immersion in Canada alone (Cummins, 1991).

Another valuable source is the common European heritage. The use of a second or foreign language as the medium of instruction has been the rule rather than the exception during the history of European education. In European schools and International schools in particular there exist well-established language programmes with a second or foreign language used for teaching (for details on these schools, see Baetens Beardsmore, 1993; Skutnabb-Kangas, 1995; Muñoz, Chapter 9, Lasagabaster, Chapter 10, this volume), and in bi- and multilingual areas forms of bi-[4] and multilingual education programmes have been established, such as the trilingual education programme in Luxembourg (LeBrun & Baetens Beardsmore, 1993).

Although these programmes have proved linguistically effective, many of them have not expanded any further because in many ways they are not real options for all children; such schools are often more expensive than 'ordinary' schools and in some cases students can only apply after having passed some kind of language- or school-oriented test. The character of an élite school is further reinforced by the fact that these schools seem to attract primarily study-oriented students or children from study-oriented homes.

However, though existing models of bi- and multilingual programmes like Canadian immersion, European and International schools can in a sense be said to be selective because they are set up under certain linguistic or other conditions, they can still provide a lot of experience, guidance and inspiration in many European situations where there is an urgent need for communicative competence in two or more languages. Within the European framework the adaptation of such models often leads from bilingualism to true multilingualism, with English often mentioned as a viable option because of its status as a *lingua franca* in many European nations. Locally there may be other language options which are both necessary and desirable. It has consequently been suggested that within Europe the linguistic goal for all citizens should be mastery of three languages: the mother tongue, the language of a neighbouring nation and an internationally widespread language (Bressand, 1990).

In Finland, discussion during the 1990s of the shortcomings of traditional language instruction has led to the introduction of a variety of bi- and multilingual education programmes (for an overview, see Helle, 1994; Nikula & Marsh, 1996, 1997; Takala & Sajavaara, 1998). All these aim at communicative competence, and as a means of achieving this goal often use the target language as a medium of instruction; this means that students' attention is focused on learning the content, not on the language *per se*. Such schemes range from minimal bilingual education programmes (with perhaps no more than songs and phrases in a second language for 10–15 minutes a week) to immersion-like ones, which are the most radical. In the school year 1996–7 it was estimated that between 3% and 8% of comprehensive schools (Grades 1–6) in Finland experimented with different types of bilingual education programme, using students' second language at least part of the time as the language of instruction (Nikula & Marsh, 1996). All these programmes are optional, since participation in them is voluntary.

## The Status of English in Finnish Society

Although three different languages (Finnish, Swedish and Sàmi) can be said to represent Finland, it is obvious that the minority status of both Swedish and Sàmi has in many areas of the nation heavily reduced Finnish-speaking students' motivation to learn these languages. Every now and then the compulsory study of Swedish sparks off a nationwide debate, since many Finnish students do not actually perceive it as a living language in their own district. The main reason for studying Swedish is often purely instrumental: high-level jobs require a knowledge of it. In bilingual areas of Finland, Finnish-speaking students still choose Swedish relatively more often as their first foreign language, but by far the most popular first foreign language overall is English (Table 11.1).

As this table shows, there is overwhelming support in Finland for the view that English is the most important international language. Although the National Board of Education has made efforts to broaden language selection in schools there was only a slight increase in the take-up of German (from 3.1% to 3.9%) and French (from 0.9% to 1.4%) in the school years 1991–2 to 1996–7, and these two languages are still far behind the position of English which many Finnish parents and students regard as a *lingua franca*.

**Table 11.1** Languages chosen as first foreign language (L2) in Finnish comprehensive schools in Grade 3 in 1991–2 and 1996–7

| Language | 1991–2 % | 1996–7 % |
| --- | --- | --- |
| English | 87.4 | 86.3 |
| Swedish | 3.9 | 3.1 |
| Finnish | 4.5 | 5.0 |
| German | 3.1 | 3.9 |
| French | 0.9 | 1.4 |
| Russian | 0.2 | 0.2 |

Older students also favour English. According to the results of a recent study of over 2000 students in vocational education (Väyrynen *et al.*, 1998), they are most highly motivated to study English and choose it over every other language, though with some small differences between branches of learning; for example German is more popular in technical branches, while French is relatively more often chosen by students who aim at service jobs. When asked to compare English and Swedish the students claimed to want to learn English, whereas many described the study of Swedish as frustrating. As a result of this preference, six out of ten students estimated that their knowledge of English was sufficiently good (or even 'excellent') to undertake jobs or studies abroad, while two out of three preferred to say nothing if asked to speak Swedish. Furthermore, two-thirds of the students claimed to have no problems with using English in everyday and professional discussions, while 62% of them estimated that they were unable to follow or take part in meetings or negotiations in Swedish.

Finnish students' motivation to learn English, combined with the fact that most of them choose English as their first foreign language at school, has of course a great impact on the development of their English skills. But English is not only in a strong ideal position in the school milieu; it can also be heard and used out of school. English TV channels are far more popular in Finland than those in other languages, and the English language has a powerful influence on both children's programmes and teenagers' pop music.

Though Finnish students' enthusiasm for learning English is a good starting-point for enhancing their communicative competence, arguments have also been put forward against the dominant position of this language. Its usefulness tends to be overestimated; many students believe that with English you can cope all over Europe. In turn, this misjudgement leads to diminished motivation to learn other languages: students become Finnish–English bilinguals and cease to aim at the expected multilingualism. The geographical position of Finland is another argument often cited as an important factor in favour of studying Swedish and the other Nordic languages. As Finland is part of the Nordic countries, closely connected in terms of both trade and culture, it is important to strengthen this unity by using a common Nordic language.

One consequence of the popularity of English among Finnish students is that it may make its status difficult to define. If time of introduction is the only criterion for defining students' L1, L2 and L3, their choice of first foreign language or L2 at school is decisive and easy to identify. But introduction time is often an insufficient criterion for L2, because another important factor in defining, for example, an L2 and an L3, is knowledge of the language. A dilemma therefore arises when students, as they very often do, rank their knowledge of English as being at or near L2 level regardless of the time of introduction. Thus among Finnish students the position of English as an L2 or an L3 can probably be reliably identified only at an individual level and within traditional language programmes. Instead of the old criteria, new and experimental bi- and multilingual programmes often have a framework within which the position of the languages learnt can be more easily defined according to the amount of exposure to each in the curriculum.

## Languages and Principles in Immersion Programmes in Finland

The bi- and multilingual programmes recently established in Finland were triggered off by an immersion programme which was started in 1987 in the city of Vaasa/Vasa on the west coast of the country. The outline of this programme strictly followed Canadian guidelines for early total immersion. It was set up for children who belonged to the majority and its aim was to the teach them the minority language by using this language as the medium of instruction. Thus the immersion programme was offered to a group of monolingual Finnish-speaking children,[5] because approximately 70% of the inhabitants of Vaasa/Vasa are Finnish-speakers and close to 30% Swedish-speakers. In terms of bilingual presence in immersion areas, only the Montreal and Ottawa areas and parts of New Brunswick in Canada have a greater bilingual presence than Vaasa/Vasa (Cummins, 1995).

The immersion children started with one year in a half-day kindergarten (four hours a day) where the kindergarten staff only used Swedish, and they then continued the programme in school, where their first language was introduced as the medium of instruction for about 15–20% of total school time, with most of the content teaching (80%) being conducted in Swedish. From Grades 5–6 onwards about half of the instruction time was in Finnish, half in Swedish. (For more details on this pioneer immersion programme, see e.g. Björklund, 1997.)

Such a radical reduction in instruction time in Finnish and the fact that almost all content teaching was conducted in Swedish deviated a lot from the National Curriculum as this stood in 1987, and had to have special permission from the National Board of Education before it could begin. Before 1987 only a few institutions with special status as 'language schools' had been allowed to use a different language from their students' first language as their medium of instruction.

Interest in this first immersion programme was enormous among parents, teachers and administrators alike and it was soon followed by similar ones in both bilingual and more monolingual areas of Finland. Today it is estimated that more than 3000 Finnish students are involved in Swedish immersion programmes. During the expansion of immersion, however, the nature of the programme has developed. In monolingual parts of Finland, Swedish as the medium of instruction is now often replaced by other languages; preferably English, but also German and French. The amount of time devoted to instruction in students' L2 and also the time of introduction can vary a lot. Whatever the subsequent variations, though, the original establishment of such programmes led at the start of the 1990s to a change in the law which enabled them to be set up without any special national permission as long as they remained optional.

One characteristic of the more immersion-like programmes in operation in Finland is their early introduction. The second language is usually brought in when children are 3–6 years of age. This trend is similar to the Catalan and Basque immersion context, by contrast with that of Germany (Wode *et al.*, 1994) and the Netherlands (Huibregtse, 1994) who have chosen late immersion. The issue of early vs. late entry is an interesting one and can naturally be discussed at length, but here we list only a few pragmatic reasons from the point of view of Finnish parents.

Although immersion studies carried out by Harley (1986) have shown that early immersion students do not necessarily master their second language any better than late entrants do, readiness and willingness to *use* the second language seem to be better among the former. This is an important factor for many Finnish parents, who have often expressed this opinion to us in the form of a very simple question: What is the use of knowing a language if you do not actively use it? In addition, as bilingual marriages become more common, more and more children in Finland today are being raised in bilingual families. In this way early bilingualism becomes more visible even in monolingual areas, and many parents comment on the 'naturalness' of the bilingual process. Furthermore, Finnish kindergartens and schools belong administratively to different national authorities. It has consequently been relatively easy to establish kindergartens that use a foreign language as the medium of instruction, whereas the same possibilities have only been granted to five or six special language schools, most of them situated in the capital area around Helsinki/ Helsingfors. In many cases children have started off in, for example, an English kindergarten, but their study of English has then been interrupted for a couple of years at school before restarting from zero (no knowledge of English) somewhere between Grades 3 and 5. This of course is a situation which has satisfied neither parents nor students.

Another characteristic of Finnish immersion programmes is the experimental status of the other languages within them. Unlike most Canadian examples, the ultimate goal of such programmes in Finland is multilingualism, which in turn is based, even in the traditional language syllabus, on the teaching of several languages. During the early years of immersion teaching in Finland, the teaching of students' L3 and L4 in the immersion context was to a large extent conducted as in traditional programmes; this meant that an L3 was not introduced until Grade 5 (at 11) and an L4 could then optionally be chosen in Grade 8 (at 14). L3 and L4 teachers used a variety of teaching approaches. Many of them used a mixture of the students' first language and the target language during lessons, and they were accustomed to having a textbook as a fundamental basis for their teaching.

In the pioneer programme in Vaasa/Vasa in 1987 it became obvious that the older immersion students were confused and even resistant to learning the new language if L3 and L4 lessons were solely built on a textbook and if L3 and L4 teachers mixed languages during the lesson. It was therefore decided that in future it would be not only L1 and L2 teachers who used a single language with their students, but that this immersion principle would also apply to teachers of L3 and L4: the L3 teacher would use only L3 and the L4 teacher only L4 as their language of instruction from the first day of L3 and L4 introduction. In practice, this means that individual teachers now function specifically as either L1, L2, L3 or L4 teachers; this is essential if the teacher is to avoid having to choose which language to use when meeting students outside the classroom, and if clear and firm boundaries for the language of communication between teacher and students are to be established.

Another change in accordance with the principles of immersion was to replace the textbook-centered teaching of L3 and L4 with more authentic and self-sourced material that followed a more communicative approach. Even where L3 and L4 lessons are restricted to one or two 45-minute periods per week the same teaching strategies as those used by L2 teachers with access to several L2 lessons each day are possible, as long as the teachers of the different languages discuss their methods with one another and adapt similar kinds of strategy to their own teaching situation.

This process of integrating L3 and L4 into an immersion context has only just begun in many immersion programmes in Finland. In many cities the focus on immersion is still heavily L2-oriented, perhaps even more so in English immersion than in Swedish. In the original pioneer immersion programme in Vaasa/Vasa the integration of L3 and L4 into the syllabus in accordance with immersion teaching principles was not considered adequate to reach functional multilingualism. Since then, in order to promote a communicative approach, the introduction of L3 and L4 has gradually been lowered. In the early years of immersion, English was introduced to the students as L3 in Grade 5; a couple of years later this was lowered to Grade 3; from 1993 it has been brought in in Grade 1. Similarly the L4 is now begun in Grade 5 (at 11). In Vaasa/Vasa, German or French can be chosen as an L4, but so far students have only opted for German. Among these changes, it is the introducion of English in Grade 1 that has probably had the most radical effect on teaching methods, because at that level children have not yet acquired either reading or writing skills. In most other Finnish immersion programmes the starting-point for L3 and L4 has not been lowered to the same extent, an exception being the Swedish immersion programme in Espoo/Esbo (near the capital), where German as L3 for the immersion students nowadays starts in Grade 1. (For a comparison between different immersion programmes in Finland, see e.g. Laurén 1998.)

## English as L3 in an Immersion Programme in Vaasa/Vasa

### Teaching procedures

In Vaasa/Vasa's immersion programme, Grade 1 introduction of English as L3 from 1993 onwards has meant a totally revised teaching approach which has necessarily had to be structured in accordance with the age of the students. Since literacy skills have not been acquired by the time English is introduced, and the teacher of English is explicitly told not to concentrate on teaching students to read and write in English (because these immersion students are already learning to read and write in Swedish, their L2, in Grade 1), the English teacher faces a whole new situation. In general, teachers of English in Grades 1–6 have been trained as classroom teachers, which means that they are qualified to teach all existing subjects in Grades 1–6, but have additionally specialised in English. For secondary grades (7–9), and sometimes also in lower ones, the training is more specialised in just one or two languages, and English teachers are qualified to teach English (plus another language) as a subject. In both cases there are compulsory periods of teaching English as a subject under the supervision of experienced English teachers and teacher trainers. All the same, the training is focused on teaching English to students who know how to read and write and consequently relies heavily on text-based material.

For the teaching of English as L3 from Grade 1 onwards the same principles and instructions as those used by L2 teachers in immersion were applied. Guidelines on immersion teaching principles collected by the research team in Vaasa/Vasa included the following:

- The immersion language is acquired naturally, since the student learns *in* another language rather than *about* another language.
- The teacher only uses the immersion language, but understands the student's first language.
- The meaning of words and expressions is complemented by facial expressions, gestures etc. (= ostensive teaching).
- The teacher acts as an adviser and expert and provides students with key words.
- The student is allowed to use his/her first language but is encouraged to use the immersion language.
- At the beginning routines are used to create a safe environment.
- Language is always visible in the classroom.
- A pupil-centered teaching approach is adopted through different activities and efficient communication.
- 'Learning-centred' teaching provides many possibilities for using the language. A wide vocabulary is achieved through natural communication.
- A 'whole-language' teaching approach is used.

- Teaching strategies include stories, rhymes, song, drama and theatre.
- Activities and culture that go beyond the classroom are used.
- Authentic materials are used.

*Grades 1-2*

English as L3 is restricted to just one lesson (45 minutes) a week, but even that short time seems to be significant, because the children are very willing to start their English studies. Teaching strategies must be carefully chosen, because the children have neither reading nor writing skills. Routine group situations create security and help with early understanding and production of language. From the beginning, words and phrases are repeated in the immersion language together and individually, though the meaning of the word is not always clear. It is like tasting the new words, the new language. Words that are important for communication (nouns, verbs, negative and positive sentences) are learnt early. Pupils also learn from the beginning that not every word has an equivalent in both languages. They are supposed to become active language users, not translators.

The immersion approach to language acquisition emphasises communication, and communication means both understanding and production. Cummins (1981) argues that the challenge of teaching students in a foreign language is to provide experiences that are both content-embedded and cognitively demanding. In addition he claims that studying a foreign language must supply experiences that provide student-to-student communication. To *learn* a language students need frequent and sustained opportunities to *produce* language, best provided through collaborative group learning activities.

Artigal, a Catalan kindergarten teacher and teacher trainer, asks (1991a): How is it possible for a child to become a user of a language that she or he does not yet know? The answer, he says, is through drama. In response to the challenge of early language teaching he created language stories.[6] These are little pieces of drama about children's everyday life. The language used in them provides vocabulary for describing family, domestic chores, friends, health and illness, seasons, time. According to Artigal (1991b) a tale has a simple plot and deals with topics akin to the experiences and fantasies of children in the target age group. It is narrated from the very start by means of a collective dramatisation in which the class actively plays all the parts that appear in the plot. Pupils take part in the performance and in all the actions, gesture, mime and intonation that teacher and pupils continuously develop together in order to make the plot comprehensible. To make the learning of the new language more varied Artigal also developed plenty of auxiliary teaching materials that help with learning the content, words and phrases; these include pictures, drawing activities, games, crosswords, competitions and songs.

For all students, but especially for the younger ones, songs play an important part in language learning. According to Fonseka (1997), songs help teacher–student interaction in a significant way, because when the teacher and the students sing together they come together in a completely stress-free atmosphere. Singing also involves memory to a large extent. The ability to sing from memory is a great potential that many children possess. Through singing a child can endlessly repeat the words and phrases and practise the rhythms of the target language. This is especially important where students have no natural contact with the target language.

Grades 3-6

A big difference in both teaching and learning strategies takes place when the students move to Grade 3 at 9 years old. Both reading and writing skills are quite fluent by that stage and this provides scope for a much richer use of language. According to the National Board of Education, at the end of junior comprehensive school students should be able to cope with everyday situations and understand simple written language in their L3 and L4 (English and German). They should be able to write short messages. To succeed in this they should have acquired the basic vocabulary needed in the linguistic situations appropriate to their age. They should also have some knowledge about the country, culture and people of the target language.

When developing educational plans for English studies in the junior immersion school, it is essential to keep in mind the guidelines for immersion teaching, instructions on the aims of foreign language teaching from the National Board of Education, and the available knowledge on language acquisition. Teaching strategies must be planned to emphasise communication. The provision of a vocabulary that is suitable for the age group must be central to the programme, and should increase in a structured manner. To guarantee the desired progress, working with texts has an important role.

The main strategy in Grades 1 and 2 is drama. A 'whole-language' approach is used; the stories are useful for developing different areas of language and often contain musical rhythm. They also comprise simple structures which can be repeated several times. They are familiar to most of the children, which facilitates understanding. During the last two years of the junior comprehensive school for immersion students (Grades 5 and 6, where the students are 11 and 12 years of age), however, both the vocabulary and the capability for using structural forms of the target language increase considerably. Strategies, both in teaching and in learning, will be different from previous years. A balance between input and output must be found, because these are closely linked in language acquisition. Input is the language to which learners are exposed; in his input hypothesis Krashen (1985) argues that acquisition will take place automatically as long as learners receive comprehensible input. On the other hand some researchers emphasise the importance of learner output, the learner's product, which includes English used in the effort to get the message across. According to Swain (1995) learner output is also an important mechanism in language learning because it enhances fluency and accuracy. In addition, output enables students to control and internalise linguistic knowledge.

The topics of the texts used at this age have to be interesting and they have to be functional. Elements that lend themselves to effective and motivated language learning, such as suspense, mystery, overcoming problems, fun, anticipation, happy endings, can all be found in adventure stories. An adventure can be authentic, it can be a legend, science fiction, a narrative, a dialogue, a cartoon, to mention just a few. Well planned and organised work with texts may even change the children's view of reading, if this is at all negative, and improve their general reading abilities. We think the best results may be achieved when several different kinds of input are used. Children may also learn a lot by watching videos and films and surfing the Internet.

Writing exercises also follow immersion principles, are communicative and have real meaning. Writing exercises are carefully started in Grade 3, with the children having their own booklets containing easy tasks. Other exercises that focus on comprehension, such as 'Listen and do' and 'Connect a picture and the word' are both useful and inspiring.

Even in Grade 4 some easy grammar is being practised, but it is more important for the children at this stage to be producing their own letters, stories, instructions, conversations and news. The same kinds of teaching strategy are also used in the upper grades of the junior comprehensive school, but there the expectations are higher and the exercises on a more difficult level. Collaborative work with other teachers is increasingly being used, particularly craft teachers. When students bring their work into the language class they use English in an authentic way to talk about materials and instruction.

It is also very common to use pair work or group work to give the students opportunities for using language for meaningful social interaction with their peers (Cummins, 1981). The teacher's role in a language class that is following immersion principles is to make the language comprehensible to the students. That means that she or he must continuously be engaged in a process of reflection on *meaning*. The teacher must also help students to make their own messages understood, and expand and refine their language. In the junior comprehensive school teachers must use simplified language and speak very slowly, employing limited structures and vocabulary.

## Research issues

The communication-based approach described above to teaching English as an L3, combined with the lowered age for its introduction, is naturally expected to result in more high-quality teaching and learning of the language. Students are likely to be motivated to study it and use it fluently and accurately. Over the first decade of the immersion programme in Vaasa/Vasa, however, the linguistic research conducted on the programme has been concentrated on the students' development of their first and second languages in immersion (see, for example, Björklund, 1996, 1997; Buss & Laurén, 1995, 1996; Laurén, 1991, 1992, 1994a, 1994b). This is only natural, since the most radical changes in the immersion programme involve an increased and intensified use of the students' L2 for both language and content instruction and reduced time for using their first language as language of instruction. Furthermore, it is the development of students' L1 and L2 in immersion that most interests both parents and administrators and which they most often bring up in discussion. Briefly, longitudinal reports on the L1 and L2 progress of these students have shown that both languages develop positively and in accordance with Canadian immersion results. Because Finland has been able to learn from previous experience and expertise, there may even be some small differences between the set-up of immersion programmes in Canada and Finland (for a comparison, see Cummins, 1995) which bring about a more positive linguistic outcome in Finland, though these factors have still to be investigated more scientifically, and there is a possible Hawthorne effect for the initial results from Finland's programmes.

The existing focus on L1 and L2 does not mean that an evaluation of L3 and L4 within an immersion programme would be of less interest or less value. In fact it could provide administrators of language programmes with important information on how to advance from bilingual to the more multilingual programmes which are needed in many European countries today.

The gradual lowering of the student age for the introduction of L2, L3 and L4 in kindergarten and school is another important and somewhat controversial issue. Nowadays there are no specific guidelines or clear recommendations on how early to start, how many languages to introduce and what language didactics to implement in language programmes, despite a great interest in and need for bringing on multicultural and multilingual students. That is, the end product is clearly defined, but how to achieve it remains to be worked out, evaluated and discussed.

In the case of the Swedish immersion programme in Vaasa/Vasa, the evaluation of L3 and L4 is especially interesting, since most immersion students and their teachers (including those with experience of 'traditional' language teaching) claim that learning and teaching L3 and L4 are 'easier' in immersion programmes. When asked to justify this statement, most of them claim that their acquaintance with and knowledge of Swedish (which is a Germanic language like English) is an effective starting-point for learning both English and German. How far do the similarities between the languages in practice affect learning? Are the efforts to make teaching methods similar for all languages worthwhile? How well do students' differing personalities fit in with the principles of immersion? This last question may be of special relevance here, since the programme is open to all students; it is not élitist or restricted to language-oriented students and it must make special arrangements for students with special needs.

Another interesting issue in the structure of this programme is the language relations between L1, L2, L3 and L4. Since much more instruction time is devoted to the students' L2, one could assume that they would acquire a higher level of proficiency in this. On the other hand neither the classroom nor the school is an isolated unit, and students will be influenced by other attitudes and trends outside school. The popularity of English among Finnish people might even diminish students' motivation to study and use the other languages in the programme.

### Students' perception of their use of English in relation to other languages

The follow-up and evaluation of English as L3 within the Swedish immersion programme is a research process which can be studied from many different perspectives. A modest start to this evaluation was initiated during the school year 1997–8, when a small-scale, cross-sectional study was conducted in order to help researchers, administrators and teachers understand students' own perceptions of their language use. A questionnaire was administered to immersion students in Grades 3, 4, 5 and 6 (Table 11.2). Of these different grades, the immersion students in Grade 6 had not been introduced to English until Grade 3, while the others had had English since Grade 1.

**Table 11.2** Numbers of immersion students

| Grade  | 3   | 4  | 5  | 6  |
|--------|-----|----|----|----|
| Number | 46* | 39 | 19 | 15 |

*The number of students in Grades 3 and 4 is greater than in Grades 5 and 6, since the programme intake has gradually been extended from one group per year to two.

In the questionnaire the students were asked simple questions about what languages they used in different situations. In general, all of them seemed to be very confident about their languages. When asked what languages they knew, the majority of the students (76.1% and 89.7%) in Grades 3 and 4 said that they knew Finnish, Swedish and English, and in Grades 5 and 6 most of them (68.4% and 80.0%) mentioned all four languages, Finnish, Swedish, English and German.

The next three questions in the questionnaire dealt with the students' use of language in three different situations – at home, in the classroom and together with friends (Table 11.3).
Surprisingly, the majority of students in Grades 3 and 4 did not use only Finnish at home, which was the expected choice since almost all of them came from monolingual Finnish-speaking homes. This seems to be an age-related question, however, as most students in Grades 5 and 6 did consider themselves to use only Finnish at home. Older students probably expect both quantity and quality in their language choices and their definitions of different language usage are most likely to include higher standards and make higher demands on language skills. The same age-related tendency was noticeable too concerning the students' choice of the languages they used with their friends. The most common choice for all students at all four grade levels was Finnish only (56.5% in Grade 3, 41.0% in Grade 4, 65.1% in Grade 5 and 86.7% in Grade 6), but among students from Grades 5 and 6 there were relatively more who spoke only Finnish with friends. The use of both Finnish and Swedish is the second most common choice except for Grade 5, where the alternative 'Finnish, Swedish and English' (26.3%) is more common than 'Finnish and Swedish' (5.3%).

In the classroom situation students perceive themselves as active speakers and users of all the languages in the programme. In Grades 5 and 6 the majority declare that they use all four languages (Finnish, Swedish, English and German), while most Grade 4 students claim to use three languages (Finnish, Swedish, English). The one-language role of the teachers may have helped to establish a communicative approach which has not been adversely influenced by the limited hours of L3 and L4 in the programme.

**Table 11.3** Language use by immersion students in three different situations

| Grades | 3 % | 4 % | 5 % | 6 % |
|---|---|---|---|---|
| At home | F 41.3<br>FSE 30.4<br>FS 23.9<br>FE 2.2<br>FSEO 2.2 | FSE 38.5<br>F 33.3<br>FS 20.5<br>FE 5.2<br>FEO 2.5 | F 68.4<br>FS 15.8<br>FSEG 10.5<br>FE 5.3 | F 93.3<br>FS 6.7 |
| In the classroom | FS 67.4<br>FSE 19.6<br>S 8.7<br>FE 2.2<br>F 2.2 | FSE 71.8<br>FS 17.9<br>F 10.2 | FSEG 73.7<br>FSE 21.0<br>FS 5.3 | FSEG 66.7<br>FSE 20.0<br>FS 6.7<br>F 6.7 |
| With my friends | F 56.5<br>FS 28.3<br>FSE 10.9<br>FE 2.2<br>FSEO 2.2 | F 41.0<br>FS 28.2<br>FSE 23.1<br>FE 5.2<br>FSEO 2.5 | F 63.1<br>FSE 26.3<br>FS 5.3<br>FE 5.3 | F 86.7<br>FS 13.3 |

F = Finnish   S = Swedish   E = English   G = German   O = Other language

As regards the relationship between L2 (Swedish) and L3 (English) it was interesting to observe that – once again – there was a discrepancy between older and younger students when they were asked what languages were used in the TV programmes they watched. 'Finnish, Swedish and English' was more common in Grades 3 and 4 than the alternative 'Finnish and Swedish' (Grade 3 FSE 52.2% and FS 10.9%, Grade 4 FSE 28.2% and FS 10.2%), while in Grades 5 and 6 the most popular choice was 'Finnish and English' (36.8% in Grade 5 and 46.7% in Grade 6). Also, at these levels no student chose the 'Finnish and Swedish' alternative.

A similar tendency regarding the linguistic relationships between L2 and L3 was demonstrated in the answers to a question about what languages students use when they think. Finnish was the dominant choice in all grades, but in Grade 3 was followed by the 'Finnish and Swedish' alternative. In Grades 4 and 5 the second and third places after the 'Finnish only' alternative were occupied by 'Finnish, Swedish and English' (17.9%) and

'Finnish and Swedish' (17.9%) in Grade 4, and by 'Finnish, Swedish and English' (10.5%) and 'Finnish and English' (10.5%) in Grade 5. This tendency for English to replace Swedish was not, however, continued in Grade 6, where the alternative 'Finnish and Swedish' was the second most common alternative. But here the time of introducing English may have been crucial, since Grade 6 students did not begin learning it until Grade 3.

In Grade 6 all students also claimed that in their dreams people spoke only Finnish. This was the prevailing choice at all levels, but 26.3% of the students in Grade 5, for example, declared that in their dreams people spoke Finnish, Swedish and English and 21.0% declared that all four languages (Finnish, Swedish, English and German) were spoken.

These results indicate that the age factor plays an important role for the students' own perception of their multilingualism. In this study the Grade 6 students tend to have a more bilingual angle, with Finnish and Swedish as the dominant languages, whereas the other students show a more multilingual tendency when assessing their language abilities. Since all students have had the same teacher and have been exposed to the same kind of communicative teaching method, the difference between Grade 6 students and the rest could be explained in terms of different grade levels for the introduction of English (Grade 6 students were introduced to English in Grade 3, the others in Grade 1). However, age also seems to be related to students' cognitive maturity and language skills. Older students in Grades 5 and 6 seem to be more restrictive in defining their language abilities than those in Grades 3 and 4.

The results of the study are tentative and still need to be complemented by refined test instruments and larger test populations. The questionnaire should be administered to subsequent immersion groups as well as distributed to the same students in a slightly modified form during Grades 7–9. As a test instrument, a simple questionnaire like the one used in this study allows a very wide variation in definitions of knowledge and use of different languages. For older students more refined test instruments may be required and developed.

## Discussion

In this chapter we have chosen to describe the position of English as a third language in a new and experimental multilingual programme in Finland. The programme is an immersion programme which has been adapted to Finnish conditions and therefore includes the teaching of several languages. English has been structurally built into the framework of the programme as the third language of the students, who after one or two early years of Swedish immersion in kindergarten continue with their Swedish immersion at school, where they are straightaway introduced to English in Grade 1. The introduction of a third language at this young age represents a new approach in Finnish education. Since teaching methods for English follow the principles characteristic of immersion programmes, these can also be considered radical and innovative for Finnish education.

Early teaching experiences of English as L3 in the youngest grades in immersion in Vaasa/Vasa have shown that both for the teaching of English as L3 in an immersion programme and for the teaching of any additional language within an immersion context, the teacher is very much an integrated part of the immersion programme. This is a view which many L3 and L4 teachers have also expressed during the in-service courses set up during the 1990s as a result of the initial immersion programmes in Finland (for in-service training of immersion teachers, see e.g. Young, 1995). It is important that the L3 or L4 teacher not only knows about the development of the L3 or L4 of the students, but is familiar with current research and theories on both individual and societal bi- and multilingualism. In the same way, linguistic awareness and acquaintance with the students' L1 and L2 facilitate the teaching of their L3 or L4, because teachers are then able to identify and modify the teaching process by observing elements which originate in other languages.

For comparative study, it is not easy to find multilingual programmes with a similar design to Vaasa/Vasa's immersion programme. On the whole there are not many studies on L3 (see Cenoz, Chapter 3) and many of these deal with transfer processes, ranging from linguistic relationships between the L1, L2 and L3 concerned (positive and negative transfer due to linguistic similarities between the languages) to more cognitively based theories of learning strategies (the more, the easier; i.e. learning how to learn new languages).

In the immersion context, Canadian double immersion programmes can be said to show certain similarities with immersion programmes in Finland. Genesee's studies (1998) indicate that there are no differences in the development of L1 (English) and L2 (French) between students from double immersion and single immersion. For the third language of the double immersion programme (Hebrew), the students from early double immersion tended to score higher than students from delayed double immersion, although both groups had been exposed to the same amount of Hebrew. Genesee suggests that this difference can be explained by the fact that the use of students' L1 during the early grades of double delayed immersion may interfere with the learning of Hebrew. This research result implies that it may be a disadvantage to have L1, L2 and L3 as languages of instruction in Grade 1 as in the immersion programme of Vaasa/Vasa. On the other hand, there are at least two points to be made. First, if L1, L2 and L3 teachers at the Grade 1 level work separately and all of them devote most of their teaching time to teach the students to read and write in L1, L2 and L3 respectively, their students are very likely to run the risk of being overloaded with too much linguistically and cognitively demanding information (in Vaasa/Vasa, learning to read and write has to be conducted in L2). Secondly, in double immersion both immersion languages (in this case French and Hebrew) have equal status as second languages, and the exposure to Hebrew is much higher in double immersion by comparison with for example English as L3 in Vaasa/Vasa (45 minutes a week). Also the status of the languages involved differs, since one of the second languages in double immersion in Canada is often a heritage language.

The status of different languages within immersion programmes is also a crucial factor to consider when comparing different European immersion programmes which have three languages included in their design, for example, those of Catalonia and the Basque Country. With respect to linguistic similarity between the L1, L2 and L3 concerned, comparable cross-linguistic influence could be extracted from the immersion programmes of Finland and the Basque Country, which both include a language structurally deviant from the others in the programme (Finnish in Finland, Basque in the Basque Country). But the status and the role of these languages differ, since Finnish explicitly represents the L1 of the immersion students and has a very clear majority position, whereas Basque does not have the same majority position and is often the L2 of the immersion students. This position as L1 is significant, at least for Finnish conditions where previous studies on the acquisition of English by Swedish-speaking and Finnish-speaking L1 students have shown that the students' L1, especially at the start of their study of English, influences their readiness to acquire the new language (Ringbom, 1987).

In Vaasa/Vasa's immersion programme the linguistic consequences of introducing English as L3 to students whose L1 is structurally very far from English but whose L2 is in many respects very similar to it, will be further exploited and evaluated over the next few years. The evaluation of English as an L3 in an immersion context has only just begun and results are still scarce. The first was an unpublished master's thesis on non-native influence on the learning of English (Heinonen, 1996) which focused on the lexical influence between the languages involved in immersion. Particular emphasis was put on the lexical relation between the students' L1 (Finnish) and L2 (Swedish) as opposed to the L3 (English). Swedish, as the students' L2, obviously affected the learning process for English at both the lexical and the syntactical level, whereas transfer from Finnish could not be detected as readily. The scope of the lexicon seems to be largely enhanced by students' previous knowledge of Swedish, but there are also examples of negative transfer from Swedish, as for example in the sentence 'Today have I a music test', where the word order is the same as in Swedish, but not as in either English or Finnish.

Alongside with this planned linguistic research, another approach which is more sociolinguistically oriented has recently been adopted, some preliminary results of which have been discussed in this chapter. This approach aims to investigate immersion students' attitudes to the use of the different languages of the programme in relation to the defined goal of the programme: functional multilingualism. First results show that here, too, the relationship between Swedish (L2) and English (L3) must be paid particular attention, as it can provide us with valuable information about how the status and 'out-of-school' dominance of a language connect to the various designs and set-ups of multilingual programmes. Interestingly enough, the bilingual presence outside school has not brought any major changes in the behaviour of immersion students outside the school milieu in Canada, where Cummins (1995) reports that immersion students' out-of-school contact with French is no greater in bilingual areas than in predominantly anglophone ones. In Vaasa/Vasa immersion students seem to be more actively involved in bilingual and Swedish activities out of school than is the case in Canada, and despite this there is also an evident interest in using English in everyday social life. Will the L2 and L3 of the immersion students eventually act as mutual support to one another, or will one language come to dominate and even hinder the development of the other one?

## The Multilingual Dimension: A Way Forward

A multilingual perspective can be said to have existed within Finland's language education policy for several decades already. Even so, this chapter has shown that the multilingual perspective can by no means be a static one, but has to be revised and renewed in accordance with changing individual and societal needs. The existing multilingual basis within the Finnish school system has, however, contributed to a readiness to apply new experimental forms of school multilingualism, which in many other European nations – where the development from a mainly monolingual base towards a more bilingual and even multilingual approach – has to pass through many different phases. In any case, the contribution of each new multilingual perspective within the school system in different areas will provide useful experience and knowledge for the common European future. Bilingual education and research on bilingualism have provided a solid foundation from which it is possible to go a step further, although the multilingual perspective may seem more chaotic, multifaceted and complicated today than in the past. Those setting up further research will have to consider many interrelated factors and run the risk of being caught between different languages, cultures, language teaching methods and linguistic research traditions. On the other hand, the challenge of putting the demands of communicative competence and functional multilingualism into practice on the European continent cannot be met unless practitioners and researchers co-operate in the search for, development and evaluation of new multilingual attempts within the different existing school systems.

## Notes

1. The statistics do not reveal the whole truth, since it is not possible to register as a bilingual speaker in Finland. Even if you are a balanced bi- or multilingual person you have to choose one language to be your mother tongue.
2. In Finland students begin school at the age of 7.
3. This chapter presents the 'standard' version of the Finnish language curriculum. Modern national guidelines now allow a variety of alternatives, and language-oriented schools may offer even more extensive language programmes.
4. Although 'bilingual education' stands for a variety of education programmes which are difficult to define in explicit terms, in this chapter we use it in the classical sense; i.e. as a form of language education where the language to be learnt is used not only for learning the language itself but at least to some extent as a language of instruction for content/subject teaching.
5. During the first years of immersion education in Vaasa/Vasa the annual intake was restricted to one group of 6-year-old children (25 children). Today the annual intake is one group of 6-year-old children and one group of 5-year-olds.
6. The stories were originally created by eight Catalan kindergarten teachers collaboratively (see Artigal *et al.*, 1984).

## References

Aikio, M. (1991) The Sàmi language: Pressure of change and reification. *Journal of Multilingual and Multicultural Development* 12, 93–103.

Artigal, J.M. (1991a) The Catalan immersion programme: The joint creation of shared indexical territory. *Journal of Multilingual and Multicultural Development* 12, 21–33.

Artigal, J.M. (1991b) *The Catalan Immersion Program: A European Point of View*. Norwood, NJ: Ablex.

Artigal, J.M., Anglada, F., Aragonès, N., Flamerich, M.D., Rall, M., Ruiz, M., Ventura, M. and Voltas, M. (1984) *Com fer descobrir una nova llengua. Proposta per a introduir el català à parvulari*. Barcelona: Eumo Editorial.

Baetens Beardsmore, H. (ed.) (1993) *European Models of Bilingual Education.* Clevedon: Multilingual Matters.

Björklund, S. (1996) *Lexikala drag och kontextualisering i språkbadselevers andraspråk.* Vasa: Vasa Universitet.

Björklund, S. (1997) Immersion in Finland in the 1990s: A state of development and expansion. In R.K. Johnson and M. Swain (eds) *Immersion Education: International Perspectives* (pp. 85–101). Cambridge: Cambridge University Press.

Bressand, J.M. (1990) A multilingual approach for Europe. *Regions of Europe* 1, 68–71.

Buss, M. and Laurén, C. (eds) (1995) *Language Immersion: Teaching and Second Language Acquisition. From Canada to Europe.* Vaasa: University of Vaasa.

Buss, M. and Laurén, C. (eds) (1996) *Kielikylpy: Kielitaitoon käytön kautta.* Vaasa: Täydennyskoulutuskeskus, Vaasan yliopisto.

Cummins, J. (1981) The role of primary language development in promoting educational success for language minority students. In California State Department of Education (ed.) *Schooling and Language Minority Students: A Theoretical Framework* (pp. 3–49). Sacramento: California Department of Education.

Cummins, J. (1991) The politics of paranoia: Reflections on the bilingual education debate. In O. Garcia (ed.) *Bilingual Education: Focusschrift in Honor of Joshua A. Fishman* (pp. 183–99). Amsterdam/Philadelphia: Benjamins.

Cummins, J. (1995) Canadian French immersion programs: A comparison with Swedish immersion programs in Finland. In M. Buss and C. Laurén (eds.) *Language Immersion: Teaching and Second Language Acquisition. From Canada to Europe* (pp. 7–20). Vaasa: University of Vaasa.

Fonseka, E.A.G. (1997) *English Children's Songs: Their Use in Promoting Oral Skills in Primary Schoolchildren in Sri Lanka.* Vaasa: University of Vaasa.

Genesee, F. (1998) Immersion and multilingualism. In J. Arnau and J.M. Artigal (eds) *Els programes d'immersió: Una perspectiva europea* [*Immersion Programmes: A European Perspective*] (pp. 151–61). Barcelona: Universitat de Barcelona.

Harley, B. (1986) *Age in Second Language Acquisition.* Clevedon: Multilingual Matters.

Heinonen, P. (1996) Non-native language influence on foreign language learning. Swedish immersion pupils learning English in Keskuskoulu Comprehensive School, Vaasa. Unpublished master's thesis, University of Vaasa.

Helle, T. (1994) Directions in bilingual education: Finnish comprehensive schools in perspective. *Applied Linguistics* 4, 197–219.

Huibregtse, I. (1994) Late immersion in the Netherlands: State of affairs and research plans. In C. Laurén (ed.) *Evaluating European Immersion Programs. From Catalonia to Finland* (pp. 137–53). Vaasa: University of Vaasa.

Krashen, S. (1985) *The Input Hypothesis: Issues and Implications.* London: Longman.

Latomaa, S. (1993) Finska och svenska som andraspråk i Finland: Utbildning, forskning och forskningsbehov. In A. Golden and A. Hvenekilde (eds) *Rapport fra det andre forskersymposiet om Nordens språk som andraspråk i Oslo den 19.–20. mars 1993* (pp. 42–61). Oslo: Universitetet i Oslo.

Laurén, C. (ed.) (1991) *Kielikylpymenetelmä: Kielen käyttö mielekkääksi.* Vaasa: Täydennyskoulutuskeskus, Vaasan yliopisto.

Laurén, C. (ed.) (1992) *En modell för språk i daghem och skola. Språkbadsdidaktik i Canada, Katalonien och Finland* [*Language acquisition at kindergarten and school. Immersion didactics in Canada, Catalonia and Finland*]. Vaasa: Fortbildnings-

centralen/Continuing Education Centre, Vasa Universitet/University of Vaasa.
Laurén, C. (ed.) (1994a) *Evaluating European Immersion Programs*. From Catalonia to Finland. Vaasa: University of Vaasa.
Laurén, C. (ed.) (1994b) *Kielikylpy: Kahden kielen kautta monikielisyyteen*. Vaasa: Täydennyskoulutuskeskus, Vaasan yliopisto.
Laurén, C. (1998) The more, the easier. Immersion for multilingualism. In J. Arnau and J.M. Artigal (eds) *Els programes d'immersió: Una perspectiva europea [Immersion Programmes: A European Perspective]* (pp. 33–42). Barcelona: Universitat de Barcelona.
LeBrun, N. and Baetens Beardsmore, H. (1993) Trilingual education in the Grand Duchy of Luxembourg. In H. Baetens Beardsmore (ed.) *European Models of Bilingual Education* (pp. 101–20). Clevedon: Multilingual Matters.
Martin, M (1992) Forskning om finska som målspråk. In M. Axelsson and A. Viberg (eds) *Första forskarsymposiet om Nordens språk som andraspråk i Stockholm 1991* (pp. 102–14). Stockholm: Stockholms Universitet.
Nikula, T. and Marsh, D. (1996) *Kartoitus vieraskielisen opetuksen tarjonnasta peruskouluissa ja lukioissa*. Helsinki: Opetushallitus.
Nikula, T. and Marsh, D. (1997) *Vieraskielisen opetuksen tavoitteet ja toteuttaminen*. Helsinki: Opetushallitus.
Ringbom, H. (1987) *The Role of the First Language in Foreign Language Learning*. Clevedon: Multilingual Matters.
Skutnabb-Kangas, T. (ed.) (1995) *Multilingualism for All*. Netherlands: Swets & Zeitlinger.
Swain, M. (1995) Three functions of output in second language learning. In G. Cook and B. Seidlhofer (eds) *Principle and Practice in Applied Linguistics* (pp. 125–44). Oxford: Oxford University Press.
Takala, S. and Sajavaara, K. (1998) *Kielikoulutus Suomessa*. Jyväskylä: Soveltavan kielentutkimuksen keskus, Jyväskylän yliopisto.
Väyrynen, P., Räisänen, A., Geber, E., Koski, L. and Pernu, M.L. (1998) *Kieliäkö ammatissa? Ammatillisten oppilaitosten kielten opetuksen nykytila ja kehittämistarpeet*. Helsinki: Opetushallitus.
Wode, H., Kickler, K., Knust, M. and Priest, B. (1994) The Schleswig–Holstein bilingual education project: A preliminary report. In C. Laurén (ed.) *Evaluating European Immersion Programmes. From Catalonia to Finland* (pp. 154–74). Vaasa: University of Vaasa.
Young, T. (1995) Professional development for immersion teachers in Finland. In M. Buss and C. Laurén (eds) *Language Immersion: Teaching and Second Language Acquisition. From Canada to Europe* (pp. 96–106). Vaasa: University of Vaasa.

## Chapter 12
# Trilingual Primary Education in Friesland

JEHANNES YTSMA

Friesland is officially recognised as the only bilingual province in the Netherlands. It has well over 600,000 inhabitants, which comes to approximately 4% of the total national population. Survey research has shown that 94% of the provincial population can understand Frisian and 74% claim to be able to speak the minority language (Gorter & Jonkman, 1995: 8). As far as literacy is concerned, 65% can read Frisian and only 17% can write in the language. A comparison of the figures for language proficiency (from 1994) with earlier research findings (dated 1980) make it clear that language relationships in the province have been remarkably stable since the early 1980s (Gorter & Jonkman, 1995: 8).

As said, a very high percentage of the total population can understand Frisian. Moreover, no less than 85% of the Dutch-speaking inhabitants of Friesland can understand the minority language too (Gorter & Jonkman 1995: 12). This has to do with the fact that Frisian and Dutch are typologically related varieties. Both are Germanic languages. Frisian and English are related as well; they belong to the branch of coastal Germanic languages. By contrast, Dutch and German are continental Germanic varieties. In historical linguistics, Frisian has been considered the language most closely linked to English.

A considerable part of the population of Friesland province uses Frisian on a daily basis. It has been found that a small majority of the inhabitants (55%) have Frisian as their mother tongue and 54% speak it at home (Gorter & Jonkman, 1995: 11–16). These figures show that the minority language only just tops the dominant language in the numerical respect. In the light of primary education, it is particularly of interest to look at the current language relationship among members of the youngest generation. It has been assessed that 53% of the children in Friesland have Frisian as their mother tongue and 39% of them have Dutch (Gorter & Jonkman, 1995: 17). The remaining 7% of the children speak a local dialect as their first language. It should also be noted that not many people living in Friesland have a foreign language as their mother tongue; this has been estimated to apply to only some 2% of the provincial population (Gorter & Jonkman 1995: 11). Despite the everyday prevalence of Frisian and Dutch, English nevertheless occupies a certain position in a number of formal domains in Dutch (and Frisian) society. That is to say that this foreign language performs an active function in 'modern' domains such as media and business. For example, there is extensive exposure to English in the mass media. De Bot (1994) remarks that 40% to 60% of the television programmes screened in the Netherlands are in English (all subtitled in Dutch). Moreover, English is increasingly used in commercial advertising; Gerritsen (1996) mentions that almost a fifth of the pages in Dutch newspapers and magazines contained English-language advertisements. Gerritsen concludes that advertisements entirely in English are now a fairly well established phenomenon in the Netherlands.

The tendency towards internationalisation has been seen as a threat to the position of Dutch in the European context (De Bot, 1994). Growing internationalisation undoubtedly strengthens the role of English as a *lingua franca* in Europe and in the long run could perhaps even marginalise the Dutch language in international terms. However, this does not directly affect the position of Dutch within its own language area, for there are no signs that English is intruding on the informal core domain of the family. In this sense it remains indeed a 'foreign' language.

## Frisian in Primary Education

Since 1980 Frisian has legally been a compulsory language in primary schooling in Friesland. Core objectives were specified for the teaching of Frisian in 1993 and were revised in 1998 (Staatsblad, 1998). The core objectives function as a guideline; they prescribe in general terms what schools are expected to achieve. The school curriculum should be designed in accordance with the core objectives. The core objectives set for the teaching of Frisian in Friesland are identical to those for the teaching of the Dutch language in the Netherlands. This means that full competence in both Frisian and Dutch (i.e. understanding, speaking, reading and writing ability) is aimed at all pupils in the province, whether they speak Frisian or Dutch at home. To attain the core objectives schools can now employ a new language course called *De Fryske TaalRotonde* [*The Frisian Roundabout*] developed by GCO Fryslân, the centre for educational advice. This course has been used by over 300 (out of some 500) primary schools in the province since its introduction in 1994. It is built round communicative use of the target language in a variety of meaningful contexts.

Current figures are not available, but an inspection conducted in the late 1980s (Inspectie van het Onderwijs, 1989) revealed the following picture of the position of Frisian in primary education. Of all schools, 10% were exempt from the obligation to teach Frisian. These schools were located in non-Frisian areas of the province. The schools which taught Frisian generally did so for one lesson per week, in all grades. The lessons were mostly given by the regular class teacher. Frisian was also used as a medium of instruction to teach other school subjects, but a fifth of the schools did not do this. In most cases, Frisian was used as vehicle of instruction for between 10% and 30% of teaching time; note that monolingual Frisian-medium (immersion) schools did not exist.

Research has shown that Frisian-speaking schoolchildren generally appreciate the use of Frisian as medium of instruction, whereas Dutch children mostly disapprove of it (Ytsma, 1995: 128). Importantly, it has also been shown that many Dutch parents overtly deprecate the use of Frisian as a vehicle of instruction in primary education (Ytsma, 1995: 136). While there is some discussion every now and then about the use of Frisian in the classroom, the use of Dutch is seen as self-evident.

The 1989 inspection also showed that pupils' attitude towards Frisian lessons was not always favourable. A third of the schools reported that their pupils were poorly motivated for Frisian schooling, in another third the children were neutral and only the last third estimated that their pupils were strongly in favour of Frisian lessons (Inspectie van het Onderwijs, 1989: 29). The new Frisian language course has possibly improved students' motivation somewhat, since a recent evaluation indicated that most children appreciated *De Fryske TaalRotonde* (Le Rütte, 1998).

In the study *Taalpeiling yn Friesland* [*Language Assessment in Friesland*] conducted in the early 1990s it turned out that the results of Frisian primary schooling were disappointing (De Jong & Riemersma, 1994). The authors concluded that there was a gap between, on the one hand, the core objectives set for Frisian and, on the other, the research results showing the command of Frisian among the oldest primary school children tested. In particular, speaking ability turned out to be low among Dutch children and writing ability was poor among both Dutch and Frisian children. Moreover, the results of a decoding test on reading ability were low for both groups of children. In view of the very modest place of Frisian within the school curriculum – both as a school subject and as a medium of instruction – these unfavourable research findings should not come as a surprise. Importantly, however, the *Taalpeiling* revealed positive outcomes regarding the command of Dutch at the end of primary education (Grade 8): in general, the performance of Frisian and Dutch primary school children in

Friesland was equal to that of schoolchildren in the Netherlands as a whole (De Jong & Riemersma, 1994: 226). In other words, it was demonstrated yet again that bilingual schooling had no detrimental effects on Dutch language proficiency. And as for reading comprehension, the Frisian schools did even better than those in the rest of the Netherlands.

## English in Primary Education

English became legally compulsory in primary education in the Netherlands in 1986. No single school is exempt from the obligation to teach this foreign language. Core objectives were set for English teaching at primary level in 1993. A revision of these objectives took place in 1998 (Staatsblad, 1998). In essence, the objectives come down to simple communicative ability in the domains of understanding, speaking and reading. English is usually taught as a school subject in Grades 7 and 8 only, i.e. from age 10 or 11 onwards. Nationwide research conducted in 1991 pointed out that just 5% of the primary schools were beginning primary English in Grade 6 (Vinjé, 1993: 34). Unlike Frisian, English, as the first foreign language at school, is not used for teaching other school subjects. In other words, content-based instruction does not occur (or only rarely occurs). English lessons are given by the regular class teacher in nearly all cases (88%; Vinjé, 1993: 34). Time available for foreign language teaching is limited. In Grade 8, the mean teaching time in 1991 amounted to 47 minutes per week, which meant most primary schools were teaching English for one or two lessons per week (Vinjé, 1993: 34).

The primary schools used various commercial language courses. A majority of 61% of the schools used a communicative course, 7% made use of a grammar-based course, and 32% of the schools employed a mixed, communicative and grammar-based course (Vinjé, 1993: 11). During English lessons the main focus was, as it still is, on listening and speaking ability and on the development of vocabulary. These figures for the position of English in primary education apply to the situation in the Netherlands as a whole, but there is no reason to assume that the situation in Frisian schools is substantially different. The fact that the latter also have to teach Frisian as an additional subject presumably has no consequences for their teaching of English.

Foreign language lessons are quite popular among primary school children. Interestingly, the older children in the Netherlands (Grade 8, age 12) picked English as their favourite school subject (Vinjé, 1993: 91). This is in line with earlier research findings from Friesland, which showed that 84% of the primary schools in the province indicated that their students were highly motivated with regard to English lessons (Inspectie van het Onderwijs, 1989: 29). The same study suggested, however, that not all primary schools in Friesland saw English as an essential part of the curriculum. In fact, although 58% of the schools indicated that English was important to them, 42% did not judge English a significant language at primary level (Inspectie van het Onderwijs, 1989: 28). It is likely that the latter schools considered the teaching of English to be really the domain of secondary schooling. This points to a general problem relative to the teaching of English at primary level: the connection between primary English and secondary English. It has been noted that secondary schools find it hard to cope with the huge spread of knowledge of (aspects of) English among their Grade 1 students (Edelenbos & Hettinga, 1993).

The 1991 national study quoted above evaluated the results of primary English in the Netherlands as a whole. Edelenbos (1993: 110) summarised the outcome as follows: reading ability moderate, understanding spoken English good; the children managed on average to get by in quite a few plain speech situations and vocabulary development scored pretty high. On the whole, the conclusion seemed to be that the results of primary English in the Netherlands were not unsatisfactory.

However, in all likelihood the relatively competent command of English displayed by the oldest primary school children tested in 1991 cannot be solely attributed to the factor of schooling. The way English functions in the wider society undoubtedly plays a significant role as well. In this respect, it is interesting to note that 45% of the children examined in the nationwide survey of primary English considered that they learnt English mainly at school. Furthermore, 33% thought that they learnt the language in school as much as outside school, and the remaining part (23%) felt that learning English chiefly took place through listening to the radio and watching television (Vinjé, 1993: 94).

## Trilingual Primary Education in Friesland

As outlined above, elementary schools in Friesland have been confronted for over a decade with three compulsory school languages: Frisian, Dutch and English. One advantage here is that the regional, the national and the foreign language are all three related, which may facilitate positive linguistic transfer. On the other hand interrelationships between languages can also involve linguistic interference (i.e. negative transfer). Furthermore, it has been pointed out that the foreign language not only has a place within the setting of the school but clearly functions within society as well. All in all, we are of the opinion that the context in Friesland is such that an innovative project on truly trilingual primary education is feasible. By 'trilingual primary education' we mean that the three languages concerned are not only taught as school subjects, but also used as vehicles of instruction.

## The Project

The new trilingual project is an initiative of the Fryske Akademy and the Frisian department of the provincial centre for educational advice (GCO Fryslân). The task of the Fryske Akademy is to follow up the project with scientific research via a longitudinal study examining the children's language proficiency (L1, L2 and L3) and their sociopsychological disposition (i.e. their attitudes and motivation) towards the three languages. The responsibility of GCO Fryslân is to develop learning material in Frisian and in English and to counsel the schools taking part. The development of additional learning material is necessary as parts of the subject of 'world studies' are in Frisian (all grades) and in English (upper grades).

In the 1997–8 academic year five experimental primary schools started working with the model in Grade 1 (at first bilingually in Frisian and Dutch), and in 1998–9 two more schools were added to the project. In the years to come the trilingual model will gradually be introduced in successive classrooms in these seven schools. This means that English is currently taught as a subject in all the project schools, and will not start to be systematically used as a medium of instruction for another couple of years. Before this it will only be used judiciously as a medium of instruction in pilot settings. At the end of each academic year the children are tested in Frisian and Dutch (and ultimately also in English) in order to gauge their progress. The schools participating in this project are small and located in villages in the Frisian countryside. It is hoped that the number of schools taking part will increase in the near future and that the project itself, like a stone thrown into a pool, has a radiating effect on other schools. In the sections below we shall look at its educational objectives and elaborate on its working methods and didactic principles.

## Objectives

Primary schools in Friesland can take the official core objectives set for Frisian, Dutch and English as their point of departure for a trilingual programme. As already mentioned, with regard to Frisian and Dutch the core objectives imply full (oral and written) language competence. For foreign language teaching, the targets imply that the objectives should be understanding, speaking and reading, albeit at a humble level. Note that writing in English is excluded from the core objectives. The approach to primary English in the Netherlands has been specified as follows:

> The purpose of offering the English language in the primary school is to make the pupils familiar with a foreign language at an early age. On the other hand, attention is also being paid to the function of English as an important international language. Pupils recognise English as a source of loan words in Dutch. These form the basis for speaking and reading the English language, starting from everyday situations. Pupils should therefore make a start with the acquisition of a vocabulary, obtain an understanding of sentence structure and be able to find out the meaning of words (SLO, 1998).

More specifically, the current attainment targets for primary English in the Netherlands are that pupils should be able to:

- understand simple conversations about everyday situations;
- understand enough English words to be able to follow spoken messages about personal information, food and drink, the living environment and time;
- talk to each other about everyday situations, using understandable pronunciation;
- understand the main issues of a simple written text; and
- use a dictionary to find out the meaning of words.

In sum, the educational objectives of the trilingual project entail full Frisian/Dutch bilingualism and biliteracy, whereas the five attainment targets listed above serve as the ultimate goal for English language teaching. Note that the targets for English are identical to those applying to all primary schools in the Netherlands, but that the project schools want to reach these goals in an optimal fashion. The next section gives an account of the way in which the Frisian trilingual project is attempting to realise the objectives set for the three languages at issue.

### Didactic and pedagogical aspects of trilingual education

The recently established Frisian multilingual project is based on the three theoretical principles listed by Cummins (1987) in relation to successful bilingual schooling. These are:

(1) additive bilingualism;
(2) linguistic interdependence; and
(3) interactive pedagogy.

The principle of *additive bilingualism*, originally proposed by Lambert (1977) says that learning another (second) language is not at the expense of the first language. Translated to our trilingual project this means that the minority language must be substantially enforced at school, not only by systematically teaching it as a school subject, but also by regularly and consciously using it as a medium of instruction.

The principle of *linguistic interdependence* implies that language proficiency in one language can be transferred to proficiency in another language (see also Lasagabaster, Chapter 10). Interdependence of language proficiency easily occurs between interrelated varieties like Frisian, Dutch and English. Besides, transfer is more likely to occur with 'deeper' aspects of language proficiency such as reading comprehension. In our project we are making use of the principle of interdependence in the sense that, for example, reading comprehension is not to be taught separately twice over (or three times), but as one single underlying ability which can be practised in more than one language. In this sense a trilingual primary school in Friesland is not actually a school that teaches three languages: it is, in fact, a 'language school'.

Finally, the principle of *interactive pedagogy* means that language learning takes place on the basis of meaningful communication. For this reason we pay a great deal of attention to the conscious and separate use of Frisian, Dutch and English as media of instruction in the classroom (see below).

The Frisian project broadly follows the concept of 'two-way bilingual education' (cf. Baker, 1996: 186ff.). Lindholm (cited in Baker, 1996: 187) describes four characteristics of a two-way bilingual programme:

(1) a minority language is used for at least 50% of instruction;
(2) in each period of instruction, only one language is used;
(3) both majority and minority speakers are present, preferably in balanced numbers; and
(4) both types of speaker are integrated in all lessons.

As regards the use of the three languages as vehicles of instruction (points 1 and 2) the model for our project means that Frisian is used as the medium of instruction for at least 50% in Grades 1 to 6. The remaining part of teaching time in these grades is in Dutch, and the two languages are deliberately separated. In the first year of the project (1997–8) the separation between the two languages has been achieved in the lower grades mostly via a division of time: using Frisian as medium of instruction one week and Dutch the next. In the case of a shared job the vehicle of instruction could be linked to the individual, one teacher consistently using Frisian, the other Dutch. In the upper grades (7 and 8) English is to be used for 20% of teaching time. In practice, this means that English will be used two days per week during the afternoon. The subjects to be taught each week in L3 are English, world studies and the creative arts. To prepare the children for the use of English as the medium of instruction, those in Grade 6 will get English lessons oriented towards vocabulary development in the areas of world studies and the creative arts.

The population of the schools which are currently participating in the project is mainly Frisian-speaking, which is not entirely in accord with the third feature of a two-way bilingual programme since it departs from the criterion of balanced numbers of majority and minority speakers. On the other hand, both Frisian- and Dutch-speaking children are fully integrated in the lessons as they are all in the same class.

One point of concern for us is the teachers' proficiency in English. As already stated, the underlying principle for language teaching in this project is that language learning takes place through language use. This means that good language learning requires proper language use. In other words, teachers should serve as a correct language model not just when they are teaching English as a language, but when they are using it as a medium of instruction, too. The teachers in the project are (almost) all Frisian–Dutch bilinguals and those who teach English in the upper grades have a fair knowledge of the language. However their English is probably not fluent and accurate enough for them to be able to use the language effectively in teaching other school subjects. A specially designed preparatory English course was therefore organised in 1998–9 to further improve oral language ability and to provide some insights into foreign language didactics in accordance with immersion principles. As part of the English course, some teachers will – as a pilot – be carefully trying out the use of English as a medium of instruction in their own classes. In this way we hope to gain an insight into the (im)possibilities of the functional use of English as medium of instruction, which should be helpful when the project schools actually arrives at the stage of trilingual schooling in the academic year 2003–4.

As explained above, for this project we have decided to teach English via delayed immersion. In doing so we are disregarding Lenneberg's well-known 'critical period' hypothesis, which suggests that one should start second language learning at a very early age (Lenneberg, 1967). We believe that this notion has not been convincingly supported by empirical evidence. As Holmstrand (1982: 64) concluded, on the basis of an extensive review of the research available, 'it is clear that the empirical findings ... unequivocally imply that the theory of the early optimal age for language learning lacks foundation'. We also tend to agree with Singleton (1989) that not much can be said with any certainty about the role of age in second language acquisition.

To us, delayed immersion has several advantages. First, introducing English in the higher grades fits in with the Dutch education system, where the first foreign language at school is normally brought in in these grades. Second, it makes use of the high motivation that generally exists among the older students. Older school children are increasingly confronted with English and become strongly motivated to learn the language, because for them it has a true instrumental value. Since it is widely assumed that motivation is an important factor regarding (second) language learning (cf. Gardner, 1985), this can also be expected to support L3 acquisition. Third, one can make use of the knowledge of English the children have already acquired spontaneously outside school. Fourth, the students have had time to become bilingual before being confronted with the third language. Remember that being bilingual may well have a positive effect on third language learning (cf. Cenoz & Valencia,1994). Postponing the introduction of English may in fact help to prevent possible linguistic confusion in children who are in the process of becoming bilingual. Note that the potential for linguistic interference increases with the number of languages learned, in particular with related varieties. The risk of linguistic confusion has also been mentioned in the Basque Country. Cenoz and Lindsay (1994) noted that when English was introduced to 8-year-olds in the Basque Country in 1993, some parents and teachers thought that the introduction of the third language at that age might confuse the children linguistically, especially since it was at precisely this age that they were learning to read and write in the second language (Basque or Castilian). As a fifth point, towards the end of elementary schooling it must be far more possible to use English functionally as the medium of instruction for teaching other school subjects. Such an immersion approach reduces pressure on other parts of the curriculum since it means that English is no longer an extra subject taking up teaching time.

The Frisian project entails a model of what one might call 'successive trilingualism'. Successive trilingualism means that the school languages (minority, dominant and foreign language) are more or less stacked. We began with a bilingual system in the lower grades and this will be extended into the middle grades. The minority and majority languages get equal attention at these stages, both as school subjects and as media of instruction. In this way minority children build on their own language and majority students are partly immersed in the minority language. Finally, the foreign language will be added for the last two grades. In these higher grades it can be used as a medium of instruction in keeping with the general principles of immersion education. Broadly speaking, our system runs from a bilingual to a trilingual teaching approach. Seen from another angle, the focus shifts from the teaching in and of the regional and national languages (L1/L2) to the teaching in and of the international language (L3). Perhaps an optimal trilingual model in Friesland should run from monolingual (minority language) teaching in the lower grades, via a bilingual scheme (minority and majority language) in the middle grades to a trilingual teaching approach (minority, majority and foreign language) in the upper grades. However, in our province there is no tradition of immersion schooling whatsoever, and primary schools still shrink from the idea of it. When we first tried to implement such a model in the project schools the school teams generally endorsed the theoretical base of such a teaching system, but feared that (Dutch and Frisian) parents would not be in favour of it.

## Conclusion

The Frisian model of trilingual primary schooling is relatively unique in the sense that the three target languages are all interrelated. This distinguishes it from other examples of trilingual primary schooling in Europe. In Catalonia and Finland one is dealing with two related and one unrelated language; the Basque multilingual primary schools are even faced with three unrelated languages (see Muñoz, Chapter 9; Björklund & Suni, Chapter 11; Lasagabaster, Chapter 10). The Frisian linguistic constellation of interrelated varieties seems to be at the same time both an advantage and a disadvantage. The relatedness between the varieties probably facilitates the occurrence of (positive) language transfer, but on the other hand it may perhaps easily lead to negative linguistic interferences (see Cenoz, Chapter 3; Bouvy, Chapter 8).

We realise that our approach to trilingual primary schooling differs from other recent trilingual initiatives taken elsewhere in Europe. We decided not to opt for an early start with primary English, as is the case in experimental programmes in Catalonia (Artigal, 1995), the Basque Country (Garagorri *et al.*, 1997) and Finland (Björklund & Suni, Chapter 11), where the teaching of L3 often starts at the beginning of primary schooling or even at kindergarten level. We think we have good reasons for postponing L3 teaching. We fully realise that we are thereby ignoring the critical period hypothesis which declares that language learning should be initiated at a very early age (Lenneberg, 1967), but we believe that this notion has not been unequivocally corroborated by empirical evidence. In any case, future research will demonstrate to what extent our model of late immersion in the foreign language actually works. If the results obtained for English fall short of expectations this may lead to a more intensive English programme in the higher grades, or alternatively to an earlier introduction of the language.

On the other hand if the outcome of the project is satisfactory we shall have to face another problem, one touched upon above, namely the potentially awkward transition from (intensified) primary English to secondary schooling. We expect the trilingual project to give the pupils a clear advantage in English language proficiency, and the secondary schools will have to cope with that. This is a tricky issue, all the more so because the project schools send their children on to a large number of different secondary schools in the province. It remains to be seen how we – or rather the reception schools – can solve this question in the future.

As well as differences, there are also some similarities between the Frisian project and the other trilingual experiments in Europe mentioned above. In all cases, English is the third language at school, which once again underlines the power of this world language. More important is the common feature of all these multilingual experiments, the communicative approach to English language teaching, the basic concept that language learning takes place through language use. In the Catalan and Basque experiments this is realised by meaningful social interaction in the target language; for instance pupils and teachers collectively dramatise stories in English. In our case the communicative approach comes into practice through the functional use of the foreign language as a medium of instruction, in keeping with the principle of immersion.

Our contribution illustrates how trilingual primary education can offer a new and fascinating opportunity for the various bilingual areas of Europe. Multilingual schooling at primary level in bilingual areas represents a challenge to express the widely known adage of 'unity in diversity', for this type of multilingual education supports the region's own language, the state language and a foreign, international language. To put it differently, trilingual schooling can prepare the present-day generation of schoolchildren to function as tomorrow's European citizens. There is clearly no single, universal, all-embracing solution for trilingual primary schooling. At the most there are some general guiding principles – such as language learning through language use – which can be applied in a variety of contexts. Whatever the context, though, in designing a suitable model for trilingual schooling all educational language planners must take into account the following aspects:

- the goals of language teaching, especially in so far as the teaching of the foreign language is concerned;

- the linguistic distances between the distinct language varieties to be taught; and
- the societal functioning of the minority language and the foreign language.

Each of these aspects may have consequences for the specific arrangement of a trilingual teaching model in a particular context. In short, Artigal (1995) seems to be right in arguing that there are 'multiways towards multilingualism'. That is not to say that each individual trilingual experiment has to find its own way, however, ignorant of the insights and experiences gained elsewhere. The present volume is evidence of that.

## References

Artigal, J.M. (1995) Multiways towards multilingualism: The Catalan immersion program experience. In T. Skutnabb-Kangas (ed.) *Multilingualism for All* (169–81). Lisse: Swets & Zeitlinger.

Baker, C. (1996) *Foundations of Bilingual Education and Bilingualism*. Multilingual Matters: Clevedon.

Cenoz, J. and D. Lindsay (1994) Teaching English in primary school: A project to introduce a third language to eight year olds. *Language and Education* 8, 201–10.

Cenoz, J. and Valencia, J.F. (1994) Additive trilingualism: Evidence from the Basque Country. *Applied Psycholinguistics* 15, 195–207.

Cummins, J. (1987) *Theory and Practice in Bilingual Education. Multicultural Education* (pp. 303–29). Paris: OECD.

De Bot, C.L.J. (1994) *Waarom deze rede niet in het Engels is*. Nijmegen: Hertogenbosch.

De Jong, S. and Riemersma, A.M.J. (1994) *Taalpeiling yn Friesland*. Ljouwert: Fryske Akademy.

Edelenbos, P. (1993) Opmaat voor kwaliteit. In M. Vinjé (ed.) *Balans van het Engels aan het einde van de basisschool* (pp. 109–12). Arnhem: Cito.

Edelenbos, P. and Hettinga, J.M.M. (1993) De aansluiting tussen Engels in het basis – en voortgezet onderwijs. In P. Edelenbos and C.J. Koster (eds) *Engels in het basisonderwijs* (pp. 78–92). Bussum: Coutinho.

Garagorri, X., Elorza, I. and Lindsay, D. (1997) Proyecto de plurilingüismo 'eleanitz' enseñanza del Inglés a partir de los 4 años. Unpublished manuscript.

Gardner, R.C. (1985) *Social Psychology and Second Language Learning. The Role of Attitudes and Motivation*. Edward Arnold: London.

Gerritsen, M. (1996) Engelstalige productadvertenties in Nederland: Onbemind en onbegrepen. In R. van Hout and J. Kruijsen (eds), *Taalvariaties. Toonzettingen en modulaties op een thema* (pp. 67–83). Dordrecht: Foris Publications.

Gorter, D. and Jonkman, R. (1995) *Taal yn Fryslân op 'e nij besjoen*. Ljouwert: Fryske Akademy.

Holmstrand, L.S.E. (1982) *English in the Elementary School. Theoretical and Empirical Aspects of the Early Teaching of English as a Foreign Language*. Uppsala: Almqvist & Wiksell International Stockholm.

Inspectie van het Onderwijs (1989) *Het onderwijs in het Fries op de basisschool: Stand van zaken 1988–1989*.

Lambert, W.E. (1977) The effects of bilingualism on the individual: Cognitive and sociocultural consequences. In P. Hornby (ed.) *Bilingualism: Psychological, Social and Educational Implications* (pp. 15–28). New York: Academic Press.
Lenneberg, E. (1967) *Biological Foundations of Language*. New York: John Wiley.
Le Rütte, M. (1998) *Evaluaasje Fryske TaalRotonde*. Ljouwert: Fryske Akademy.
Singleton, D. (1989) *Language Acquisition. The Age Factor*. Clevedon: Multilingual Matters.
SLO (1998) Home page, Stichting Leerplan Ontwikkeling: www.slo.nl.
Staatsblad (1998) Besluit 354.
Vinjé, M. (1993) *Balans van het Engels aan het einde van de basisschool*. Arnhem: Cito.
Ytsma, J. (1995) *Frisian as First And Second Language. Sociolinguistic and Socio-Psychological Aspects of the Acquisition of Frisian among Frisian and Dutch Primary School Children*. Ljouwert: Fryske Akademy.

## Chapter 13
# Teaching English as a Third Language to Hungarian–Romanian Bilinguals

TATIANA IATCU

The earliest known inhabitants of Romania were the Thracians, who occupied a wider area of the south-east of Europe. Later, around the sixth century BC, the tribes that populated the approximate territory of present-day Romania were known by the Roman people as the Dacians. This was also the old name for the country, Dacia. Historically the Romanian people inhabited three large provinces: Moldova in the north-east, Tara Romaneasca or Wallachia in the south, and Transylvania in the central and north-west part of modern Romania. In 1856 came the first unification, between Moldova and Tara Romaneasca. After the First World War, in 1918, came the second, between the United Regions of Moldova and Tara Romaneasca and Transylvania.

Transylvania's southern and eastern borders had been colonised by the Hungarian kings during the twelfth century. Today the Hungarian population is mostly centred on the counties of Mures, Harghita and Covasna (in the central and south-eastern part of Transylvania) and in the north-west of the country. There are also some people of Germanic origin who live mainly in the counties of Brasov and Banat.

The formation of the Romanian language, which is a Romance language, was also a long-drawn-out process. It was a development of the common Latin language spoken in the territory between Dacia, the Balkan Mountains and the Black Sea. The major influence on it was however the Slavonic language, and up to 20% of the Romanian lexicon consists of words of Slavonic origin. Evolution of the common Latin language to Protoromanian and then to Romanian was unitary until the Slavonic invasion, following which the Dacian Roman dialect subdivided into three other dialects found south of the Danube: Aromanian, Istroromanian and Meglenoromanian. These four dialects were established during the ninth and tenth centuries. (Pascu, 1992: 271). Hungarian and Romanian thus have different origins:

Hungarian is a Finno-Ungric language and Romanian comes from Latin. And they both differ from the English language, which is Germanic.

Apart from Latin and Greek, which until the second half of the eighteenth century were very influential, no other languages were taught in Romania until the Romance languages began to be introduced somewhere between 1830 and 1850. Until the end of the Second World War the most important foreign language was French. After the Second World War, however, the *lingua franca* of all the communist countries was Russian, which became the chief compulsory language in all Romanian schools until 1989. In fact for a period of almost 20 years it represented 80% of the foreign languages taught in Romania. The teachers were of Russian origin or had previously studied in the USSR.

Although everybody learnt Russian for about eight years in school the paradox was that nobody spoke the language. Those who taught it belonged to the old generation, trained during the 1950s and 1960s, and were fairly numerous. Replacing them with teachers who taught other foreign languages was a real problem, carrying both human and social implications. As van Essen says (1995: 5–6):

> during the Cold War knowledge of the target culture was often interpreted as knowledge of the Soviet Union, irrespective of the language that was taught. In what was formerly the Eastern Bloc, English is currently ousting Russian from its position of privilege, and in order to cope with the massive demand for English tens of thousands of former teachers of Russian are being retrained.

Nevertheless some other foreign languages were being taught prior to 1989, and in 1963 the Romanian Government decided to found an institute for foreign languages and literature attached to the University of Bucharest. Thus the teaching of foreign languages at a high academic level acquired official status and many students were sent off to study abroad. The main aim in studying a foreign language at that time was to be able to read a newspaper, a literary book or scientific review, rather than to communicate directly (Braescu,1966: 29).

There is not much information avilable on the position of English as a foreign language before 1800, but its use is thought to have been limited to the main ports and routes. Motivation for its learning must have been mostly instrumental (van Essen, 1995: 4). Between the two world wars it was taught sporadically in Romania, by both native speakers and foreigners, in business schools.

In 1989 Romania was among the last countries to undergo a major upheaval in its political regime. From being a communist country under a totalitarian government it became almost overnight a democratic political body, struggling hard to catch up with the developed countries of the world. Romania opened its frontiers, and foreign languages other than Russian immediately became more important. Romania can now benefit from the many different activities sponsored by the Council of Europe: international conferences on language teaching, the publication of monographs and books about language teaching, scholarships both for teachers and learners. As van Essen (1995: 5–6) points out:

> With the increase interdependence of European countries came the need for greater efforts to teach adults the major languages of the European Common Market and the Council of Europe. The need to articulate and develop alternative methods of language teaching was considered a high priority.

## The Role of Languages in Romanian Education

Our school system comprises 12 years of study: Grades 1–4 in primary school (age 7–11); Grades 5–8 in secondary school (age 11–15); Grades 9–12 in high school (age 15–19). Primary and secondary school are compulsory. After leaving school, education can be continued in universities (from four to six years of study) or colleges (three years). There are both state and private institutions. The type of knowledge, skill and ability to be acquired in each subject at each different level is specified in official guidelines and curricula drawn up by the Ministry of National Education. The curriculum lays down the framework of organisation for schools: the subjects to be taught, their introduction in different grades and the number of hours to be assigned to each.

Before the late 1970s English (or another first foreign language) was taught in secondary schools for three hours per week, starting in the fifth grade, the total amount of hours during four years of study being 384. New school regulations brought in in 1964 also allowed schools the possibility of teaching some of their subjects in a foreign language (Braescu 1966: 82). In schools where foreign language teachers were available a second foreign language was generally introduced in Grade 2, or else as the first foreign language in Grade 5.

Teaching foreign languages has always played an important role in our schools and this can be seen in the structure of the curriculum. Like all the other domains of social, political and economic life, education in Romania is undergoing major changes in order to keep up with the rest of the European countries. Scholars, teacher trainers and teachers are now working to improve the curriculum and to achieve school autonomy.

Table 13.1 shows the number of hours per week allowed for foreign languages and the mother tongue in primary and secondary schools today.

**Table 13.1** Language tuition in primary and secondary schools: hours per week

| Primary school grade | 1 | 2 | 3 | 4 |
|---|---|---|---|---|
| **Romanian pupils:** | | | | |
| Romanian | 8 | 5 | 5 | 5 |
| 1st foreign language | — | 2 | 2 | 2 |
| **Hungarian pupils:** | | | | |
| Hungarian | 8 | 6 | 6 | 5 |
| Romanian | 4 | 5 | 5 | 5 |
| 1st foreign language | — | 2 | 2 | 2 |
| Secondary school grade | 5 | 6 | 7 | 8 |
| **Romanian pupils:** | | | | |
| Romanian | 5 | 4 | 4 | 4 |
| Latin | — | — | — | 1 |
| 1st foreign language | 2 | 2 | 2 | 2 |
| 2nd foreign language | — | 2 | 2 | 2 |
| **Hungarian pupils:** | | | | |
| Hungarian | 5 | 4 | 4 | 4 |
| Romanian | 5 | 4 | 4 | 4 |
| Latin | — | — | — | — |
| 1st foreign language | 2 | 2 | 2 | 2 |
| 2nd foreign language | — | — | — | — |

Source: *Planul de invatamant pentru invatamantul primar, gimnazial si liceal* (1994)

It is now possible for schools in Romania to introduce intensive English classes provided they have teachers trained to teach them. Intensive English means approximately seven hours of language teaching, including two in which English is the language of instruction. Subjects to be taught in English are as follows: geography of the UK and USA in the ninth grade, history of the UK and the US in the tenth grade and culture and civilisation of the UK and USA in the eleventh and twelfth grades.

Table 13.2 shows a tentative scheme of languages for the new curriculum. The presence of languages in the curriculum is ranked according to the amount of hours taught (37% for the primary school and 28% for the secondary school).

**Table 13.2** Language tuition in the new curriculum: hours per week

| Grades | 1 | 2 | 3 | 4 | 5 | 6 | 7 | 8 |
|---|---|---|---|---|---|---|---|---|
| **Compulsory:** | | | | | | | | |
| Romanian | 7 | 7 | 6 | 6 | 4 | 3 | 3 | 4 |
| 1st foreign language | — | — | 2 | 2 | 2 | 2 | 2 | 2 |
| **Optional:** | | | | | | | | |
| Romanian (for Hungarian pupils) | 1 | 1 | 1 | 1 | | | | |
| 2nd foreign language | 2 | 2 | 2 | 2 | | | | |

*Source: Lansarea dezba terii publice asupra nouluy plan de invatamint (1998)*

The Romanian educational system has up till now been a teacher-centered process, based mainly on memorisation and the reproduction of knowledge. The proposed educational reforms place students at the centre of the teaching process instead. Here they will be guided in the acquisition of skills such as analysis, synthesis, comparison, problem-solving and the application of information. As far as primary school pupils are concerned, the main aim of the new curriculum is to provide them with a general elementary education, building up their personality and stimulating the development of effective and creative relationships with the social and natural environment. For secondary school pupils (*Lansarea dezbaterii publice asupra noului plan de invatamant*, 1998: 15), teaching will be aimed at enabling them to:

- communicate efficiently in real situations, using either their mother tongue or other languages;
- adapt themselves to and integrate with society, showing tolerance, responsibility and friendship; and
- choose their future profession and discover a motivation for learning

in a changing society.

## Teacher Development

Prospective English teachers have to study for four years at a university and be awarded a bachelor's degree. After three years of teaching experience they must then pass a compulsory exam in order to become fully qualified as teachers. There are further exams to certify qualified teachers. The traditional teacher training route has been one of individual study and scientific research, pedagogical activities within a school or in a group of schools (in the same field of research or the same area of location), sessions of presentation of scientific papers and periodical training courses organised by universities (Benta 1974: 23). Publications include the *Educational Journal* and the *Pedagogical Review*, and each university has its own printing-house. There are also publications for teachers at a national level.

Today, as well as the old forms of scientific activity we have conferences organised by all the main universities in the country. There are also summer camps and courses in teaching grammar and literature organised by the Ministry of National Education and the British Council. In 1998 there were summer camps on the following topics: young learners, young teacher development, varieties of language, literature and mentor training (*Together*, 1998: vols 3–4).

Before the revolution few teachers or students had the chance to go abroad to study English. Now the situation has changed; Romania is participating in some of the European educational projects such as ERASMUS, SOCRATES, Lingua and Comenius and has many opportunities to exchange both information and people with other countries. Through visiting other countries, both teachers and learners come into contact with other civilisations and, as van Essen (1995: 8) says:

> even if learners are not successful as far as the language is concerned they will hopefully lose some of their ethnocentric beliefs, through the contact with a different variety of European culture. I would add that the cause of linguistic and cultural tolerance is perhaps much better served, or at least considerably furthered, by putting into the language curriculum a special space for the discussion of language itself.

## Teaching Methods and Materials

The specific aims of teaching foreign languages depend on the level of the class and/or on the pupils' age, and on the required scope of the teaching – whether it is just for conversation, for writing or for reading purposes.

For younger children (aged 7–10) the main target is speaking and understanding. As they get older more and more reading and writing skills are taught.

The methods traditionally used in Romania for teaching English kept pace with those used in the other European countries. Thus in the early twentieth century the grammar–translation method was used. After the Second World War teachers began to make use of the direct method; between the 1930s and the 1960s the oral approach or situational language teaching were introduced, and in the 1970s the audiolingual method (Richards & Rodgers, 1994).

Today's teachers of English are mostly still using the audiolingual method; very few have been educated to be intercultural learners and communicative classroom teachers. The communicative method was only introduced after the political changes at the end of 1989, under the guidance of the British Council, an institute that provides native English teachers, training courses for Romanian teachers, and teaching materials. Of these last, textbooks are the main material whatever the level or age of the group. Textbooks used up to the sixth grade are the same as those used in other European countries, but those for Grades 7 and 8 were written in 1983 and revised in 1990. The teachers use additional materials such as reading books, computers, pictures, drawings, charts, tapes and videos.

In common with other European countries, we have found in Romania that young children are generally highly motivated to learn English. Some are interested in English songs and almost all of them like cartoons and films and watch them on TV. Others learn English because it is fashionable – only a very few because it might be useful to know a foreign language for a future profession. Older pupils, from the fifth grade onwards, naturally perceive different goals. Some pupils just want to pass a test, to get a better mark, to please their parents or to show off. Others wish to get a better job, to use English when travelling abroad or even to get a job in another country.

Primary school pupils can take extra English classes after school or at weekends. In these classes they learn short poems and play games, perform short plays for children, solve puzzles and crosswords, read easy texts and fairy-tales and at the end of the school term or the school year organise a festival. Pupils from the secondary schools organise reading workshops, set up drama clubs, write poems or short pieces of prose. Their meetings are based on shared literary experience and conversation (Galateanu & Comisel, 1975: 117–18). Native speakers are a great help, enriching pupils' vocabulary and providing information on the English language, culture and civilisation. They usually belong to various organisations like the Peace Corps, SOL (Services for Open Learning), APSO (Agency for

Personnel Skills Overseas) and others. SCROLL (Scotland–Romania Language Link) was set up with 40 students in 1991, has gone on every summer since with over 90, and holds four-week courses in many towns in and around Iasi. In 1998, 100 students from Scottish universities came to Romania and worked in schools in Arad, Bistrita, Onesti and other areas. SCROLL is a highly organised group whose sole interest is to offer a mutually beneficial experience to both countries, one that will ensure that links are made for future generations of Romanians. All Scottish students apparently arrive home saying that Romania has given them as much as and often more than they have given themselves (Wood-Lamont 1998: 101).There are also travel agencies that organise three-day trips outside town, led by native speakers of English, on which pupils can enjoy themselves and practise their English at the same time. In addition we have English–Romanian inter-educational projects such as the one started in 1992 at Liviu Rebreanu High School, Bistrita. This project arranges exchanges for both students and teachers and is rated a very enriching experience (Botezatu, 1997–8: 96).

## English as a Third Language for Hungarian–Romanian Students

The curriculum used in our schools has never made any distinctions in teaching pupils from the minorities who live in our country. The most numerous of these is the Hungarian community, one-tenth of the population, who live in the centre of Romania. This was once called the Autonomous Hungarian Region, but at the Ninth Congress of the Communist Romanian Party in 1968 it was separated into three counties: Mures, Harghita and Covasna. Hungarian pupils may have either Romanian or Hungarian teachers; the latter prefer to teach Hungarian pupils if they are given the choice. Hungarians and other linguistic groups in Romania can be taught in their own language provided the groups are large enough for a class and there are teachers available. When Hungarian is the language of instruction Romanian is introduced as a second language in the first grade. Some children already know some Romanian, but if they are living in a Hungarian-speaking community they usually have a very low level of proficiency in Romanian when they first go to school. Hungarian may be used as the language of instruction in both primary and secondary education, but Romanian is the language of instruction at university, with a few exceptions such as Babes-Bolyai University in the city of Cluj-Napoca where Hungarian is used as the language of instruction in some colleges.

In counties where both Romanians and Hungarians live there are schools that use only Hungarian as the teaching language, only Romanian, or both. As already explained, most Hungarians live in Transylvania, mainly in the counties of Mures, Harghita and Covasna. In these counties there are schools in which Hungarian is the language of instruction for all subjects except the Romanian language; these schools can accept both Hungarian- and Romanian-speaking children. For example Mures county has 203 primary schools, of which 68 use Hungarian for teaching, and 240 secondary schools, of which 35 use Hungarian. The total number of primary school pupils is 35,523, of whom 11,735 are Hungarian. The total number of pupils studying a foreign language is 27,273 and the languages they study are English (9096), French (15,062), German (2974) and Russian (141).

The total number of secondary school pupils is 27,377, of whom 8771 are Hungarian. All the pupils study a first foreign language and 12,829 pupils also study a second foreign language. The number of pupils studying each of the languages available can be seen in Table 13.3.

**Table 13.3** Number of secondary school pupils studying English, French, German and Russian in Mures

| Foreign language | English | French | German | Russian |
|---|---|---|---|---|
| First | 8,212 | 15,584 | 3,144 | 437 |
| Second | 7,546 | 3,424 | 1,138 | 721 |

The data indicate that we still have more students studying French than English as a first foreign language, which is simply due to the fact that there are not enough teachers of English available. The number of English teachers in Mures in the academic year 1996–7 was 277. Only 118 of them were university-trained and qualified to teach English and of these, 59 taught in schools that used Hungarian as their teaching language (Mures County Educational Inspectorate, 1998).

Though we do not have enough research data, results from the first grades of primary school suggest that Hungarian pupils learn English more slowly than their Romanian peers and retain a stronger accent from their mother tongue. This could be due to the fact that they begin studying Romanian and English at the same time, both languages being foreign to them. Table 13.4 shows the percentages for the marks obtained for English by Romanian and Hungarian pupils at a specific school in Grades 2 to 8. Marks in Romanian education range from 1 to 10, 10 being the highest. Due to the mobility of foreign language teachers after 1989 and frequent changes in the curriculum, language studies show some gaps.

**Table 13.4** Percentages of students obtaining different marks

| Grade | Origin | Mark | | | | | |
|---|---|---|---|---|---|---|---|
| | | 10 | 9 | 8 | 7 | 6 | 5 |
| **Primary school: English as a first foreign language** | | | | | | | |
| 2 | Romanian | 45.45 | 27.72 | 18.18 | 4.54 | — | — |
| | Hungarian | 27.27 | 31.81 | 22.72 | — | 4.54 | 13.64 |
| 3 | Romanian | 36.36 | 22.72 | 9.09 | 22.72 | 9.09 | — |
| | Hungarian | 27.27 | 22.72 | 4.54 | 13.64 | — | 13.64 |
| 4 | Romanian | 21.42 | 25.00 | 17.85 | 10.71 | 14.28 | 10.71 |
| | Hungarian | 38.88 | 27.77 | — | — | 5.55 | 27.72 |
| **Secondary school: English as a first foreign language** | | | | | | | |
| 5 | Romanian | 17.85 | 14.28 | 35.71 | 14.28 | 10.71 | 7.14 |
| | Hungarian | 23.80 | 28.57 | 28.57 | 14.28 | 4.76 | — |
| 6 | Romanian | 44.11 | 32.35 | 11.76 | 11.76 | — | — |
| | Hungarian | 10.00 | 40.00 | 20.00 | 20.00 | — | — |
| **Secondary school: English as a second foreign language** | | | | | | | |
| 6 | Romanian | 13.51 | 27.02 | 24.32 | 16.21 | 10.80 | 8.10 |
| | Hungarian | 10.71 | 17.85 | 17.85 | 39.28 | 14.28 | — |
| 7 | Romanian | 13.33 | 70.00 | 13.33 | — | 3.33 | — |
| | Hungarian | 5.71 | 37.14 | 37.14 | 11.42 | 8.54 | — |
| 8 | Romanian | 9.09 | 45.45 | 31.81 | 4.45 | 9.09 | — |
| | Hungarian | 11.76 | 17.64 | 29.41 | 5.88 | 35.29 | — |

*Source:* Scoala Generala Nr. 10, 1995–8

The data show an improvement in the Hungarian pupils' results over the course of time. This could be due to the positive influence of Romanian which is closer in grammar patterns and vocabulary to English than Hungarian is. The methods used for teaching both Romanian and Hungarian are 'traditional', i.e. a mixture of structuralist, situational, audiolingual and Latin grammar-based. For teaching English the communicative approach is becoming more popular. There are no differences in the teaching methods used for English as a first or a second foreign language.

When English is taught as a third language to Hungarian pupils some differences have been observed by comparison with Romanian students. For example, when teaching speaking and pronunciation there are differences between the phonetic systems of Hungarian and English that must be taken into account. Sounds such as /i/, /æ/, diphthongs and triphthongs which do not exist in Hungarian, can only be produced correctly after hours of practice. /ʌ/ and /ð/ can be taught through comparison with Romanian because these do exist in the Romanian phonetic system. However consonants like /θ/ /ð/ or /w/ are absent from both Hungarian and Romanian and can best be produced when demonstrated several times and practised both on their own and in words. The word 'three', for example, is usually first pronounced either like 'tree' or 'free' or just /sri/. /w/ is often mispronounced /v/ by Hungarian learners. Stress is another quite difficult matter to teach because in Hungarian it is always on the first syllable. Repetition of minimal pairs, individually or in groups, and making sentences that contain the sounds involved give the best results (Doff 1996: 44). In the case of grammar, it has been observed that Hungarian pupils often place the adjective after the noun as in Romanian. If they are told that in English, adjectives are placed the same way as in Hungarian, mistakes are less likely. Another problem that can be easily solved, this time using Romanian, is when children have to choose between 'to be' and 'to have'. In Hungarian possession is expressed syntactically with the verb 'to be' plus the accusative, so instead of 'to have' they would use 'to be'. However in Romanian possession is expressed lexically as in English, so the distinction between the two verbs can be emphasised through Romanian.

## Conclusion

The Romanian educational system is part of a society in transition which is currently seeking the best way to integrate itself into the main educational trends developed by the European Community. New teaching methods and more qualified teachers, along with all the new opportunities for travelling abroad, will certainly improve Romanian knowledge of English in the near future.

Romania is a country populated by speakers of different languages, chiefly Romanian and Hungarian, and English is rapidly becoming the most popular foreign language. This situation provides an excellent opportunity for analysing the differences between second and third language acquisition where the learners involved are speakers of languages with different structures and origins.

## Acknowledgement

Special thanks to Cristian Lako for his contribution in writing the part concerning teaching English to Hungarian pupils.

### References

Benta, V. (1974) *Citeva consideratii despre metodologia predarii limbilor straine.* Iasi Inspectoratul Scolar Judetean.
Botezatu, R.(1997–8) *Working Together* (Part 3). Together Educational Center SRL. Bucharest: Oxford University Press.
Braescu, I. (1966) *Modernizarea metodelor de studiere a limbilor straine.* Bucharest: E.D.P.
Doff, A. (1996) *Teach English.* Cambridge: Cambridge University Press.
Galateanu, G. and Comisel, E. (1975) *Indrumator metodic pentru predarea limbii engleze in scoala generala.* Bucharest: EDP.
*Lansarea dezbaterii publice asupra noului plan de invatamant* (1998). Buletin informativ nr. 9. Bucharest: Ministerul Educatiei Nationale.
Pascu, St. (1971) *Voievodatul Transilvaniei* (Vol. 1). Cluj-Napoca: Dacia.
*Planul de invatamant pentru invatamantul primar, gimnazial si liceal* (1994) Bucharest: Editura Didactica si Pedagogica R.A.
Richards, J.C. and Rodgers, T.S. (1994) *Approaches and Methods in Language Teaching.* Cambridge: Cambridge University Press.
*Together* (1998) (Vols 3&4). Together Educational Center SRL. Bucharest: Oxford University Press.
van Essen, A. (1995) *English among the Other European Languages.* The British Council, Crown Press.
Wood-Lamont, S. (1997/8): *SCROLL: Scotland–Romania Language Link.* Together Educational Center SRL. Bucharest: Oxford University Press.

*Chapter 14*
# Expanding the Scope
## Sociolinguistic, Psycholinguistic and Educational Aspects of Learning English as a Third Language in Europe

JASONE CENOZ AND ULRIKE JESSNER

The purpose of this chapter is to summarise and evaluate the evidence reported in this book, with all its implications for the study of English as a third language, both in the European context and elsewhere. In many European countries the role of English is being reassigned these days, with the language gaining more and more the status of *lingua franca* for the whole of Europe. According to Crystal (1995: 454) a *lingua franca* is 'a medium of communication for people who speak different first languages': with respect to the situation in Europe, as described in this volume, we would like to add 'and different second languages'.

As stated in the Introduction, in our book we try to integrate theory, research and practice with respect to questions of the learning of English as a third language on the European continent. Our purpose is at least threefold; our aims are to:

- present the latest research on theories of third language acquisition;
- describe some of the research and language planning carried out in several multilingual educational settings where English is taught as a third language; and
- provide a focus on the special role of English today in a changing Europe.

We describe and discuss a collection of linguistic situations in various European countries. Apart from English, these include the following European languages: Basque, Catalan, Dutch, Finnish, French, Frisian, German, Hungarian, Polish, Romanian, Russian, Spanish and Swedish. These languages have different degrees of relationship with the English language and vary in terms of their vitality within their specific community, discussed in this volume, and their spread outside these specific communities. French, Spanish and German are important international languages; Basque and Frisian are less widely used even in their own communities. In other cases, national languages become minority languages when spoken in contact with other languages outside their national territory, as is the case of Hungarian in Romania or Polish in Germany.

In terms of typology, the languages involved present different origins: Dutch, Frisian, German and Swedish are Germanic languages, as is English; Spanish, Catalan, French and Romanian are Romance languages; Finnish and Hungarian are Finno-Ungric languages; Polish and Russian are Balto-Slavonic languages; and Basque is typologically unrelated to all the others. This diversity is reflected in the different typological patterns found when English is acquired as a third language. For example in Friesland, the three languages involved in the educational system (English, Dutch and Frisian) are closely related to each other; this is not the case in Hungary, where Hungarian, Russian and English are not typologically related. The question of typology is an important factor for consideration in the study of third language acquisition, specifically when analysing the role of the L1 and L2 in the acquisition of the L3.

## Sociolinguistic Aspects

In the European context the English language, by virtue of its extensive and ever increasing use, is developing into a sort of European English or even a number of European Englishes. According to Charlotte Hoffmann (Chapter 1) we can speak of societal and individual 'multilingualism with English' in Europe, because an ever-increasing number of people are not only using the language as a vehicle of communication with native speakers of English, but also as a *lingua franca* in their contacts with speakers of other languages. This spread of English and the growth of multilingualism with English has resulted in an increased demand for English tuition in most European educational systems.

At first sight ETL (English as third language) might appear to be simply a variant of EFL (English as foreign language), but in fact the more it is used as a *lingua franca* (in the European context, on a more or less daily basis) the more it seems to be developing differing characteristics from EFL. In many countries it appears to be losing its 'foreignness' altogether; as McArthur says (1996: 10), 'English is no longer really foreign, but a strong second language that is steadily becoming nativised'. Consequently the foreign–second distinction should really be reconsidered, as already suggested by Berns (1990: 4), who introduces a continuum for language status that has 'foreign' at one pole and 'second' at the other. Viereck's model of European English (1996: 16) also makes use of this dichotomy, presenting English in northern Europe as a second language or *lingua franca*, in southern Europe as a foreign language, in central Europe as EFL but becoming a *lingua franca*, and in eastern Europe as having gained importance since the fall of the Iron Curtain.

Whether such a dichotomy is useful in the context of third language learning will have to be discussed. In this volume, Allan James (Chapter 2) suggests a reconsideration of some of the analytical dichotomies used in research on learning English. Drawing on the trilingual reality in the Alpine-Adriatric region of Carinthia–Friuli–Slovenia, where English is used as *lingua franca*, he makes some interesting typological and qualitative reflections on ELF as a *variety*. And he concludes that this variety of ELF has characteristics of a register, rather than a dialect, a conclusion which might lead to considerable discussion in the future. All in all, investigations into the nature of the *lingua franca*, whether English or not, seem to offer challenging aspects to future research.

## Theoretical and Psycholinguistic Aspects

From a theoretical point of view, learning a third language (TLA) differs in many respects from learning a second language (SLA), and these differences establish the importance of carrying out some linguistical research on the former. In many respects, although interest in multilingualism dates back at least to Vildomec (1963), this type of research can be seen as a fairly young discipline. Theoretical aspects of multilingualism in language acquisition have often either been neglected or else subsumed into research on SLA. The topic of learning several languages has been of some interest in applied linguistics, but primarily in the area of exceptional language learning (Naiman *et al.*, 1978), although in recent years TLA and trilingualism have aroused more interest in the international academic community (Bensoussan *et al.*, 1995; Hufeisen & Lindemann, 1998; Cenoz & Genesee, 1998a).

In Chapter 3 Jasone Cenoz describes the history of research on TLA and the characteristics of a trilingual system by drawing on various examples of English as L3 in the language learning process. Her discussion focuses on a definition of multilingualism and multilingual acquisition which is accompanied by the distinction between *product* and *process*, a dichotomy of whose crucial role in language acquisition research many scholars seem not be aware, but which is fundamental in discussions of multilingual contexts. In the study of TLA the diversity and complexity of the parameters involved in language acquisition become even more obvious than in SLA. An issue of interest to scholars, apart from different orders of acquisition (as in early trilingualism, or bilingualism with a third language), has been the nature of the influence that bilingualism may exert on the learning of an additional language. As most studies in this area have pointed out, a positive influence poses questions concerning the degree of proficiency in L1 and L2 and how this might lead to a positive effect on TLA in relation to the latter's individual and contextual factors. The phenomenon of transfer in TLA in both natural and instructional settings forms an essential part of studies on TLA, as we suggest below.

Cenoz also mentions that in a multilingual speaker, linguistic requirements might be subject to change. This is particularly important in the multilingual context, as the linear concept of language acquisition that is still widely prevalent turns out to be questionable in the field of multilingual research. Focusing on changes in individual language development, Philip Herdina and Ulrike Jessner add the aspect of *dynamism* to Cenoz's description of TLA. In Chapter 5 they point out the differences between monolingual and multilingual systems and adopt a holistic and dynamic view of multilingual phenomena. Following a systems-theoretical approach, they discuss the dynamics of the growth or development of individual language systems by comparing them to biological systems and identifying characteristics of the multilingual psycholinguistic system. These include stability, non-linearity of growth, maintenance and loss or reversibility and change of quality in language learning. Most of the features discussed have been of only minor interest in dominant language acquisition research paradigms so far. Systems theory presents a new approach to psycholinguistics, but has become well known in other scientific discussions in biology and psychology; it is helpful for both linguistics and applied linguistics to start thinking in new paradigms.

So far TLA has been presented in this book as a complex and dynamic process. In subsequent chapters the characteristics of a trilingual system are described through paying special attention to multilingual competence with English as a third language. Multilingual competence shows characteristics such as enhanced metalinguistic awareness which are not shared by monolingual systems (Cenoz, Chapter 3; Herdina & Jessner, Chapter 5). In Chapter 6, Istvan Kecskés and Tunde Papp, investigating differences between trilingual and bilingual speakers in Hungary, identify an important component of multilingual competence, *metaphorical competence*. In previous research these authors have discussed a common underlying conceptual base (CUCB) in multilingual speakers. This base, which at first sight might bring to mind parallels with Cummins' concept of common underlying proficiency, forms part of a multilingual language processing device (LPD) that has developed as a link between two or more constantly available interacting systems (CAIS). Drawing on Danesi's work (1992) on conceptual fluency, Kecskés and Papp see bilingual cognition as concept-grounded, rather than code-dependent, and metaphorical competence as an important – though not the only – constituent of conceptual competence. CUCB develops through experience in discourse, a process which is both linguistically and culturally grounded. In TLA, conceptual fluency can be described as dominated by the dominant language, but CUCB is also influenced by the levels of proficiency attained in L2 and L3.

Kesckés and Papp also touch upon the issue of the role that gender plays in language acquisition by identifying lower levels of risk-taking in the learning style of girls. Gender presents a very challenging aspect which has not so far been investigated in any satisfactory way, the difficulty being that ideally, research should combine expert knowledge in both areas. In the very few studies that exist the focus has been on individual factors of language acquisition that include gender (Ehrman & Oxford, 1995), and on gender differences in language learning strategies (Green & Oxford, 1995). In most studies gender has been discussed simply as a by-product of other results.

Another aspect of multilingual competence is investigated in Chapter 7 by Ute Schönpflug, who presents a psycholinguistic study on word completion tests in Polish/German/English trilinguals. In her experiment on the contrasting ways in which abstract and concrete words are stored, she identifies differences in trilinguals for abstract as opposed to concrete words and for English as opposed to German words. This supports Paivio's (1986) dual-coding theory. Schönpflug considers that both lexicons and their translation equivalents seem to be activated during word recognition. She also points to the difference between language processing in TLA and SLA because of the greater number of translation equivalents supporting early word completion in the third language. Although differing in methodology from the rest of the book this study investigates a fascinating perspective of multilingual processing and contributes to our knowledge of the multilingual lexicon. We are definitely in considerable need of more research on the bilingual lexicon, as evidence in some areas of research is still scarce (Bialystok, 1991; Harris, 1992), which means that research on the tri- or multilingual brain is still in its infancy. Schönpflug's study raises the important issue of conceptual processing vs. lexical processing in multilinguals; this could be considered in relation to Kecskés and Papp's investigations into conceptual fluency in Chapter 6.

Another kind of interaction between the languages of the trilingual learner is discussed in studies on what has become widely known as *transfer*. The focus on errors that learners make during the learning process dates back to the early days of contrastive analysis, but has not lost its importance in language teaching. The corpus analysis carried out on the transfer problems of French-speaking Dutch/ or German/English learners in Belgium indicates that learner mistakes were of a syntactic, morphological and lexical nature. The latter category was most numerous. Christine Bouvy suggests in Chapter 8 that the errors were largely performance-based and not as systematic as transfer from the L1. Furthermore she proposes that L3 transfer should be viewed as a compensatory performance phenomenon rather than as a phenomenon of intellectual compensation, which is how one might describe L1 transfer. Cross-linguistic influence is defined as a largely unconscious interaction phenomenon between sets of imperfectly acquired structures, where only those elements are transferred which the learner regards as transferable. Learner strategies are described as elaborative, evolutive, selective and mixed processes, which may be reinforced by various factors such as the activation level of L2, relative knowledge of both L2 and L3, the linguistic despecification of the candidates for transfer, the degree of linguistic constraint implicit in the context of production and the communication pressure. Above all, cross-linguistic influence reflects the *psychotypology* of the language systems involved, i.e. perception of similarities and differences between L2 and L3. As several chapters in this book (Cenoz, Chapter 3; Bouvy, Chapter 8) suggest, research on cross-linguistic influence in multilingual settings requires a different approach to phenomena of language contact in a trilingual speaker to the approaches familiar from SLA studies (see also Cenoz & Genesee, 1998b; Hufeisen & Lindemann, 1998).

Another aspect which is gaining more attention in the field of TLA is the labelling of cross-linguistic phenomena through the use of specific terminology. Jessner and Herdina (1996) argue for a theory of cross-linguistic interaction (CLIN) that goes beyond the dominant concept of cross-linguistic influence (CLI) proposed by Kellerman and Sharwood Smith (1986). CLIN also focuses on the cognitive advantages resulting from contact with several languages, such as enhanced metalinguistic awareness, communicative sensibility and flexibility in thinking, to name but a few (see also Herdina & Jessner, Chapter 5). But this would only become possible if methodology and terminology in the two research areas of SLA and TLA or bi- and multilingualism were combined.

Some recent work in the field of language transfer (Kasper & Kellerman, 1998) seems to suggest a change in terminology by talking about 'communication strategies' in the speaker/learner, rather than cross-linguistic influence or transfer problems. With regard to the issue of transfer in multilingual education, Lindemann (1998) suggests a more learner-centred analysis of strategies used in the language classroom, one that goes beyond error analysis. In addition, multilingual education should try to enhance positive transfer between individual language systems by paying more attention to the similarities between L1/L2/L3 (Köberle, 1998; Jessner, 1999).

## Educational Aspects

Over the past 20 years, research on bilingual education has been strongly influenced by Jim Cummins' BICS/CALP distinction. He detected that educators' ignorance of these aspects of language proficiency in English created academic problems for immigrant/minority students. Such students take approximately two years to catch up on conversational English, but it is some five to seven years before they attain grade norms in academic aspects of the language. Later on, Cummins elaborated his distinction into two intersecting continua highlighting the range of cognitive demands and contextual support involved in particular language tasks or activities. He distinguished between context-embedded/reduced and cognitively undemanding/demanding tasks. Chapter 4 in this book represents his answer to critiques of his framework which have been made on the grounds that it is based on the results of standardised tests, and that it ignores the social context of literacy and language development (Edelsky *et al.*, 1983; Edelsky, 1990; Wiley, 1996). Critics have also disparaged the encouragement of skill-oriented teaching forms and the perceived closeness of Cummins' concept to a deficit theory, similar to semilingualism.

Cummins responds by discussing social relations, and by describing language proficiency as an intervening variable mediating children's academic development. He analyses the construct of CALP via three components (cognitive, academic, language) and suggests that a strong bilingual (or trilingual) programme should provide a focus on message, a focus on language and a focus on use. His chapter goes a long way towards clarifying the embeddedness of social, educational and linguistic parameters in multilingual acquisition. It also shows that sociopolitical issues are strongly linked to power relationships in bilingual education (see also Cummins, 1996).

A new dimension in educational efforts to provide students with linguistic knowledge other than their first language(s) was created some 30 years ago in Canada with the introduction of immersion schooling. In Europe, the tradition of bilingual schooling has been gaining importance in several countries in recent decades (Baetens Beardsmore, 1993; Arnau & Artigal, 1998). All around Europe there is growing interest in developing efficient language programmes, as the supranational characteristics of politics and economics increase and communication barriers based on language have to be overcome. Several studies in this book present the role of English as a third language in the multilingual classroom. They range from immersion schooling in the Basque Country and Finland to discussions of the age problem in Catalonia and Friesland and the situation in a diglossic area of Romania.

In the Basque Country the bilingual situation has given rise to three models of linguistic education in which English is taught as a third language. David Lasagabaster's study, described in Chapter 10, compares levels of competence in Spanish, Basque and English in the three programmes. His findings support the developmental interdependence and the threshold hypotheses, originally presented by Cummins, on contact between two languages. A significant relationship between all three languages was found, with Spanish turning out to be more influential on the development of English than Basque. This result raises the question of typology again and confirms, for instance, the results from a study by Cenoz (1998) on linguistic distance or psychotypology between English and these two other languages. She found that more words were borrowed from Spanish than from Basque, independently of their primary language. Lasagabaster also considers a central issue of trilingual education to be the importance of metalinguistic awareness as one of the cognitive advantages that bi- or multilinguals develop (see Cummins, Chapter 4; Herdina & Jessner, Chapter 5)

The developmental interdependence hypothesis was also tested by Carmen Muñoz (Chapter 9) in a different language environment in the Spanish region of Catalonia, where the age for starting to learn English was lowered from 11 to 8. Muñoz researched the relationship between age, rate and eventual attainment in the context of learning English as a third language. In parallel with Lasagabaster, high levels of competence in students bilingual in Catalan and Spanish turned out to correlate highly with their level of proficiency in English. In multilingual acquisition the question of a critical period in language learning is an important issue, as is the belief that more gradual and flexible, multiple 'sensitive periods' allow for the differences observed between the language components. In her research study Muñoz was interested in the question of how long the period of instruction must be in order for the younger children to overtake the older learners. Singleton (1995: 3) had proposed that 18 years in a formal instructional setting were needed for older learners' initial advantage to begin to disappear. Muñoz's hypothesis that 12-year-olds will have significantly higher results than 10-year-olds (both after 200 hours of instruction) was also proved. Her study demonstrates yet again the importance of the age issue in language learning. A considerable amount of research is needed to shed some light on the problem, but many scholars involved in foreign language programmes still seem to be convinced of the 'the younger the better' hypothesis. Another question that must also be tackled in further research is the quality of instructional input.

In Jehannes Ytsma's study on English in Friesland (Chapter 12) the focus is on a different age group, one learning three closely related Germanic languages. In this, the only bilingual province of the Netherlands, the teaching of English in primary schools was introduced in 1986. In Friesland successive trilingualism, i.e. a bilingual system in the lower grades with extension in the middle grades, is considered more efficient; it is felt that transfer problems will be minimised in a delayed immersion programme, where English is not used as a medium of instruction until the higher grades. In the Frisian model the focus shifts from teaching in and of the regional and national languages (L1/L2) to teaching in and of the international language (L3). This trilingual schooling concept draws on the principles of *additive bilingualism, linguistic interdependence* and *interactive pedagogy*. According to Ytsma, in bilingual areas multilingual schooling at the primary level represents a challenge to fulfil the request for 'unity for diversity' expressed by the European Community: this means that any concept of adequate multilingual education should include the region's own language, the state language and a foreign, international language.

In 1987 an immersion programme was set up in the bilingual region of Vaasa/Vasa wherein Swedish started to be used as the medium of instruction. English is the most popular first foreign language in Vaasa/Vasa and was introduced in an experimental programme in Grade 1 in 1993. In Chapter 11, Siv Björklund and Irmeli Suni describe the teaching goals and methodology of the teaching of English as a third language and report the results of a small-scale study on students' own perceptions of their use of English at home, in the classroom and with friends. These authors express some kind of scepticism in asking whether L2 and L3 used in immersion will promote eventually one another's existence, or whether one language will come to dominate and even hinder the development of the other one. At the same time they regard the contribution of each new multilingual perspective from within the school systems of different areas as providing useful experience and knowledge for future education across Europe.

Finally, in Chapter 13, Tatiana Iatcu offers some interesting information on the teaching of foreign languages in Romania, where as a consequence of the social and political changes of recent decades English is now replacing Russian and French as the preferred foreign language. Iatcu also provides information about the Hungarian minority who acquire English as a third language, and mentions an interesting point based on her own perception regarding the comparable development of L2 and L3. Though research evidence is still needed to confirm the initial advantages of L2 learners over L3 learners and the subsequent disappearance of these advantages, her point illustrates the dynamics of multilingualism and TLA already pointed out by Herdina and Jessner in Chapter 5.

This book focuses on sociolinguistic, psycholinguistic and educational perspectives on English as L3 in Europe and contains various theoretical and methodological orientations which can be explained in terms of the differing disciplines and research traditions that converge in the study of language acquisition. It includes no more than a few of the situations in which English is acquired as a third language in Europe, but together these give rise to several relevant issues for language acquisition in other European and world contexts.

It is clear that further research is desirable on the spread of English in Europe and on third language acquisition in general. First, there are several aspects related to the spread of English in Europe. These include the relationship between the spread of English and the different European cultures, and the social psychological implications of the use of English on existing forms of European identity (Berns, 1995; Norton, 1997). Second, another interesting area that deserves further development is the examination of the linguistic characteristics of non-native European English at the phonetic, lexical, morpho-syntactic, discourse and pragmatic levels. Such research could provide interesting insights into common characteristics shared by European non-native speakers of English, as compared to non-native speakers of English from other parts of the world. And third, we need to analyse the effect of the spread of English on less widely used languages at all levels, linguistic, sociolinguistic and social psychological. This analysis should also include a comparison between the European and the non-European sociolinguistic contexts.

Research on the specific characteristics of TLA is still in its infancy and all the areas which are relevant in the study of language acquisition need further attention (see also Cenoz & Genesee, 1998b; Hufeisen & Lindemann, 1998). For example, it is necessary to analyse in more detail the role of the L1 and the L2 in different areas of TLA, and the role of metalinguistic awareness and learning strategies on different aspects of L3 development.

Research on this new sociolinguistic situation created as a result of the spread of English, including specific research on L3 acquisition, will have important implications at the educational level regarding the variety of English to be used in education, curriculum design involving more than two languages, learners' own awareness, and the development of efficient learning strategies. The relationship between research on TLA and education is bidirectional, because educational experiments in TLA and trilingualism can also provide very useful information for researchers and language planners. The examples of TLA in school contexts presented in this volume, together with other well-known examples of multilingual education such as the Foyer project, the European schools of educational system in Luxembourg (Byram & Leman, 1990; Hoffmann, 1998), provide interesting research data and can also be adapted to other contexts in education where more than two languages are being used. This volume covers a wide range of cultural and social European contexts which illustrate the diversity of European Englishes, but it is also intended to contribute to the theoretical discussions on second and third language acquisition that are relevant for other parts of a multilingual world where English is in contact with a large number of languages.

## References

Arnau, J. and Artigal, J.M. (eds)(1998) *Els programes d'immersió: Una perspectiva europea* [*Immersion Programmes: A European Perspective*]. Barcelona: Universitat de Barcelona

Baetens Beardsmore, H. (ed.) (1993) *European Models of Bilingual Education*. Clevedon: Multilingual Matters.

Bensoussan, M., Kreindler, I., and Mac Aogáin, E. (1995) (eds) *Language, Culture and Curriculum* 8 (2). Special Issue: Multilingualism and Language Learning.

Berns, M. (1990) 'Second' and 'foreign' in second language acquisition/foreign language learning: A sociolinguistic perspective. In B. van Patten and J. Lee (eds) *Second Language Acquisition/Foreign Language Learning*. Clevedon: Multilingual Matters.

Berns, M. (1995) English in Europe: Whose language, which culture? *International Journal of Applied Linguistics* 5, 193–204.

Bialystok, E. (ed.) (1991) *Language Processing in Bilingual Children*. Cambridge: Cambridge University Press.

Byram, M. and Leman, J. (eds) (1990) *Bicultural and Trilingual Education: The Foyer Model in Brussels* (pp. 30–56). Clevedon: Multilingual Matters.

Cenoz, J. (1998) Linguistic distance and cross-linguistic influence in bilinguals' oral production in English as a third language. Paper presented at the Eurosla Conference, Paris.

Cenoz, J. and Genesee, F. (eds) (1998a) *Beyond Bilingualism: Multilingualism and Multilingual Education*. Clevedon: Multilingual Matters.

Cenoz, J. and Genesee, F. (1998b) Psycholinguistic perspectives on multilingualism and multilingual education. In J. Cenoz and F. Genesee (eds) *Beyond Bilingualism: Multilingualism and Multilingual Education* (pp. 16–32). Clevedon: Multilingual Matters.

Crystal, D. (1995) *The Cambridge Enclycopedia of the English Language.* Cambridge: Cambridge University Press.
Cummins, J. (1996) *Negotiating Identities: Education for Empowerment in a Diverse Society.* Los Angeles: California Association for Bilingual Education.
Danesi, M. (1992) Metaphorical competence in second language acquisition and second language teaching: The neglected dimension. In J.E. Alatis (ed.) *Georgetown University Round Table on Languages and Linguistics* (pp. 489–500). Washington, DC: Georgetown University Press.
Edelsky, C. (1990) *With Literacy and Justice for All: Rethinking the Social in Language and Education.* London: Falmer Press.
Edelsky, C., Hudelson, S., Altwerger, B., Flores, B., Barkin, F. and Jilbert, K. (1983) Semilingualism and language deficit. *Applied Linguistics* 4, 1–22.
Ehrman, M. and Oxford, R. (1995) Cognition plus: Correlates of language learning success. *Modern Language Journal* 79, 67–89.
Green, J. and Oxford, R. (1995) A closer look at learning strategies, L2 proficiency, and gender. *TESOL Quarterly* 29, 261–97.
Harris, R. (ed.) (1992) *Cognitive Processing in Bilinguals.* Amsterdam: North Holland.
Hoffmann, C. (1998) Luxembourg and the European schools. In J. Cenoz and F. Genesee (eds) *Beyond Bilingualism: Multilingualism and Multilingual Education* (pp. 143–74). Clevedon: Multilingual Matters.
Hufeisen, B. and Lindemann B. (eds) (1998) *Tertiärsprachen. Theorien, Modelle, Methoden.* Tübingen: Stauffenburg.
Jessner, U. and Herdina P. (1996) Interaktionsphänomene im multilingualen Menschen: Erklärungsmöglichkeiten durch einen system-theoretischen Ansatz. In A. Fill (ed.) *Sprachökologie und Ökolinguistik* (pp. 217–27). Tübingen: Stauffenburg.
Jessner, U. (1999) Metalinguistic awareness in multilingual speakers: Cognitive aspects of third language learning. *Language Awareness* 8 (3&4), 201–9.
Kasper, G. and Kellerman, E. (eds) (1998) *Communication Strategies. Psycholinguistic and Psycholinguistic Perspectives.* London: Longman.
Kellerman, E. and Sharwood Smith, M. (1986) *Crosslinguistic Influence in Second Language Acquisition.* Oxford: Pergamon Press.
Köberle, B. (1998) Positive Interaktion zwischen L2, L3, L4 und ihre Applikationen im Fremdsprachenunterricht. In B. Hufeisen and B. Lindemann (eds) *Tertiärsprachen. Theorien, Modelle, Methoden* (pp. 89–110). Tübingen: Stauffenburg.
Lindemann, B. (1998) L2–L3 und ihre zwischensprachliche Interaktion. Probleme und Herausforderungen in bezug auf Untersuchungsdesigns. In B. Hufeisen and B. Lindemann (eds) *Tertiärsprachen. Theorien, Modelle, Methoden* (pp. 159–68). Tübingen: Stauffenburg.
McArthur, T. (1996) English in the world and in Europe. In R. Hartmann (ed.) *The English Language in Europe* (pp. 3–15). Oxford: Intellect.
Naiman, N., Fröhlich, M., Stern, H. and Tedesco, A. (1978) *The Good Language Learner.* Toronto: Ontario Institute of Studies in Education.
Norton, B. (1997) Language, identity, and the ownership of English. *TESOL Quarterly* 31, 409–28.
Paivio, A. (1986). *Mental Representations: A Dual-coding Approach.* New York: Oxford University Press
Singleton, D. (1995) Introduction: A critical look at the critical period hypothesis in second language acquisition research. In D. Singleton and Z. Lengyel (eds) *The*

*Age Factor in Second Language Acquisition* (pp. 1–29). Clevedon: Multilingual Matters.
Viereck, W. (1996) English in Europe: Its nativisation and use as a *lingua franca*, with special reference to German-speaking countries. In R. Hartmann (ed.) *The English Language in Europe* (pp.16–23). Oxford: Intellect.
Vildomec, V. (1963) *Multilingualism. General Linguistics and Psychology of Speech.* Leyden: A.W. Sythoff.
Wiley, T. G. (1996) *Literacy and Language Diversity in the United States.* Washington, DC: Center for Applied Linguistics and Delta Systems.

# The Contributors

**Siv Björklund** has a PhD from the University of Vaasa (Finland) and is now professor of second language acquisition at the Centre for Immersion and Multilingualism at the University of Vaasa. Her major interests are immersion and bi- and multilingualism and she has actively been involved in the first immersion programme in Finland. She has published several articles on immersion, multilingualism and second language acquisition.

**Christine Bouvy** is Senior Lecturer in English at the University of Liège, Belgium. Ever since she started working in the ESP department of the University of Liège, she has taken a lively interest in the various processes involved in second language development and vocabulary acquisition. She wrote several papers on error analysis and transfer in second-language acquisition and is currently concentrating on specialised vocabulary acquisition.

**Jasone Cenoz** is Associate Professor of English Linguistics at the University of the Basque Country (Spain), where she teaches applied linguistics and psycholinguistics. She has published books and articles in the fields of second language acquisition, bilingualism, multilingualism and interlanguage pragmatics. She is currently coordinating a research project on the acquisition of English as a third language by Basque–Spanish bilingual children.

**Jim Cummins** is Professor in the Department of Curriculum, Teaching and Learning of the University of Toronto. He has published widely in the areas of language learning, bilingual education, educational reform, and the implications of technological innovation for education. Among his latest publications are *Brave New Schools: Challenging Cultural Illiteracy through Global Learning Networks* (with Dennis Sayers, St Martin's Press, 1995) and *Negotiating Identities: Education for Empowerment in a Diverse Society* (California Association for Bilingual Education, 1996).

**Philip Herdina** is Associate Professor of English Linguistics at the University of Innsbruck (Austria). He has published on the philosophy of language, multilingualism, computer-assisted language teaching and

English literature. His publications include a bilingual (German–English) dictionary of philosophy.

**Charlotte Hoffmann** is Senior Lecturer and Associate Director of the European Studies Research Institute at the University of Salford (United Kingdom) where she teaches German, sociolinguistics and bilingualism. She is the author of *An Introduction to Bilingualism* (Longman) and editor of *Language, Culture and Communication in Contemporary Europe* (Multilingual Matters) and has published articles on child trilingualism, trilingual competence, language maintenance, language planning and language and nationalism.

**Tatiana Iatcu** is Assistant Professor at the Department of History Philology at the 'Petru Maior' University, city of Tg. Mures (Romania), where she teaches English grammar and semantics. Her interests include English teaching methodology and gender studies. She has published two books on English grammar and two exercise books. She is currently working on the English phrasal verb and a book on teaching English in Romania.

**Allan James** is Professor of English Linguistics at the University of Klagenfurt (Austria), where he teaches a varied range of subjects within theoretical and applied linguistics and is coordinator of the interdisciplinary group on multilingualism. He has published widely on second language acquisition, phonetics and phonology and is currently piloting a large-scale project on English as a *lingua franca* in the Alpine-Adriatic region.

**Ulrike Jessner** is Associate Professor of English Linguistics at the University of Innsbruck (Austria) where she teaches courses on general linguistics, psycho- and sociolinguistics. She has published on second language acquisition, bi- and trilingualism, gender issues and the meaning of silences. She is currently co-authoring a book on multilingualism and writing a book on the metalinguistic awareness of trilingual speakers.

**Istvan Kecskés** is Professor of Linguistics at the State University of New York, Albany where he teaches second language acquisition, pragmatics and bilingualism. His research focuses on multilingualism, conceptual fluency and transfer in multilinguals, and situation-bound utterances in L1 and L2. His latest publications include several articles and the book *Foreign Language and Mother Tongue* (Erlbaum).

**David Lasagabaster** was a school teacher of English for several years and is currently Associate Professor of English Studies at the University of the Basque Country, where he teaches applied linguistics, English language and literature. He has published on second language acquisition, bilingualism, trilingualism and the use of literary texts in the foreign language classroom. He is working on a research project on the acquisition of English as an L3 and conducting a study on attitudes towards trilingualism.

**Carmen Muñoz** is Associate Professor of English Linguistics at the University of Barcelona (Spain), where she teaches Applied Linguistics and Second Language Acquisition. She has published books and articles in grammar, applied linguistics, and first and second language acquisition. She is currently coordinating a research project on the influence of age on the acquisition of English by Catalan–Spanish bilingual school children.

**Tunde Papp** is affiliated with the State University of New York at Albany where her research focuses on the effect of foreign language learning on the development of mother tongue skills, and metaphorical competence in second language acquisition. She co-authored the book *Foreign Language and Mother Tongue* (Erlbaum).

**Ute Schönpflug** is Associate Professor of Developmental Psychology at Martin-Luther-University, Halle/Saale, in Germany. Her special research interests are first and second language development and learning. Her current approach is to extend research on bilingual to trilingual language processing and to look at personal resources enhancing bilinguals' discourse (text) processing. Her publications in this research domain cover bilingual children's concept formation, language and culture, and processes of translation.

**Irmeli Suni** has a degree from the University of Jyväskylä and worked as a teacher of Finnish and Swedish in Finnish lower comprehensive schools. She also worked as a teacher of English as a third language in immersion schools from 1992 to 1999. She retired in 1999 but still works as a consultant for the teaching of a third language in Swedish immersion.

**Jehannes Ytsma** is working as a researcher at the Fryske Akademy (The Netherlands), where he is currently involved in a longitudinal study into trilingual primary education. His thesis was on the acquisition of Frisian as first and second language among primary school children. His research interest is in bilingualism among children, bi- and multilingual education and language attitudes.

# Index

## Author Index

Abunuwara, E. 121, 122
Adler, M. 31
Agnoli, F. 100
Ahmad, F. 9
Ahukanna, J.G.W. 42, 50
Aikio, M. 199
Altwerger, B. 56, 67, 70, 72, 75, 254
Ammon, U. 23, 25, 26
Anglada, F. 219
Appel, R. 194
Aragonès, N. 219
Arenas, J. 158
Arnau, J. 158, 173, 254
Arnbert, L. 43
Artigal, J.M. 208, 219, 232, 234, 254
Au, K.H. 69
August, D. 61
Baetens Beardsmore, H. 16, 200, 254
Baker, C. 14, 43, 44, 84, 85, 93, 229
Balke-Aurell, G. 45, 47
Barik, H. 184, 254
Barkin, F. 56, 67, 70, 72, 75
Barron, N.S. 24
Bartelt, G. 50
Baschek, I.L. 127
Basden, B.H. 125
Basden, D.E. 125
Bates, E. 85, 95
Bel. A. 158, 159
Bensoussan, M. 250
Benta, V. 241
Berns, M. 161, 163, 249, 257
Bhatia, T.K. 84
Bialystok, E. 85, 252
Biber, D. 64, 78
Bild, E. R. 42, 44, 45, 49, 183, 184
Björklund, S. 204, 211
Boix, E. 160
Bonilla-Meeks, J.L. 125
Botezatu, R. 243
Bourhis, R.Y. 42
Bouton, L. 105

Bouvy, C. 147
Braescu, I. 237, 238
Bredenkamp, J. 127
Bressand, J.M. 201
Brodbeck, D.R. 124
Brosnahan, L.F. 5
Bruner, J.S. 57
Bulwer, J. 15
Burstall, C. 165, 174
Buss, M. 211
Byram, M. 193, 194, 258
Cabré, M.T. 163
Campos, J. 69
Cancino, H. 57
Carroll, S. 42, 50
Carter, R. 35
Cenoz, J. 41, 44, 45, 47, 50, 170, 179, 180, 181, 183, 184, 193, 195, 231, 250, 253, 255, 257
Challis, B.H. 124
Cheshire, J. 24
Clark, J.M. 125
Cline, T. 56, 79
Clyne, M. 8, 11, 42, 50, 121, 123
Cohen, S.P. 45
Collier, V. P. 64
Comisel, E. 242
Convery, A. 14
Cook, G. 24
Cook, V. 99
Cooper, R.L. 5
Corder, S.P. 144, 151
Corson, D. 54, 64, 66
Crystal, D. viii, 248
Cummins, J. 32, 46, 54, 55, 56, 57, 63, 64, 70, 71, 73, 76, 77, 78, 80, 170, 174, 184, 193, 195, 200, 204, 208, 210, 211, 218, 228, 254
Danesi, M. 103, 104, 105, 110
Davine, M. 45
De Avila, E. A. 184
De Bot, C.L.J. 223
De Bot, K. 99
De Jong, S. 224, 225

# Index

De Temple, J. 57
DeHouwer, A. 43
Delpit, L. D. 70
Denison, N. 8, 10, 11, 28
Doff, A. 246
Dogançay-Aktuna, S. 8, 9, 17
Dollerup, C. 11, 23 , 24
Donaldson, M. 57
Dörnyei, Z. 89
Doutriaux, C.W. 45
Dufour, R. 121
Duncan, S. E. 184
Durmüller, U. 23
Edelenbos, P. 226
Edelsky, C. 56, 67, 68, 69, 70, 72, 73, 75, 76, 254
Edwards, H.P. 45
Ehrman, M. 252
Eisenstein, M. 184
Ellis, R. 41, 84, 88
Elman, J. 85, 95
Elorza, I. 232
Enomoto, K. 45, 184
Espi, M. J. 183, 193
Eubank, L. 164
Evans, M. 14
Ezzaki, A. 47
Ferguson, C. 28
Fielding, L.G. 66
Fishman, J. 5, 6, 25, 28, 29
Flamerich, M.D. 219
Fletcher, P. 84
Flores, B. 56, 67, 70, 72, 75, 254
Fonseka, E.A.G. 209
Frederickson, N. 56, 79
Freire, P. 74
Freixa, J. 163
Fröhlich, M. 93, 250
Fu, L. 45
Gabiña, J. J. 181
Galateanu, G. 242
Garagorri, X. 232
García, M.P. 162
Gardner, R. 95, 231
Geber, E. 202
Gellert-Novak, A. 23
Genesee, F. 41, 42, 184, 193, 195, 250, 253, 257
Gentile, J.R. 42, 50
Gerritsen, M. 223
Gentner, D. 100
Gentner, D.R. 100
Gibbons, J. 65
Gibbons, P. 59, 60

Giles, H. 42
Goncz, L. 184
Goodman, S. 24
Gorostidi, R. 181
Gorter, D. 222
Graddol, D. 23, 24
Green, J. 252
Green, S. 14
Gregg, K.R. 164
Grosjean, F. 27
Gulutsan, M. 49
Hakuta, K. 61
Halliday, M.A.K. 32, 33, 65
Hammarberg, B. 50
Hansen, N. 49
Harding, E. 43
Harley, B. 91, 174, 204
Harris, R. 252
Hart , D. 44, 47, 91, 194
Hartfiel, V. F. 187
Hasan, R. 65
Heinonen, P. 217
Helle, T. 201
Helot, C. 43
Herdina, P. 90, 93, 253
Heredia, R. 88
Hettinga , J.M.M. 226
Hoefnagel-Höhle, M. 165
Hoffmann, C. 16, 23, 27, 28, 30, 31, 43, 44, 258
Holmstrand, L.S.E. 230
Hudelson, S. 56, 67, 70, 72, 75, 254
Hufeisen, B. 29, 93, 250, 253, 257
Hughes, A. 169
Hughey, J. B. 187
Huibregtse, I. 204
Humboldt, W. von 101
Hunt, E. 100
Hurd, M. 45, 49
Irujo, S. 105
Iruretagoiena, R. 181
Isasi, X. 180
Jacobs, H. L. 187
James, A.R. 30
Jaspaert, K. 45
Jessner, U. 90, 93, 94, 253, 254
Jilbert, K. 56, 67, 70, 72, 75, 254
Johnson, M. 85, 95, 100, 104
Jones, S.P. 43
Jonkman , R. 222
Jordan, C. 69
Kachru, B.B. vii, 5, 6
Karmiloff-Smith, A. 85, 95
Kasper, G. 253

Keatinge, R. 69
Kecskes, I. 102, 106, 110, 113, 114, 118
Kellerman, E. 152, 155, 253
Kessler, C. 184
Kettemann, B. 30
Kickler, K. 200, 204
Klapper, J. 17
Klein, E.C. 45, 184
Klesmer, H. 64
Knust, M. 200, 204
Köberle, B. 254
Kodzopeljic, J. 184
Koski, L. 202
Kövecses, Z. 103, 105
Krashen, S. 78, 79, 164, 210
Kreindler, I. 250
Kroll, J.F. 121, 122
Krueger, N. 49
Kuhs, K. 88
Labrie, N. 25, 26
Lado, R. 152
Lakoff, G. 100, 104
Lambert, W. E. 45, 46, 125, 193, 228
Lapkin, S. 44, 47, 194
Larsen-Freeman, D. 41, 184
Lasagabaster, D. 44, 45, 49, 170, 174, 181, 184, 186, 194, 195
Lascar, E. 65
Latomaa, S. 198
Laurén, C. 211
Laver, J. 10
Le Rütte, M. 224
LeBrun, N. 200
Leman, J. 193, 194, 258
Lemmens, G. 45
Lenneberg, E. 101, 164, 230, 232
Lewis, E. G. 183, 184
Lightbown, P. 165
Linblad, T. 45, 47
Lindemann, B. 29, 250, 253, 257
Lindsay, D. 183, 193, 231, 232
Loban, W. 114, 115
Locke, J. 100
Long, M. 41, 164, 185
Lorge, I. 127
Lund, N.J. 42, 50
Lyon, J. 14
Mac Aogáin, E. 250
Macaro, E. 14
MacWhinney, B. 84
Madigan, S. 127
Mägiste, E. 123, 137
Margoret, A. 95
Marsh, D. 201

Martin, M. 198
Martin-Jones, M. 56, 67, 68, 75
Massad, C. E. 183, 184
Maturana, H. 90
May, W. 102
McArthur, T. 6, 23, 249
McCarrey, H. 45
McCarthy, M. 35
McLaughlin, B. 49, 88
Meijers, G. 44, 45
Mellor, J. 14
Michael, E. 122
Mikes, M. 44
Miron., M. 102
Modiano, M. viii,
Möhle, D. 50, 174
Moser, L.-M. 24
Muñoz, C. 162, 175
Muysken, P. 194
Naiman, N. 93, 250
Nation, R. 49
Nayak, N. 49
Nikula, T. 201
Norton, B. 257
Nunan, D. 86
Nussbaum, L. 162
Obler, L. 49, 91
Oehrle, B. 127
Olaziregi, I. 181, 187
Oller, J. 57, 169
Olson, D.R. 57
Orpwood, S. 183, 184
Ortiz, A.A. 55
Osgood, C. 102
Oxford, R. 252
Paivio, A. 125, 127, 136, 252
Papp, T. 106, 110, 113, 114, 118
Paradis, M. 100
Parasher, S.N. 28
Parisi, D. 85, 95
Pascu, St. 236
Patkowski, M. 164
Pavlenko, A. 100, 117
Pearson, P.D. 66
Penfield, W. 164
Perales, J. 179
Pernu, M.L. 202
Phillipson, R. 163
Plunkett, K. 85, 95
Poe, E.A. 66
Priest, B. 200, 204
Quell, C. 25, 26
Quinn, M. E. 184
Räisänen, A. 202

# Index

Rall, M. 219
Ramirez, J.D. 78
Reixach, M. 160
Reyes, M. L. 70
Richards, J. C. 242
Riemersma, A.M.J. 224, 225
Riley, P. 43
Ringbom, H. 50, 217
Ritchie, W. 84
Rivera, C. 67
Rodgers, T. S. 242
Roedinger, H.L. 124
Romaine, S. 56, 61, 67, 68, 75
Rosenbaum, Y. 5
Rosenthal, D. 42
Roukens, J. 10
Rowen, N. 44, 47, 194
Ruiz, M. 219
Sajavaara, K. 201
Sanders, M. 44, 45
Sapir, E. 101
Scarcella, R. 164
Schachter, J. 152
Schley, S. 57
Schönpflug, U. 125
Scovel, T. 164
Searle, J. 101
Serra, J.M. 158, 159, 173
Sharwood Smith, M. 39, 253
Sierra, J. 181, 187
Singh, R. 42, 50
Singleton, D. 50, 164, 165, 230, 255
Skehan, P. 88
Skutnabb-Kangas, T. 56, 200
Smith, M.C. 125
Snow, C.E. 57, 165
Solé, E. 163
Spada, N. 165
Spratt, J.E. 47
Stern, H. 93, 161, 250
Stewart, E. 122
Street, B.V. 74
Swain, M. 42, 44, 45, 47, 49, 67, 73, 183, 184, 194, 210
Sweetser, E. 100, 101
Szabo, P. 103, 105
Takala, S. 201
Tarone, E. 152
Taylor, J.R. 102
Thomas, J. 44, 45, 46, 184, 194
Thorndike, E.L. 127

Todesco, A. 93, 250
Torras, M.R. 162
Torres, J. 176
Toukomaa, P. 56
Tragant, E. 162
Tremblay, P. 95
Troike, R. 63, 67
Tucker, R. 45
Valencia, J.F. 44, 45, 231
Valeva, G. 104, 105
van Essen, A. 237, 238, 241
van Geert, P. 86, 94
Varela, F. 90, 95
Väyrynen, P. 202
Ventura, M. 219
Verhoeven, L. 54
Viereck, W. 249
Vila, I. 158, 159, 173
Vila, X. 160, 173
Vildomec, V. 250
Vinjé, M. 225
Voltas, M. 219
Voorwinde, S. 121, 123
Vygotsky, L.S. 101
Waddington, C.H. 86, 87, 88
Wagner, D.A. 47
Wald, B. 61, 67
Wandruszka, M. 8, 11
Wardhaugh, R. 5, 18
Weldon, M.S. 124
Wells, G. 69, 70, 72
Whorf, B.L. 101
Widdowson, H.G. 34
Wierzbicka, A. 101
Wightman, M. 45
Wiley, T. G. 56, 67, 74, 75, 78, 254
Williams, S. 50
Winner, E. 104
Wippich, W. 127
Wode, H. 200, 204
Wood-Lamont, S. 242
Wormuth, D. R. 187
Yates, J.R. 55
Young, T. 216
Ytsma, J. 224
Yuille, J.C. 127
Zinkgraf, S. A. 187
Zobl, H. 45

## Subject Index

abstract words 125, 127, 129, 133, 138
academic achievement 78, 79
achieved bilingualism 3, 31-32
additive context (see additive bilingualism)
additive bilingualism 185, 194, 228, 256
age ix, xi, 48, 91, 92, 163-166, 167, 170, 172-175, 182, 186, 188, 211, 213, 215, 230, 255, 255, 256
American English viii, 7, 19
anxiety 89, 95
applied linguistics x, 84, 96
aptitude 48-49, 89, 95
Arabic 122
ascribed bilingualism 31
attitudes 13-14, 27, 48, 95, 169, 218, 224, 227
audiolingual method 242
Australia vii ix
Austria 8, 13, 22, 36
Austrian German 8
autochthonous languages viii, 158
autodynamic system 94
average metaphorical density 108
balanced bilingualism 19, 85, 184, 185, 193, 194, 195
Basque viii, xi, 42, 45, 47, 158, 167, 179-197, 217, 231, 248, 249, 255
Basque Country 9, 13, 42, 44, 179-197, 217
Belgium viii ix, 8, 9, 13, 15, 145, 253
Benelux 8
Berber 43
Basic Interpersonal Communicative Skills (BICS) xi, 11, 32, 54-83, 254
biculturalism 20
bilingual competence 27-28, 46-47
biological growth 86
Breton viii
Britain (see UK)
Brittany 44
British English viii, 19, 182
British Isles 3
Cognitive Academic Language Proficiency (CALP) 11, 32, 54-83, 93, 195, 254
Canada vii ix, 44, 163, 200, 211, 217, 218
Canadian immersion 55, 200
Cantonese 4
Castillian (see Spanish)
Catalan viii, xi, 43, 157-178, 248, 249, 255
Catalonia 9, 44, 157-175, 217, 232
Central America ix
China vii
cloze test, 171, 172
code-switching 44

cognition 79
cognitive advantages (see cognitive effects)
cognitive deficits 70
cognitive demands 57, 58-61
cognitive effects 44-45, 77, 93, 184, 253
cognitive-linguistic interdependency 101
cognitive mechanisms 103
cognitive style 48
cognitivism 95
common underlying conceptual base (CUCB) 99, 101, 111, 116, 251
common underlying proficiency 185
communication strategies 161-162, 169, 253
communicative ability 162, 225
communicative approach 233, 242, 245
communicative course 225
communicative competence 104, 105, 199, 201, 203, 213
communicative methodology 111
communicative sensitivity 48
communicative skills 163
compensatory performance 143
competence x, 89, 94, 163, 166, 170, 173, 175, 186, 187, 188, 194, 227
conceptual fluency 103-104, 110, 111-113, 117, 252
conceptualisation 103,
conceptual processing 124, 125, 126, 136, 138
conceptual thinking 112
concreteness 125, 127, 129, 132, 136
concrete words 125, 127, 129, 133, 136
connectionism 95-96
Constantly Available Interacting Systems (CAIS) 252
content teaching 204
Costa Rica 128
creativity 48, 49
critical pedagogy 74
critical period 164, 230, 232, 255
cross-linguistic influence xi, 44, 49-50, 145, 253
cross-linguistic interaction 253
cross-linguistic transfer 143-156
Cyprus 4
cultural bilingualism 31
culture 101
declarative knowledge 100
deficit theory 67, 72
Denmark 9, 23, 25
dialect 32-34
dictation 169, 171, 172, 174
diglossia 8, 28-29,

direct borrowing 147
discourse 175
double immersion 45, 216-217
drama 208
dual-coding theory 251
Dutch viii, xi, 7, 44, 45, 123, 143-156,
   222-235, 248, 249, 253
dynamic model xi, 94-96
dynamic processes 84, 251, 257
early multilingualism 42-44
early trilingualism 43
Eastern Europe 25
elaborative transfer
elite bilingualism 3, 31
England, *see* UK
English for academic purposes (EAP) 24
English as a *lingua franca* (ELF) 22-38, 250
ESL programmes 67
English for science and technology (EST) 24
English for special purposes (ESP) 34
error(s) 128, 143-156, 252
error corpus 145, 153
error rate 131, 133, 136, 137
esteem 89
Estonian 198
ethnolinguistic vitality 42, 48
exposure 165
Euro-English viii
European Englishes 249, 258
European Schools 15, 200, 258
European Union/Community vii, viii, 2, 11,
   12, 13, 15, 16, 20, 23, 24, 181, 200
Eurospeak 24
family bilingualism 12, 205
field independence 95
Finland 42, 198-206, 211, 232
Finnish viii, xi, 123, 198-221, 248, 249
Foyer project 45
France ix, 15, 18, 25, 128, 179
French viii, ix, xi, 5, 11, 13, 14, 25, 32, 41, 42,
   43, 44, 45, 46, 50, 99, 106-117, 143, 145,
   161, 162, 181, 201, 202, 204, 206, 216, 218,
   237-244, 248, 249, 253, 256
Friesland 44, 222-235, 256
Frisian viii, xi, 222-235, 248, 249
Friulian 23
Galician 158
gender 108, 110, 113-116, 117, 186, 188, 252
generalisation 149
German ix, xi, 7, 8, 11, 14, 17, 23, 25, 26, 43,
   44, 121-142, 143, 144, 146, 209, 213, 215,
   244, 248, 249, 252, 253
Germany ix, 4, 7, 8, 13, 15, 17, 25, 44, 128,
   163, 204

grammar 246
grammar-based course 225
grammatical competence 104, 105
grammaticality judgement tasks 45
grammar-translation method 111
Guarani ix
Hawthorne effect 211
Hebrew 42, 122, 216
heritage language 217
holism 84, 95
Hungarian xi, 99, 107, 108, 113, 116,
   236-247, 248, 249
Hungary 105, 110
identity 14, 257
idiom(s) 35, 102, 105
immersion 32, 107, 109, 111, 117, 160, 181,
   194, 198, 200, 203-206, 207, 208, 211, 212,
   214, 216, 217, 224, 230, 231, 232, 254-255,
   256
immigrants, ix, 2, 6, 27, 59, 63, 198
independence 121-123
India vii
indigenous minority language 1
individual bilingualism 2, 27, 30-31
individual differences 47-49, 88-90,
input 160, 210
in-service courses 216
interactive pedagogy 228-229, 256
interdependence 46, 47, 92, 101, 121-123,
   138, 173, 184, 228, 229, 255, 256
interference 121, 122, 144, 150, 155, 231
interlanguage 151
International Schools 15, 200
intertranslatability 101
intelligence 188
interactive pedagogy 228
IQ 48, 49, 55, 70, 73, 186
Ireland vii, 3, 163
Irish 3, 43
Israel ix
Italian ix, 23, 42
Italy ix, 13, 15, 22, 25, 36, 128
Japan viiix
Kenya ix
language attrition 88, 91, 92
language awareness 77, 93, 216
language deficits 70
language dominance 123
language growth 85-90, 92
language maintenance 90, 93
language processing device 99-100
language proficiency 227
language similarity (*see* typology)
language use 123, 180, 205, 213, 214

latency 122
Latin 157, 239
learning style 70
legal English 24
lexeme copying 148
lexeme matching 148
lexical access 124, 125, 126, 136, 137
lexical errors 146
lexical interference 152
lexical processing 138
lexical repertoire 123
lexicon 66-67, 71, 78, 102, 121-142, 144
linear process 85-86
*lingua franca* vii, x, 1, 5, 22-38, 162, 181, 200, 201, 223, 248, 249, 250
lingualism 29, 30
linguistic demands 58-61
linguistic distance (*see* typology)
linguistic interdependence ix
linguistic normalisation 158
linguistic relativism 100-102,
listening comprehension 129, 170, 172, 174, 175, 182, 186, 189, 190
literacy 47, 62, 69, 71, 72, 74, 78, 79
Loban Number 114
long words 135, 137
Luxembourg 15, 41, 200, 258
Luxembourgish 41
majority language 193, 222, 229, 232
Malta 3
Maltese 4
Mauritius ix
mainstream classes 67
markedness 155
mental lexicon (*see* lexicon)
metalinguistic awareness ix, 48, 49, 93, 94, 143, 152, 162, 194, 251, 255, 257
metaphor 100
metaphorical competence xi, 99-120, 117, 251, 252
metaphorical density 47, 105, 106, 108-109, 117
metaphorical thinking 112
metaphorical system 102
methodology 182, 194, 245
Middle/Far East 5
minority language(s) viii, ix, 1, 4-5, 46, 173, 193, 194, 195, 222, 229, 232, 249
minority language speakers 56, 63, 65, 67, 68, 70, 72
mixing 154
mode 65
Mohawk ix
monolingual acquisition 85

Montessori Schools 16
morphological errors 146
morph-syntactic code-mixing 146
morpho-semantic code-mising 146
motivation 19, 48, 71, 89, 95, 116, 162, 169, 188, 202, 203, 210, 211, 212, 224, 226, 227, 231, 237, 242
Mozambique ix
multicompetence 99-100, 101, 111
multilingual acquisition x, 39-53, 96
multilingual competence ix, 27-28
multilingual language processing device 251
multilingual lexicon xi, 252
multiple choice grammar test 170, 174
Netherlands ix, 8, 9, 13, 15, 23, 44, 54, 163, 204, 222, 223, 225, 226
New Zealand vii ix
Nigeria vii, ix
non-indigenous minorities 4
non-linear patterns 86
non-native varieties vii
non-native European English 257
Norway 9, 23
output 210
Panjabi 4
passive competence 137
pedagogical strategies xi
perceived language competence 89
perceptual overlap 124, 136
personality 48
Philippines vii
Poland 128
Polish 123, 128, 248, 249, 252
popular bilingualism 3, 19, 31
pragmatic skills 105
primary education 223-234
priming 124, 125
proficiency x, xi, 44, 45-47; 54-83, 112, 164, 193, 194, 230, 251
pronunciation 175, 246
psychotypology 143, 255
pupil-centered teaching 207
quechua ix
reaction times 127
reading 68, 69, 73, 79, 129, 160, 175, 186, 190, 206, 227
register 32-34, 65
resident errors 152
Romania xi, 233-247, 256
romanian 236-247, 248, 249
Romance languages 8, 236
Russia 128
Russian vi, 9, 26, 99, 106, 107, 110, 111, 112, 116, 198, 237, 238, 256

Sami viii, 198, 199, 201
Sardinian viii
Scandinavia 8, 13, 163
Scandinavian languages 7
school bilingualism 13-18 (*see also* immersion)
second language acquisition ix, 39-41, 47-48, 50, 84-85, 250
self-confidence 95
self-rated competence 128, 129
semilingualism 254
sensitive periods 164
short words 135, 137
sign language 198
societal bilingualism 23, 27, 28, 30-31
speaking 129, 182 190, 191
spelling interference 147-148
Slavonic language 236
Slovenia 22, 36
Slovene 23
social classes 169
socioeconomic status 48, 188
societal bilingualism 23, 27, 28, 30-31
South America vii ix
Spain 9, 13, 157, 163, 179
spanish viii, xi, 3, 5, 14, 43, 45, 46, 47, 69, 124, 125, 144, 157-175, 179-197, 231, 248, 249, 255
speaking 129, 160, 227
Spread of English vii-x, 1-21, 24-26, 257
strategies ix, 48-49, 93, 95, 117, 169, 209, 253, 257, 258
stress 246
Stroop Colour Test 121, 122
structural well-formedness 108, 114
subtractive contexts 46
successive trilingualism 231
Sweden 9, 23, 56, 123
Swedish viii, xi, 42, 198-221, 248, 249, 256

Switzerland 13, 15, 23, 24, 31
system stability 91
systems theory 251
teaching materials 208, 241-243
teaching methods 206, 215, 241-243
teaching strategies 206, 207, 209
test-taking skills 174
teacher training/development 207, 241
textbook-centered teaching 206
textual variation 64-65
threshold hypothesis 184, 195, 255
transfer 11, 154, 155, 251, 252, 253, 256
transfer errors 152, 152
transformative pedagogy 73
translation 126, 145
two way bilingual education/program 229, 230
Turkey 8, 13, 17
Turkish 9, 44
typology 41-42, 44, 49-50, 123, 153, 174, 195, 222, 234, 249, 256
UK vii, 12, 13, 15, 18, 25, 163, 239
Ukraine 128
underlying cognitive mechanisms 105
Universal Grammar 73
uniqueness 127
US(A) vii, ix, 5, 54, 55, 74, 163, 239
USSR 237
Vaasa/Vasa viii, xi, 203-219, 256
Wales 4, 6, 44
Weighted index of subordination 114
Welsh 4, 14, 41
whole language teaching 207, 209
word fragment completion 121, 124, 125, 126, 127-138
world Englishes 6
writing 80, 105, 106, 111, 129, 145, 160, 189, 206, 228

For Product Safety Concerns and Information please contact our EU Authorised Representative:

Easy Access System Europe

Mustamäe tee 50

10621 Tallinn

Estonia

gpsr.requests@easproject.com

www.ingramcontent.com/pod-product-compliance
Lightning Source LLC
Chambersburg PA
CBHW022010300426
44117CB00005B/118